CHINESENESS) *across Borders*

Renegotiating Chinese Identities

in China and the United States

ANDREA LOUIE

Duke University Press Durham and London 2004

2nd printing, 2004

© 2004 Duke University Press. All rights
reserved. Printed in the United States
of America on acid-free paper ∞
Designed by Amy Ruth Buchanan.
Typeset in Scala by Keystone Typesetting,
Inc. Library of Congress Cataloging-in-
Publication Data appear on the last
printed page of this book.

An earlier version of chapter 2 originally
appeared in the journal *Identities: Global
Studies in Culture and Power* in 2001,
published by Taylor and Francis (http://
www.tandf.co.uk). An earlier version of
chapter 5 originally appeared in the journal
American Ethnologist, copyright American
Anthropological Association 2000.
Reprinted from *American Ethnologist,*
volume 27, number 3.

DUKE UNIVERSITY PRESS GRATEFULLY
ACKNOWLEDGES THE SUPPORT OF THE
CHIANG CHING-KUO FOUNDATION,
WHICH PROVIDED FUNDS TOWARD
THE PRODUCTION OF THIS BOOK.

For my parents

CONTENTS

ACKNOWLEDGMENTS

This book could not have been completed without the assistance of individuals who were instrumental to both the research and writing portions of the project. There are too many individuals to be able to mention all of them here. Without the experience of having been a participant in the In Search of Roots program and, later, the cooperation of its organizers and fellow interns, this project would not have been possible. I have the deepest gratitude to Al Cheng, Him Mark Lai, Albert Lowe, Jeff Ow, Tony Tong, and others I interviewed, for sharing their words and experiences, which have come to shape the central focus of this book.

I began this project as a graduate student under Laura Nader, whose guidance has been instrumental to my development as an anthropologist. I also thank my other committee members who supported me throughout the project in various ways—Gerald Berreman, Jack Potter, Frederic Wakeman, and Ling Chi Wang. Numerous friends and colleagues have provided valuable feedback on different portions of this work. Connie Clark shared adventures in the field with me and gave me invaluable comments as I began to write about my research. Susan Brownell not only provided me with insightful feedback at various stages of writing this book, but also with general guidance on the publishing process. I also thank Martin Manalansan, Laurie Medina, and Diane Mines for their helpful comments on portions of the manuscript.

The China portion of this project would not have been possible without the friends, relatives, and colleagues who hosted me during my various trips to China. I thank the Guangdong Provincial Office of Overseas Chinese Affairs for hosting the Roots program's activities in China and for sponsoring the Youth Festival, as well as the local officials and tour guides who facilitated the Roots group's travels in China. I thank the teachers and staff at Shenzhen

Experimental School for their hospitality and for supporting my use of their school as a base for parts of my research. Chen Li Peng, Yang Lie Feng, He Xin, and Xing Qingsheng set up and accompanied me on many interviews. Other teachers and staff, in particular Liu Hui Fang, Liang Bi Xia, and Li Yingjie, provided friendship in the field. Also in Shenzhen, Mr. Lin He Ping shared with me many valuable insights about overseas Chinese policies.

In Guangzhou, members of the Huaqiao Huaren Yanjiu Suo (Institute of Overseas Chinese Studies) at Jinan University, particularly Zhang Ying Long and Huang Zhao Hui, patiently and excitedly discussed their ideas about overseas Chinese research. I am particularly grateful to Zhang Chang for introducing me to friends and relatives in her home village in Zhongshan.

I would also like to thank my Aunt Gladys and Uncle Eddy Y. H. Chan for opening their home to me during my many visits to Hong Kong. Not only did they welcome me like a daughter, the conversations I had with them about Chinese culture and society greatly enriched my research. My relatives in Guangzhou—Yi Suk Gung, his wife, their three daughters, and their spouses (in particular Lu Ping and Zhang Guolin)—were welcoming and generous. I am fortunate that doing this research allowed me to spend time with them and get to know them better.

Thanks also to Madeline Hsu for inviting me along on her research trip to Taishan County in 1995, and to Chen Xiao, my former student from ninth-grade spoken English in Shenzhen, now a graduate student in Michigan, who showed me around Shenzhen on my most recent trip.

The Chinese American portion of this research was funded by the Wenner Gren Foundation. I am also grateful to the Department of Anthropology at Michigan State University for giving me a course reduction to work on this manuscript; to Robert Edmondson for help scanning slides; to Jon Carroll for creating the map; and to the members of the department's Culture, Resources, and Power Concentration for helping to provide a vibrant intellectual atmosphere within which to explore new ideas.

I am also grateful for Ken Wissoker's support of the project, and for the able editorial assistance of Fiona Morgan and Christine Dahlin. Thanks also to Justin Faerber for his patience and flexibility during the production process. The anonymous reviewers for Duke University Press provided encouraging and constructive feedback that greatly improved the manuscript. I would be remiss in not adding that I alone am responsible for the ideas contained within the book.

Finally, I could not have written this book without my husband, Adán Quan, who over the years not only patiently read and commented on numerous dissertation, article, and book drafts but also encouraged me in his uniquely understated way throughout this project.

INTRODUCTION: ON BOUNDARY CROSSINGS

Village Encounters (Beginnings)

In July 1992, on summer break from graduate school, I visited my paternal grandfather's village in Heshan County, Guangdong Province, for the first time, accompanied by my fellow participants in the In Search of Roots program.[1] This program, run by organizations in Guangzhou and in San Francisco, provided an opportunity for young adults (ages seventeen to twenty-five) of Cantonese descent to visit their ancestral villages in China. My second great-uncle, Yi Suk Gung, whom I had met only a few days earlier, took the bus from Guangzhou to meet our group at the Heshan County seat and lead the village tour.

On first impression, the village could have come straight out of the nineteenth century. To the Chinese American visitors, the village was a maze of narrow alleyways, old brick houses, and open sewers, surrounded by rice paddies. However, a closer look revealed electric power lines, radio cassette players, and three-story homes of gleaming ceramic tile. Yi Suk Gung took us to the ancestral home that my great-grandfather had built on returning from the United States where he worked to build the railroad[2] along with a village watchtower (c. *lau jai, pao lau*)[3] constructed jointly with his four brothers for protection against bandits. My great-grandfather's picture remained on the wall of the house, somehow having survived years of Communist reform. I paid respects at the house's altar, made special note of the open window (*tianchuang*) in the ceiling of the house that I remembered my father mentioning, and had my picture taken innumerable times by fellow interns helping me to record "the moment." The group proceeded by van to a hillside that was a fair distance from the village, then hiked up

The village watchtower in my ancestral village of Tiegang, in Heshan County, Guang-dong Province. My great-grandfather's picture on the wall of our ancestral home.

through tea bushes and small pine trees until we reached a clearing that contained the horseshoe-shaped graves of my great-grandfather and his wives.[4] After Yi Suk Gung and I paid our respects (c. *bai san*) he lit an amazingly long and loud string of firecrackers and we returned down the hill. Later, we toured a blanket factory that proudly displayed the colorful fleeced acrylic blankets produced there, a special product (*techan*) for which the area was well known, and attended a banquet hosted by local officials from the village and from the Office of Overseas Chinese Affairs (Huaqiao Shiwu Ban).

I returned a second time to the village in February 1993 while on break from teaching English at a Chinese high school, this time with Yi Suk Gung and his daughter as well as with my parents who were visiting for a couple of weeks. It was the first time my father had been back to the village since he had lived there as a boy for a year in 1948. His father had sent his American-born children to China in two waves. The first group left in 1931 from Akron, Ohio, where the family ran a hamburger joint. The six children, ranging in age from a few months to seven years old, lived in the village for nine years, accompanied by their parents for the first two years, and later taken care of by close relatives living in the village. My grandfather wanted

The ancestral grave of my great-grandfather.

Yi Suk Gung (my great-uncle) setting off a string of firecrackers during my first visit to the ancestral village in 1992.

them to receive a Chinese education (without which one could not be considered truly Chinese).[5] However, the Japanese invasion in 1939 cut their visit short, and the group fled to Hong Kong and returned to the United States through the immigration station in Seattle, Washington. Although they were U.S. citizens and still had the birth certificates and certificates of identity that their mother had sewn into the backs of their clothing, they were interrogated in Chinese (they had forgotten any English that they had known) and temporarily detained by immigration officials, as was common under the Chinese Exclusion Acts. Racial identification as Chinese alone was grounds for interrogation. In my family's Immigration and Naturalization Service (INS) files obtained from the Seattle archives there are records of the process of interrogation. The system was designed to identify those trying to enter the United States under false identities. However, the detailed questions that immigration officials asked the detainees were difficult to answer "correctly," even if one was telling the "truth." The group of six children was detained because one had insisted that their kitchen table was round, instead of square. It turned out that the family ate around two tables, one round and one square.

The second group, consisting of the children who had not yet been born when the first group departed, was sent to China in 1948 in another instance of unfortunate timing, only to return a year later when the Communists took the area. My father, twelve at the time, was part of that group. As a young child in Easton, Maryland (the family had relocated there and now ran a laundry), he had not even realized that he had a group of older siblings in China until one day his mother told him to wash his hands because they were having guests for dinner. The "strangers" piled out of the laundry truck, one of the older sisters chasing my understandably afraid aunt, then two years old, around the block in an effort to pick her up. My father recalls his surprise that they never did leave after dinner.

My father's return to the village in 1993 unfolded with much less fanfare than my own visit the previous summer. We rented a van in Guangzhou and drove to the village for the day. The weather was quite cold (for southern China) and very few people were around, perhaps because it was during the Chinese New Year period, the busiest travel time of the year, rather than harvest season. We walked around the small village, took pictures, and listened as Yi Suk Gung showed a three-story "modern" style house in the village built with US$20,000 donated by people from overseas. He encouraged my father to consider pitching in with his ten siblings to do the same ("then you'll have someplace to stay when you come back"). In actuality, members of my father's family had visited the village only a few times since they lived there as children. During the years between 1949 and 1979 travel to China was nearly impossible. One group of siblings returned in the early 1980s for a tour of China, stopping by the village on their way back to Hong Kong. Another group visited in the early 1990s. However, they would have never considered actually spending the night in the village, and the family did not visit the village (or Yi Suk Gung) at all in subsequent trips to other tourist destinations in China.

We peered into the windows of the thick-walled fortress, where my father and his brothers had slept after the family received a mysterious ransom note intended to preempt a kidnapping that had not yet taken place.[6] The key to the building had been lost long ago. I remember as a child asking my father about his memories of his year in China, and they were few and select: how dirty the village was; how much he missed playing baseball, eating Hershey bars, and reading comic books; and how his pet dog "disappeared" (into a dish on his aunt's dining table, he discovered later) while he was away in Guangzhou. He recalls struggling to learn enough Chinese to write a letter home to his father—the benchmark indicating that he had become sufficiently educated in Chinese to return to the United States—and hoping that his older brothers, aged eighteen and nineteen, would heed their father's wishes and find wives so that they could all go home.[7] He remembers the culture shock he experienced on arrival at the village: his baseball glove was mildewed, there were no flush toilets, and the village children made fun of him by chanting "ABCD."[8] He recalls being scolded by relatives for stubbornly standing on the stoop at the entrance to the house, and not understanding why they thought this would bring bad luck. He also remembers fondly the kindness of his village relatives, playing near the fish pond, and going to school.

When I asked him later what he thought about during his 1993 trip back, he said that the brief visit had evoked memories of his earlier time there. He had been surprised to see that after forty years very little had changed. When I inquired whether he would like to go to China again to spend more time in the village, he replied that although he would not resist going back again, it would be mainly because seeing the village evoked his past experiences there. There were no longer any people that he knew in the village, and the physical structures themselves had no meaning apart from these memories.

My own visit as part of the In Search of Roots program had been characterized by an emotional intensity carried by the group as a whole throughout our journey to ten ancestral villages. An expectant air, created through months of research on family history and genealogy and magnified through youthful energy and curiosity, permeated the atmosphere at each participant's village visit. Would we be able to find the village? Would the ancestral house still be standing? Would there be any relatives, or perhaps a geneaology book, left in the village? This mood was not diminished by the lack of firsthand connections and memories that characterized the experiences of our parents' and grandparents' generations who had spent time in the villages. In many ways, the power of experience that was necessary to give these old physical structures meaning was derived from our sense of anticipation coupled with the careful orchestration and preplanning by both the mainland Chinese and the Chinese American organizers. One of the Chinese American organizers remarked once to me that "unless someone tells you what connection this place has to you, all you see is a dirty old place." Indeed, a fellow intern and I mused that we had no way of telling for sure whether or not these places were really our ancestral villages.

Rethinking the Experience

I have realized that the family history that brought me to China as a participant in the In Search of Roots program, with a subtext of anthropological curiosity, reflects the multiple ways that people craft relationships with China and the multiple formations of Chineseness that I have come to examine as a central part of my research. For each generation described above—mine, my father's, my grandfather's—"returning" to China carried very different significance, and the "return" experience itself was shaped by the particularities of the social and political events of the time. My grandfather, who was born in China, thought nothing of sending his children "back" for a Chinese education in the village, and he traveled to China numerous times himself in the continuation of a pattern of return migration that had long characterized life in emigrant villages in southern coastal China (see Hsu 2000; Watson 1975).[9] My father's generation, although raised speaking the village dialect at home, found themselves temporarily uprooted from their lives in the United States, only to be placed into an unfamiliar village setting during a dramatic period of change in China. Still, a number of continuities—family connections, a basic knowledge of the language, and participation in local educational institutions—marked the relationship of this generation to their ancestral homeland.

My own "return" occurred in the context of China's reopening to the outside world, during a period of massive social, political, and economic change in which overseas Chinese were cast in a central role by the People's Republic of China (PRC) government.[10] It was also framed by a politics of multiculturalism in the United States that celebrated diversity and a return to cultural origins. Many American-born Chinese Americans, like myself, felt ambivalent toward China because it was both a place to which we were often attached (both voluntarily out of interest in family heritage and involuntarily when we were racialized as Chinese) and a place that we knew little about. We were not culturally Chinese enough to be considered Chinese by many people in China, yet also not American enough to be seen as Americans by many people in the United States. Even if the links of my generation to our ancestral villages had been firmly entrenched in our family histories, what we hoped to see there had been created primarily through our imaginations and facilitated by media images.[11]

I chose to begin this book at this very specific time and place—a visit to my ancestral village in China as part of the In Search of Roots group—because while this ethnography focuses on Chineseness as negotiated across locales, ideas about place remain essential to these very conceptualizations of Chineseness. This ethnography takes as its core a set of multistranded and often diffuse relationships around which people of Chinese descent in China, the United States and other locations negotiate identities across national borders. Increasingly, complex and multifaceted flows of media, information, capital, and migrants create new connections between peoples and places around the globe. These linkages are changing the ways that "Chineseness" becomes salient as a social, political, and cultural identity in today's world. But rather than focusing on mobile transmigrants who easily negotiate national borders, I explore the highly mediated and indirect relationships between two populations that have been separated across generations and seldom interact directly: mainland Chinese and American-born Chinese Americans. These two communities are linked not so much by contemporary social networks and shared cultural or political beliefs as by myths of common origins that define Chineseness as a mixture of racial, national, and territorial identities. Within these interactions exist possibilities not only for varied connections and relationships based on shared heritage but also new forms of difference.

Indeed, as I will discuss later, genealogical and historical connections to ancestral villages provide the basis through which transnational formations of Chinese identity are crafted over time and across space. That both Chinese Americans and the mainland Chinese government are invested in producing territorialized Chinese identities in this era of globalization is a question that is central to this book. But perhaps even more interesting than the ways in which these discourses of Chinese culture are created based on shared history and ancestry are the new forms of identity that are produced out of these contemporary interactions. Whether through inclusion or exclusion, these constructions of Chinese identity are mediated by both U.S. and PRC state projects of cultural citizenship that shape Chinese identities. However, rather than producing firmly rooted and unambiguous Chinese identities, these transnational interactions more often result in encounters with unfamiliar ways of being Chinese. Ironically, transnational connections reveal disjunctures that are created in part by other conjunctures created by global flows between Chinese and Chinese Americans. The interaction between state constructions of identity for its citizens (and sometimes noncitizens) and transnational flows circulating more broadly has implications for transnational theories that discuss the role of the state within transnational projects.

The Mobile Anthropologist: Piecing Together a Study of Chineseness

The themes in this book have emerged ethnographically. My exploration of productions of Chinese identity has required a mobile, multisited ethnographic approach that provides insight into the complex and ever-changing nature of the diffuse relationships through which meanings of Chineseness are being renegotiated. However, it would be misleading to imply that the project unfolded neatly and methodically because anthropological fieldwork almost never does. Below, I present three narratives focusing on overlapping experiences in China that were integral to the development of my project in a way that could not have been preplanned: my research with the In Search of Roots program in the San Francisco Bay Area and in China (from 1992 to 1995); my year teaching English and conducting fieldwork in Shenzhen from 1992 to 1993; and the fieldwork period I spent in various places throughout the Pearl River Delta region in 1995. The process of developing my field site and research problem brings out some of the methodological and theoretical difficulties of taking on the transnational question of Chinese diaspora identities. The cohesiveness of the concept as an academic or intellectual construct is betrayed by the actual diversity within it, making it nearly impossible to study the Chinese diaspora as an undifferentiated whole. Yet both the academic frameworks and the identity-making projects I studied worked within a transnational framework that sought continuities between homeland and diaspora populations.

Each of these experiences illustrates broader themes or questions that I wish to emphasize in the study. All are to various degrees informed by my positionality as a Chinese American ethnographer within a multisited exploration of Chineseness, in which at times I am the only consistent feature. Each illustrates various processes through which Chinese from abroad are contextualized as "Chinese" in China, and how this relates not only to the ways that mainland Chinese conceive of overseas Chinese but also of their own changing identities in the context of China's opening up to the outside world.

A Note on Ethnographic Methods

My fieldwork on Chinese identities employed a type of mobile anthropology aimed at examining various parts of a "relationship" being forged anew across national boundaries that draws on metaphors of shared heritage and place.[12] In my investigation of "Chineseness" I conducted participant observation and interviews in San Francisco with Chinese American participants of the In Search of Roots program, as well as later in China when they visited their ancestral villages and participated in government-sponsored Youth Festivals. I conducted fieldwork in the San Francisco Bay Area; in the Pearl River Delta region of Guangdong, China; and in Hong Kong, all sites of Chinese (particularly Cantonese) cultural production. In China, I researched from a number of bases the shifting attitudes of Chinese living in the Pearl River Delta region of Guangdong, including a village in the emigrant region of Zhongshan County, the Taishan region, and a middle school in the Special Economic Zone of Shenzhen. I interviewed people in their homes, dorms, and apartments; in cafés, culture centers, and McDonald's restaurants; and in rural Chinese villages and on jet planes, focusing on various moments and contexts of interaction within which multiple and often discrepant discourses of Chineseness are brought together. Given the fluid nature of transnational processes, and the fact that identity is always situated, under negotiation, and never complete (Hall 1990), the exploration of identity at specific sites and at specific moments of contact was to become more important to me than delineating a fixed geographical site. It was necessary to trace connections, following the contours of ideas and social actors by moving among these people and ideas that were also in motion. Through conducting fieldwork from multiple sites and on multiple Chinese subjectivities, I used my own privilege of mobility to investigate from a number of angles the numerous and flexible ways of identifying and being identified as Chinese. By positioning myself and being positioned within a number of different contexts—as a former participant in the Roots program interviewing a friend about their experiences, or as an American-born Chinese (*mei ji hua ren*) teaching English in China—I investigated the question of Chinese identities (as a relational concept) from different and changing perspectives. Willingly or not I was a subject of my own research, if only in the ways that others perceived and interacted with me.

The In Search of Roots Program:
Beyond "Buffet-Style" Chinese Culture[13]

The Roots program is a product of China's reopening to the outside world in the post-Mao period as well as an effort to reach out to the Chinese community abroad for economic and political support. It is jointly sponsored by organizations in the San Francisco Chinese American community (the Chinese Culture Center and the Chinese Historical Society of America) and by the PRC's Office of Overseas Chinese Affairs (Qiao Ban, the state apparatus for relations with the Chinese abroad).[14] The program's Chinese American and mainland Chinese portions are connected only during the two-week journey to China, where Chinese American participants visit their ancestral villages in the Pearl River Delta region of Guangdong, China. Their agendas correspond only to facilitate their village visits and to meet the shared goal of helping participants search for their ancestral roots (*xungen* is the Chinese name of the program used both in China and by the Chinese American organizations).

The program's Chinese American portion has its origins in the shifting demographics of the Chinese American population in the San Francisco Bay Area, catering to the second-, third-, and fourth-generation descendants of Cantonese immigrants. It was formed as part of an effort by Chinatown cultural organizations to reconnect to the suburban Chinese community, and it was designed for Chinese Americans who know little about China or their family heritage. Prior to their participation in the In Search of Roots program, many of these Chinese Americans had not given much thought to their origins in China. The majority of participants belonged to families that had moved away from Chinatown, and whose children had gone to college and entered professional positions. Many lived in the Richmond district of San Francisco, or in the East Bay, South Bay, or Marin County areas. Although some spoke Cantonese or a village dialect quite fluently, having learned it from their parents or from living in China or Hong Kong as small children, most did not know how to read or write in Chinese, and the majority had never been to China and did not speak Chinese well or at all.

For example, Adam Chan, a fourth-generation Chinese American who grew up in Marin County, had been active since he was a child in a lion dance troupe organized by his father. However, when he was growing up he had never thought much about being Chinese or about China. For him, China was "the place that Bugs Bunny dug through to if he kept digging from here." He, like many other participants in the program, had become involved in the year-long In Search of Roots program as a young adult curious about his heritage.

At one point during Roots program activities, another participant, Fred Chang, conducted an informal poll of the nine others in the group. He arrived at the conclusion that his parents were the only ones who had strong objections to his participation in the Roots program and the trip to China. His father, for reasons that Fred was not entirely aware, was estranged from his relatives in China. After the death of Fred's grandfather, who had emigrated from China, the family had stopped sending money to the village. Fred's mother, who was born in China, didn't understand why he wanted to visit China; after all, Fred did not speak the language and there were no longer any close relatives there. Indeed, Fred himself had reservations about participating in the program. He was a student activist who identified strongly with the larger "Asian American" political movement, which since the Third World Student Strike in 1968 had pushed for the recognition as Americans of people of Asian descent in the United States. Researching his Chinese heritage seemed a contradiction to his belief in a larger, pan-ethnic (Espiritu 1992; S. Wong 1995), U.S.-based identity politics. Still, some of Fred's friends had participated in the Roots program and had found it to be a worthwhile experience. Despite some diversity, the group was largely self-selected in terms of class background and of personal interest in issues of heritage. Like Fred, most of the Roots interns were American born (second, third, or fourth generation) and of Cantonese descent. This was a program requirement because logistics limited group travel to a region of China that could be covered by ground transportation over a period of a few weeks. In addition, there is a historical connection between San Francisco Chinatown and this region (see Chen 2000).

Participants came to the program in a variety of ways: some found out about it through friends or classmates; others had family members or friends involved with the Chinese Culture Center, which sponsored the program. One high school student mentioned the program over her school's intercom during morning announcements for two weeks before it dawned on her that she qualified for it. Another college student heard about it in his Mandarin Chinese class at a private California university, quickly realizing that he was the only student of Cantonese descent in the room.

For some families and individuals, financial concerns were a factor in the decision to participate. The program required a fee of $450 plus airfare to China, which usually ran about $900. Cost is also an issue in the fact that the program received little interest from first-generation migrants living in Chinese ethnic enclaves. However, as I will discuss later, another issue may be that first-generation migrants are subject to a different set of racializing practices and societal barriers than generations born and raised in the

United States who have limited knowledge of their Chinese heritage. Still, assumptions that one is not a citizen, does not speak English well, or insinuations that one should "go back to China" (even if one has never been there) constitute a set of racist behaviors that frame perceptions of all Chinese Americans as perpetually foreign and "other" to mainstream U.S. society.

Since the early 1980s the Chinese Culture Center had made efforts to reach out through its programs to the largely English-speaking suburban Chinese American population. Its leadership viewed its Roots program as an opportunity to educate American-born "assimilated" generations about Chinese culture, with the idea that this education would preserve the knowledge of culture for future generations. Further, program leaders felt that giving American-born Chinese opportunities to explore their family's past would provide them with a solid grounding as Chinese Americans. The In Search of Roots program pairs roots searching with family history, as in the traditional Chinese expression, *xungen wenzu* ("searching for roots and looking for ancestors"). The program focuses on the researching and writing of family histories and the narratives of identity exploration that trace family roots back to emigrant villages in China. This is done with the aid of detailed history lessons provided by a noted Chinese American historian as part of the program's bimonthly meetings. The history lessons begin in the emigrant regions of the Pearl River Delta, from which the ancestors of Roots participants originated. The lessons continue by tracing the history of Chinese immigration to the United States and the experiences of Chinese in the United States up to the present. The course chosen for this historical narrative is significant because it emphasizes a continuity between China and Chinese Americans that until recently has been neglected in discussions of Chinese and Chinese American history.[15] Although the program focuses on family history and genealogy, it also references the present in its emphasis on identity exploration. In doing so it allows participants to bring together the history of past transnational connections to China within a contemporary, transnational Chinese American context.

Instructors teach participants techniques of oral-history interviewing and bring them to the National Archives in San Bruno, California, to search for the immigration files of their relatives who passed through Angel Island Immigration Station during the period of legal exclusion.[16] Understanding this history of exclusion is essential to providing the larger sociopolitical context shaping a family's story of emigration. For example, awareness of this context helps explain why immigrant ancestors assumed "paper names," that is, the use of purchased citizenship papers or birth certificates that was necessary to skirt unfair immigration laws designed to restrict the entry of Chinese laborers.[17] Knowledge of this historical background allows participants to understand what seem to be idiosyncrasies and particulars of their family's stories as part of broader historical, political, and social patterns. Through this process, interns can recontextualize "illegal" acts such as entering the country under a false name as reasonable and creative responses to an unjust system. Such actions can be redefined as collective acts of resistance that connect one's own family history to a shared Chinese or Asian American history (see Wong and Chan 1998). "Roots" interns are taught that although much of the information found in the INS files may consist of fictional information taken from the "coaching books" used to gain information for entry, these stories and processes were integral to shaping their family's history.[18]

In contrast to other programs for Chinese Americans organized in the United States, the Roots program is based on a pedagogy of participatory learning through experience. These learning goals are followed throughout the trip to China and culminate in a public presentation and display of family history and genealogical information at the Chinese Culture Center the following Chinese New Year. The vision of the program extends beyond the intern's year-long participation: its organizers hope that it will be a powerful, life-changing experience that will produce future Chinese American leaders who will create and implement new visions of Chinese American culture.

My research with the Roots program involved attending activities prior to and after the China trip. These activities included formal classes on Chinese and Chinese American history and genealogy, research trips to the National Archives, organized outings to Angel Island and other destinations, as well as more informal social gatherings over lunch or dinner. I also accompanied Roots groups twice on their trip to China, once in 1992 as an intern, and a second time in 1994 as an observer. These trips not only included visits to the interns' ancestral villages in rural Guangdong, but also attending the Chinese government-sponsored Youth Festivals activities. These three-day events bring together various groups of visiting overseas Chinese youth for numerous banquets, performances, and tours of the city. I saw the evolution of these activities over three years (in 1992, 1994, 1995), and I have communicated with interns, many of whom are now friends, through an e-mail network, and arranged both formal and informal meetings with them for interviews. They have been generous in sharing their personal narratives with me and the rest of the group. The program's leaders have been similarly accommodating in discussing with me the program and its goals.

Shenzhen City, in Guangdong Province, China

My first experience living in China was in 1993 when I spent a year teaching English in the Special Economic Zone of Shenzhen while on a hiatus from graduate school after my participation in the Roots program. While there, I began conducting preliminary fieldwork for my study. I taught in the Shenzhen Experimental School, which was a model public school that had been erected among the newly built multistory apartment complexes on land that a mere ten years earlier had been farmers' fields. The school was a microcosm of the new Shenzhen. The students who attended the school were the children of the relatively privileged class of professionals who immigrated to the city to fill its growing industrial and service sectors. The majority of the school's employees—from teachers and administrators to kitchen and janitorial staff—hailed from northern provinces, although some were from places in Guangdong and Fujian. In this setting where almost everyone, except the Hakka farmers who originally inhabited the area, was from somewhere else, notions of nativeness, place, and identity took on new meanings.

As I was introduced around the school as the "new foreign English teacher," some points of confusion became evident. Because I am phenotypically Chinese based on hair, eye, and skin color, I did not look the part of a foreign English teacher, especially since the previous teacher had been a young, tall American man of European descent. But although I spoke English more fluently than Chinese, because I didn't look "like a typical foreigner" my "not-foreign-enough" appearance ruled me out of profitable opportunities to teach English at various night schools around the city. At the same time, my lack of native fluency in Chinese initially made me the subject of snickers or bewilderment on the part of some employees who had never before seen someone who looked Chinese but who could not skillfully negotiate the cultural and linguistic terrain of Chinese society. Some teachers or staff spoke to me loudly, as though I were slightly deaf. Some talked with others around me as if I weren't present or were incapable of understanding anything they said. Still others addressed their questions (in Chinese) to the person with whom I was speaking. Often that person would turn around and repeat the question again in Chinese, the language in which we had been communicating.

It soon became obvious that I was in many ways a walking contradiction, or as Doreen Kondo (1990) terms it, a "conceptual dilemma" or "living oxymoron" who fits neither into the category "foreigner" (*waiguoren*) nor "Chinese" (*zhongguoren*). "Racially" I was Chinese, a "descendant of the dragon" (*long de chuan ren*), by virtue of my "black hair and yellow skin." One old teacher said that I looked "more beautiful" from drinking the water of my home country (I'm sure she meant this metaphorically, because the water in Shenzhen was often brownish in color and like all water in China had to be boiled before drinking). This assumed bond to the soil and water of China implied an organic, naturalized connection to China, a place to which I had been for the first time only recently. However, I learned that I also was not considered an overseas Chinese (*huaqiao*), which carried implications of Chinese extraterritorial rule (see L. Wang 1995), but rather a person of Chinese descent with American citizenship (*meiji huaren*). The terms in English—Chinese, overseas Chinese, and Chinese American—did not reflect the complex racial, legal, and political subtleties contained within the Chinese terms *zhongguoren, huaren, meiji huaren, huaqiao,* and *hua yi.*[19]

As a *mei ji hua ren* in an immigrant city in the mid-1990s, I learned that a variety of contradictions and complexities were attached to the category of the Chinese abroad, stemming from racialized and descent-based ideas of Chineseness that were extrapolated to Chinese living abroad, as well as from more "official" views of overseas Chinese as patriotic, put forth by the Chinese government. At the same time, in this city of immigrants I observed other processes of categorization. Everyone at the school knew where everyone else was from, not where they came from most recently but also the location of their "hometown" or ancestral village (*zuji, jiaxiang*). In addition, these understandings of place provided the basis for solidarities, in the form of informal social networks and divisions fed by stereotypes, around groups of *tong xiang* (hometown mates).[20] I was included in this categorization as someone from Guangdong Province, Taishan County, a region known for its emigrants.[21] When Mr. Liu from Taishan entered the room, other teachers would point out that we were "hometown mates," and he would nod politely in response.

My experiences in China of being inserted into the newly forming social order of Shenzhen were indicative of the massive changes experienced by Chinese society as a whole in the postsocialist period. Shenzhen is a place characterized not only by its immigrant population but also by the emerging class divisions and regional distinctions made between those with official urban residency (*hukou*) status versus temporary or illegal status. As China reopens to the outside world, and the old Maoist order unfolds onto fast-changing, outward-looking, capitalist-influenced terrain, identities are being reworked. Categories of class, rural versus urban origins, north versus south, foreigner versus Chinese, and Chinese versus overseas Chinese are being renegotiated. The collaborative sponsorship by the Chinese government and the Chinese American cultural organizations of the In Search of Roots program can be seen as part of this larger process.

A Second Look

In 1993, after my year of teaching English in China following my participation in the Roots program, I returned to graduate school intending to continue my research on these culturally and politically rooted conceptions of "Chineseness" from both sides of the Pacific. I decided to focus on the two groups—American-born Cantonese Americans and Guangdong Chinese— who were brought together around the idea of roots searching by the Chinese government. Throughout my various attempts to conceptualize this research problem, I struggled to find a framework that would connect the various geographically and culturally scattered parts of the project. I was not studying a physically, politically, socially, or culturally bounded community. In fact, few American-born Chinese had spent an extensive amount of time in mainland China and, with the exception of Hong Kong Chinese, few Guangdong Chinese had come into close contact with the Chinese born abroad, especially those of the third and fourth generations. The extent to which this could even be referred to an "imagined community" (Anderson 1983) was sketchy. Asian American identity politics advocated empowerment through U.S.-based identities with an aversion to petty subgroup loyalties that were divisive to common goals as minorities in the United States. A large number of American-born Chinese saw themselves as "Americans" who had, like generations before them, "melted" into U.S. society. At the same time, many Guangdong Chinese would claim that they knew little about the Chinese abroad, other than that they were probably rich and that some had returned to invest in China. The racial constructions of Chineseness that fueled modern Chinese nationalism were extended to conceptions of overseas Chinese in often subtle, ambivalent, and unconscious ways.

Both Chinese Americans and mainland Chinese formed conceptions of the Chinese or Chinese American "other" at a distance, not through direct contact and interaction but rather with secondhand information filtered through Chinese government constructions of the Chinese abroad and Western discourses on the "Orient." Linkages had to be sought more through shared histories and genealogies than through shared political or cultural ideals, thus rendering this attempt at structuring a community vulnerable to deconstruction should its parts actually be brought together for a kind of "first contact" (Schieffelin and Crittenden 1991). At this point, I realized that roots searching required a structure and a context in order to be meaningful to its participants. I also began to question the implicit emphasis on connections and continuities within transnational theories.

In 1995 I returned to the Pearl River Delta area of Guangdong to continue with my research, hoping to further investigate people's attitudes toward the Chinese abroad, as well as the more abstract topics of roots searching and native-place ties. I planned to find out to what extent socialist reforms had brought about new forms of social identity through the suppression of tradition, and through bureaucratic practices and controls that had supplanted more "traditional" closed-community, lineage-based forms of identification. Had shared urban identities controlled through the *hukou* (household registration system) and *danwei* (work unit) system made ties to native place less significant? I wanted to see through what mechanisms and practices links to overseas Chinese relatives and friends were viewed if not through more historically rooted ties of shared place, property, and ancestors. On what foundation were these relationships perceived as being based—other than obligations as kin? How were status and power relations enacted within these kinship relations? In conducting fieldwork in an urban setting where relations and trust depended largely on personal networks it was difficult to know where and how to start asking questions about such abstract issues. I needed to ground my fieldwork in issues more relevant to people's daily lives.

More informants in Guangzhou, on initial inquiry, would say they knew little about overseas Chinese and that, for example, I should really talk to someone else, who had a brother in Indonesia. However, further inquiries led to more complex and nuanced conceptions of the Chinese abroad discussed in relation to their own status in China. I was told that overseas Chinese were no longer considered as special as they once were. Since the Open Policy more people have had opportunities to emigrate. The phrase *nanfeng chuang* ("window to the southern breeze"),[22] formerly used to represent the window of opportunity provided by having a relative abroad, was no longer in fashionable use because these opportunities were no longer as pronounced. Previously, having relatives outside mainland China gave one access to the privilege of buying duty-free goods such as televisions and washing machines, which brought status to the families who owned them. Now these items were available openly on the market to anyone who could pay for them.

Many Guangdong residents from more prosperous areas of the Pearl River Delta have reflected on changes that have occurred in their understanding of the lives of their friends and relatives abroad. "Outside" (overseas) used to be seen as a "heaven" (*tiantang*), but now many said, they know that things aren't necessarily better overseas. They can be "first-class citizens" (*diyi denggongmin*) in China. They know that in the United States, Chinese have to work long hours washing dishes and are targets of discrimination. Ten years ago they were very poor, but now they can make money in China. They say that some people are choosing to stay. These shifts in attitudes coexisted and sometimes conflicted with pre–Open Policy attitudes toward the Chinese abroad.

Statistics dramatically demonstrate the economic growth in Guangdong associated with the Open Policy. While the real economic growth for China between 1981 and 1991 averaged 8.8 percent per year, Guangdong's growth was 12.8 percent. Guangdong's GDP (gross domestic product) grew 7.12 times during this period. In 1978 the difference in wages between Guangdong and neighboring provinces was 10 percent greater, but by 1990 it ranged from 35 percent to 70 percent greater. The result has been massive labor migration to Guangdong's industrial areas from poorer areas within Guangdong and from other provinces.[23]

It was evident to me that the Guangdong Chinese were in the process of reworking old conceptualizations of overseas Chinese as privileged sons who had flexibility of movement and opportunities to earn foreign capital and attain higher living standards. These conceptions, which in the past made them the object of blind envy (*xianmu*) to those who felt they had been left behind, have been tempered by increased access to information about the "outside" world combined with improvements in living standards at home. In turn, these changes have resulted in more multidimensional assessments of the status of overseas Chinese, fostering a sense of relativism about the development of China in relation to the West and a critical reassessment of the type of lifestyle that might personally be most appropriate. Living as a minority in a non-Chinese country might not be a situation that many Chinese would choose.

Rethinking the Problem

My fieldwork period in China made me realize that the the the separation of the Chinese abroad from China during much of the Communist revolution complicated the terms of roots searching, and indeed of what it meant to be Chinese. While Chinese Americans sought to find roots in China in order to place themselves within American society, mainland Chinese were struggling to stake a new position for themselves as modern Chinese after the Open Policy. At the same time, these processes did not occur totally independently from one another. American-born Chinese Americans—even those who (at an extreme) are not sure whether they are Cantonese or Mandarin, who think *ju yuk beng* (md. *zhurou bing*) is a type of meatloaf, and who learn about Chinese culture from kung fu films—are increasingly connected to mainland China through processes accompanying globalization. The rise of the Pacific Rim as a significant global arena; the appearance of China in the news regarding issues of trade and human rights; the increase in the number of immigrants from the Pacific Rim and controversies over "illegal" immigration to the United States; and the accelerated flow of information and people across national borders have brought the image of mainland China to the forefront of the American public imagination.

Historically rooted orientalist images of the "Far East" continue to shape ideas about China on another level—as an exotic, mysterious, and underdeveloped region. For those generations of Chinese Americans who in many ways learn more about "Chinese culture" outside the home than from their parents, these discourses have a heightened impact. Ien Ang, an Indonesian-born Dutch citizen of Chinese descent, comments, "I have always had to see it [China] as my country, if only imaginarily" because "throughout my life, I have been implicitly or explicitly categorized, willy-nilly, as a 'Chinese'" (1994: 5). Regardless of the degree to which the Chinese abroad choose to identify as "Chinese" or with China as a place of origin, there is, according to Ang, a "pressure toward diasporic identification with the mythic homeland" that problematizes the label of Chineseness for the Chinese abroad (5). Ang proposes a reconceptualization of this label, as encompassing multiple meanings, to free people of Chinese descent from this forced identification.

Producing Chinese Identities: U.S. and Chinese Contexts

My initial and rather personal discovery of the changing relationships between Chinese Americans and their ancestral place in China has evolved into a broader investigation of the renegotiation of Chinese identities under globalization. This book brings together two themes that present themselves through my multisited ethnographic study of Chinese identities in the United States and China. The first theme derives from the ways that Chinese identities are renegotiated across national borders, as mainland China reopens to the outside world and as increased transnational flows of people, ideas, capital, and goods allow people of Chinese descent around the world to interact with one another (or impressions of one another) in new ways. These interactions may not only produce a revival of ethnic (and racial) identity and affinity but also sets of contrasting identities based on differences in language, culture, and regional or national identity that contradict race-based constructions of Chineseness. They may also produce contrasting relations between transnational formations and state attempts to shape identities.

The second theme relates to the continued importance of notions of place and rootedness to these various constructions of Chinese identities by both mainland Chinese and Chinese Americans. Mainland China holds great power as the symbolic center to which Chinese identities both in China and outside of China are metaphorically attached through state-sponsored identity-making projects (see Ang 1994; L. Wang 1995).[24] Put together, these themes reflect a tension, although I argue that it is a productive one, between processes of globalization and the rooting of identities in place. It is my intent in this book to flesh out these tensions and contradictions as they result in new possibilities for the production of diverse Chinese identities within and across national borders. These identities are characterized by a type of bifocality derived from constructing relationships with places both near and far.[25] As my ethnographic case reveals, ironically, as opportunities arise for interactions between mainland Chinese and Chinese from other parts of the world, forms of Chinese identity based on regional affinities or distinctions of status increasingly emerge. New information about the existence of these forms of identity disrupts the continuity of racial, cultural, and national identities that is often assumed in both U.S. and Chinese government narratives about the relationship between mainland and overseas Chinese.[26]

As my fieldwork reveals, the production of Chinese identities does not occur in a vacuum. Nor can we assume that Chinese identities are significant in and of themselves, independent of the projects shaping them or the efforts of Chinese people themselves to reshape them. This book focuses on "Chineseness" as a dynamic formation, as Chinese identities are produced simultaneously on local, state, and transnational levels.[27] In the following chapters I will address in further depth the question of what is revealed by the participation of Chinese Americans, mainland Chinese, and their governments in the production of Chinese identities. In particular, I will examine how state mobilizations of Chinese culture and heredity interact with other notions of culture that are in circulation, such as those produced by the movements of Chinese people, capital, and media and popular culture across national borders. Key to this analysis is the question of how these productions are mediated on multiple levels, as well as what is produced out of these interactions as people encounter unfamiliar ways of being Chinese.

As will be seen, multiple ironies emerge as transnational connections both bring together and further differentiate Chinese people from different parts of the world.

Thus, far from being produced in a vacuum, Chineseness is used as both an inclusive and exclusive concept, empowered as racial discourse, used to reinforce a sense of rootedness, or turned into a commodity within the contexts discussed above. At times, Chineseness can be stretched to include the many people of the diaspora, and at other times to distinguish one group within the category from another. Chineseness, like all axes of identity, is not a fixed or bounded category, and its meaning only becomes relevant as people use it as a tool to define themselves in relation to others. Like Ang, I take Chineseness to be an open signifier, a fluid and contested category that encompasses a diversity of political, "racial," and ethnic meanings within varied and shifting contexts. This is not to say that Chineseness is an amorphous essence waiting to be recovered, claimed, and formed into a basis for identification, but rather it is a dimension of identity that is contested and shaped within power relations and becomes salient in different ways in various contexts.[28] In fact, it is often only when discrepant ideas or competing claims about Chinese identity are brought together, and the fiction of common origins or shared interests is dissolved, that the meaning of being Chinese (or not Chinese) is questioned or becomes problematic.[29]

In some contexts, Chineseness becomes a form of cultural capital that is shaped through transnational discourses that are negotiated by social actors within various regimes of control (Ong 1999: 6). Ideas about degrees of authenticity as Chinese, which are seen as derived from links to territory and knowledge of "traditional" Chinese culture, have become a basis through which diaspora Chinese define themselves in relation to one another. These processes are inseparable from the unequal flows of capital that have shaped processes of Chinese immigration and created differentials of wealth and status within and between diaspora and mainland Chinese. At the same time, both mainland Chinese and American governments produce discourses of citizenship that are both inclusive and exclusive based on conceptualizations of Chineseness that equate "race," culture, and membership in the nation (Ong 1999; Lowe 1991). On reopening to the outside world, mainland China has invoked Chineseness as a racial category to reign in the ethnic Chinese capitalist networks of diaspora Chinese, while the United States has recast Chinese Americans variously as potential spies, as corrupters of democratic politics, and as an illegal tide of refugees.[30] These official discourses overlook the complex ways in which Chineseness as a form of identification can work as both a unifying and differentiating factor, and the ways in which patriotism, cultural identification, and "racial" categorizations are not always neatly correlated.

In the following sections I examine some broader questions framing the transnational processes of Chinese identity construction to lay out a background for themes I expand on later in the book. More specifically, I discuss the investment of Chinese Americans, mainland Chinese citizens, and their respective governments in shaping Chinese identities through projects such as the In Search of Roots program and the Summer Camps for Overseas Chinese. Both U.S. and PRC state efforts to shape Chinese identities take place as part of nationalist projects that define cultural citizenship through processes of inclusion or exclusion in the nations' membership. Thus, the U.S. state provides a context for shaping Chinese American identities on a number of levels: in its foreign policy toward China and Taiwan, in its historical treatment of Chinese immigrants, and in its current politics of multiculturalism that define relations between different immigrant and minority populations and the nation in particular ways. At the same time, the PRC state has its own culturally, historically, and politically rooted framework for defining Chinese identities that has taken on interesting new forms following the Open Policy (*gaige kaifang*) of the early 1980s. As the nation has opened up to the outside world it has combined socialist ideologies with pre-Communist ideals in the process of market reform. In seeking to define a national direction that is both Chinese and modern, the PRC has reached out to reencompass the Chinese abroad, including those of foreign nationalities, in its development projects.

Chinese Americans and mainland Chinese citizens are also invested in defining Chinese identities. For Chinese Americans, this is in large part because they have been excluded from U.S. cultural citizenship on the basis of their Chineseness at the same time that they continue to be both voluntarily and involuntarily associated with China. The "Chineseness" of Chinese on the southern coast of Guangdong has long been highlighted in contrast to the various foreign influences they have encountered either at home or as emigrants abroad. Perhaps for these reasons the Guangdong Chinese have historically played a central role in defining modern Chinese national identities (of how to be both modern and Chinese), whether as revolutionaries (Sun Yat Sen) at the turn of the twentieth century or as beneficiaries of the Open Policy. As a "window to the southern breeze" (*nanfeng chuang*) Guangdong has been at the front lines of both foreign influence and socialist experimentation and has played the role of mediator between China and the West.

This is not to imply that racially or culturally derived aspects of Chinese identities take precedence over class, gender, or regional dimensions. In fact, as will be discussed later, these factors are inextricably linked to both productions and negotiations of Chineseness. However, racialized and territorialized conceptions of Chineseness form the primary building blocks for state productions of cultural citizenship that define the boundaries of the nation through both inclusion and exclusion. Thus, the Chinese origins of Chinese Americans, and the symbolic markers of foreignness and cultural difference that accompany them, result in the sense of displacement that motivates Chinese Americans to seek their roots in China. And similar essentialized conceptions of the racial and cultural origins of Chinese Americans form the basis of their inclusion in Chinese government nation-building programs.

In Search of Roots in the Context of U.S. Racial Politics

As stated previously, the In Search of Roots program is a collaboration between a particular segment of the Chinese American community, with a specific mission to recover Chinese American family histories, and the Chinese government, with its agenda to incorporate the Chinese abroad into its nation-building projects. As I will discuss below, it becomes important for Chinese American organizers, participants in the program, and the mainland Chinese government to bring Chinese Americans to China to visit their ancestral villages. For each side, the program's goals are formally encapsulated within the idea of "searching for roots" (*xungen*), based on the cultural and racial origins of Chinese Americans in China. At the same time the unspoken dimensions that define the significance of roots-searching activities within contemporary contexts help place into perspective the vast resources put into these programs. The specific political, social, and economic contexts framing each side's interests extend beyond their desire to acknowledge the shared history and territorial origins of Chinese Americans and mainland Chinese in the Chinese countryside. Thus, while their agendas cross during the Roots interns' trip to China, closer examination of the Roots participants' experiences with the program, as well as those of Chinese citizens, reveals disjunctures where these agendas diverge. As I will describe later, these areas of divergence are produced through transnational linkages between mainland Chinese and Chinese Americans in areas that extend beyond state control.

The Roots program can only be understood when placed within its historical and political contexts.[31] The investment in identity production and the means through which it is achieved are specific to Chinese Americans of a certain generation living within a particular historical era marked by a state-sponsored politics of multiculturalism (see Rouse 1995) and transnational flows. As described earlier, the program's focus on genealogy and family history originated from the San Francisco's Chinese Culture Center leaders' realization that immigrant generations of the Cantonese American population were passing away, while their grandchildren had little knowledge of their family history. It also was initiated by an offer of the Chinese government to sponsor a group of Chinese Americans to visit China. But the question of what actually motivates Chinese Americans themselves to participate in the program is complicated—particularly, as we shall see, if we try to move beyond the idea that roots-seeking is a natural activity.

Willingly or not, American-born Chinese Americans are defined within U.S. society through their Chineseness. They are on the one hand cast as perpetual foreigners in a society where achieving status as a true "American" is attached to racial and class background in addition to legal citizenship. On the other hand they are expected to have and display their Chinese "culture" in this era of multiculturalism. Aihwa Ong defines cultural citizenship as the "cultural practices and beliefs produced out of negotiating the often ambivalent and contested relations with the state and its hegemonic forms that establish the criteria of belonging within a national population and territory. Cultural citizenship is a dual process of self-making and being-made within webs of power linked to the nation-state and civil society" (1996: 78). Drawing on her ethnographic work with both Hong Kong elites and Cambodian immigrants living in the United States, Ong describes the specific institutional and political processes by which they are cast, as immigrants and refugees respectively, in relation to the majority populations. She adds critical complexity to the idea of a pan-ethnic Asian American population by detailing the "contrasting dynamics of the subjectification" of these two groups, which positions them at opposite ends of the black-white racial politics of the United States. As she notes, "Cambodian refugees and Chinese business people did not arrive as ready-made ethnics" (75).

Ong's profile of "Asian" immigrants on opposite ends of the class and racial spectrum creates a space for an analysis of where the Chinese Americans in my study fit (or rather, don't fit) into these politics. As fluent speakers of English living in primarily middle-class neighborhoods and headed for white-collar employment positions, they may at first glance appear to be firmly entrenched in U.S. society. The myth most often applied to them is that of the model minority, a concept that refers to Asian cultural values, social networks, and possibly even genetic predispositions that result in their success in U.S. society. In combination with a "rags-to-riches" ideal of the of the American dream, this myth only serves to exaggerate their perceived success and "mainstream" status, while undermining any difficulties they may experience as minorities in U.S. society. Although in many respects the American-born generations of Chinese Americans may no longer face language barriers or economic difficulties to the same degree as their immigrant ancestors, their apparent entry into mainstream American multicultural society may in fact serve to mask the actual precariousness of their position.

This precariousness stems from the fact that while the Chinese Americans in my study do not fit into the dominant discourses surrounding Asian immigrants in U.S. society, they are nevertheless caught within these discourses without an effective means of creating their own political or social space. The existing immigrant-focused discourses of Chinese (or more broadly, "Asian") culture in circulation exclude them. American-born Chinese Americans with roots that are generations deep in the United States do not fit into the discourse of cultural citizenship crafted for the Hong Kong "astronauts," (Ong 1999)—mobile entrepreneurs who move between both Pacific coasts and whose cultural citizenship is made questionable on the basis of their mobility, lack of participation in U.S. institutions, and relative wealth. Nor do they fit into discourses of cultural citizenship crafted for Cambodian refugees, whose "exotic" cultural practices and use of the welfare system give the impression that they are not playing by the same rules. While in some ways their marginal position may liberate them from the disciplining practices of the state that attempt to control these populations, it also leaves them on their own to carve out a place within a rapidly changing U.S. society focused on newly arrived immigrants and refugees.

The contemporary discourses in circulation surrounding Asians in the United States construct all people of Asian descent as newcomers to U.S. society with sustained contacts with the homeland and traditional cultural practices that make their investment in U.S. society questionable. The complex terms of U.S. multiculturalism simultaneously celebrate cultural difference while they reshape and co-opt this diversity for state projects (Rouse 1996). As I will discuss in chapter 3, the Chinese Americans in my study are on the one hand seen as perpetual foreigners or as too "Asian," and on the other hand as not Asian enough in a U.S. society that celebrates symbolic diversity and parades ethnicity. Thus, they feel compelled to demonstrate Chinese cultural competence and cultural authenticity, even in asserting their "Americanness."

At the same time, transnational flows of people, capital, and culture bring not only new immigrants from the Asia-Pacific region but also popular culture and commodities. Through these flows, Chinese Americans are increasingly exposed to other ways of being "Asian" while also being subject to the backlash against these immigrants. They struggle to create identities as "modern" Chinese Americans, which in the context of the contemporary politics of cultural citizenship and multiculturalism ironically involves demonstrating their cultural legitimacy through their knowledge of "tradition." For example, they are expected to know how to communicate in Chinese and know about Chinese foods and holidays. In a sense, these Chinese Americans are similar to the Guangdong Chinese in my study in that they are a generation on the cusp of great societal change while state-sponsored discourses remain inadequate to explain their sense of displacement.

Mainland Chinese Roots Searching

Since before the turn of the twentieth century, Chinese national identity has been defined through its struggles with becoming modern yet remaining Chinese. China's socialist experiment, which began in 1949, was an effort to develop internally following a form of Chinese socialism. Mao's plan not only isolated China from the outside world but also attempted to eradicate traditional social structures and feudal practices that were thought to be impeding China's development. As I will discuss further in chapter 4, the Open Policy and economic reform implemented in the early 1980s after Mao's death represented a radical departure from this strategy. It produced a brand of socialist reform that incorporated elements from both preliberation society and from capitalism, and called itself "socialism with Chinese characteristics." The Chinese government's adaptation of socialist ideology to market-based reforms unleashed a set of rootless ideologies that selectively drew on the past. However, the plan did not fully address the complexities of the socialist legacy or the changes that had occurred in the "traditional" relationships it was attempting to draw on.

The Cultural Revolution (1966–1976) was to have removed associations with feudal superstitions including those of family-based social structures and ancestor worship. The Open Policy and economic reform attempted to draw on these very attachments in attracting the overseas Chinese back to China. Overseas Chinese capitalists were key to the development of "socialism with Chinese characteristics"—an indigenous form of hybrid capitalism—because in the government's eyes they were undeniably Chinese yet also experienced in dealing with the outside world (see Ong 1999). But this radical departure from Maoist projects of socialist reform, which included a new focus on the urban as opposed to the rural (Chen et al. 2001) and on experimentation with capitalism, was built on a shaky structure. As will be seen in chapter 4, while Deng Xiaoping's economic reforms have no doubt been successful in opening up China socially and economically to the out-side world, there remains a mismatch between China's rapidly changing society and these ideas rooted in an idealized Chinese past.

This mismatch has resulted in fragile discourses of Chinese culture that are problematic and easily complicated or even contradicted by other dis-courses of Chineseness in global and local circulation. These alternative narratives of Chineseness, which include the idea that Chinese in other countries are victims of discrimination and that the Chinese abroad have lost touch with their cultural heritage, crosscut the ideas on which the Chinese government's economic reform are based. These ideas, equating Chinese heredity with patriotism for the motherland, were seemingly cre-ated in a vacuum that did not take into account the changing relationship between mainland China and the Chinese abroad. So while economic re-forms have unleashed various opportunities for development, they have not yet addressed the issues of how to be modern yet remain Chinese that plague modern Chinese nationalism.

Economic reforms also do not take into account the many ways of being Chinese in mainland China and abroad. Guangdong Chinese are increas-ingly being exposed to different ways of being Chinese caused by the ac-culturation of the Chinese abroad to the societies they live in and by regional and class variation within China. These capital and media flows are also creating massive internal changes in China such as floating populations, detachment from hometowns, the separation of families caused by internal migration, and the creation of new towns without histories.

The example of the Shenzhen Special Economic Zone illustrates this problem. On a recent trip there I had an opportunity to meet the director of the Shenzhen Museum. After touring the museum we walked down the street on the way to a dim sum restaurant, passing the famous billboard commemorating Deng Xiaoping's southern tour. When I pointed out the sign, the director responded by saying that people in Shenzhen love Deng Xiaoping. He said that, indeed, without Deng Xiaoping there would be no Shenzhen.

Shenzhen people live a privileged lifestyle, with housing conditions and salaries that outrank most of the rest of China. Yet at the same time, I thought about the other sides of Shenzhen that did not fit neatly into this picture, including the displaced migrants from inland China who moved there to do manual labor, work in factories, or serve as nannies (*baomu*) for local families. And on the museum tour I had caught a glimpse of yet another problem that lay beneath the surface of Shenzhen. My former students who had brought me to the museum had commented as we entered the compound that "people used to think that Shenzhen did not have a history." In a sense this had appeared to be the case because a little over twenty years ago Shenzhen had consisted only of rural villages occupied by Hakka farmers.

The Shenzhen Museum's new exhibitions offer a corrective to the rootless past of Shenzhen. The first room that we entered portrayed Shenzhen in the Neolithic era, displaying the pre-Han tools and funerary objects excavated by local archaeologists. The room also featured Shenzhen's history as a port town through the exhibition of trade items such as porcelain painted with large-nosed Caucasian figures. The next room skipped forward in time to the Opium War, featuring Shenzhen's role in the defense of China against the British imperialists, then brought us through the founding of modern China, the war with Japan, and finally Communist Liberation in 1949. It is perhaps significant that the exhibit seemed to skip the period of Communist reform from 1949 through 1978. Instead, the rest of the museum's rooms featured an exhibit titled "Shenzhen, a Newly Rising City: The History of Shenzhen in the Reform and Opening to the Outside World and Its Achievement in Construction". Complete with scale models of the developing city (past, present, and future), the exhibit focused on the success of Deng Xiaoping's project by highlighting the modernity of Shenzhen. However, by placing this exhibit within the context of Shenzhen history, this recent era of economic reform appeared to be less a departure from Shenzhen's past as much as the logical continuation of its history at the leading edge in establishing China's position in relation to the outside world. The exhibit concludes with the following words: "As the Window and Proving Ground of China's reform and opening policy, Shenzhen since its very birth has attracted [the] attention of the whole country as well as the world. Till today, twenty years have passed and this special zone has experienced numerous hardships and made brilliant achievements as well. Shenzhen with its success in the practice has clearly manifested the soundness of Deng's theory on the construction of socialism with Chinese characteristics."[32]

Thus, in a way, the Chinese state sponsorship of Chinese Americans to find their roots in China may actually be part of its broader project of seeking its own contemporary path in the world, as represented in Shenzhen's rediscovery of its own history. In fact, the Shenzhen City Office of

Overseas Chinese Affairs sponsors roots-searching projects of its own where the modern features of Shenzhen stand in for China's economic development more broadly.

Genealogy and Territory as Transnational Formations

Both Chinese American root-seeking projects and the Chinese government's efforts to facilitate their roots searching may perhaps seem even more extraordinary because these activities invoke historically rooted attachments to place in an era that is increasingly marked by globalization.[33] However, as I will show, although based on roots metaphors these projects are simultaneously both localized and transnational and employ the flexible and mobile identities that accompany global processes. These state projects mobilize Chinese culture in specific ways that bolster their respective goals. At the same time, these projects depend on the conflation of culture and race within the transnational imagination, based on inferred continuities of race and place, to accomplish these goals.

The shared cultural, genealogical, and territorial origins of Chinese Americans and Guangdong Chinese that I trace through my family history at the beginning of this chapter are a potentially rich resource for the construction of contemporary Chinese identities. The relationship between overseas Chinese and their ancestral places in China appears to be a natural point from which to begin a broader examination of Chinese diaspora identities and transnational relations with the homeland. As the main point of historical linkage between diaspora Chinese and mainland Chinese, the ancestral village remains salient as a symbolic nexus for relations between mainland Chinese and overseas Chinese, both past and present. Native place continues to serve as the basis for the racialization of overseas Chinese in late-socialist China. Overseas Chinese, in their perceived ability to successfully negotiate capitalist markets while remaining essentially Chinese (Ong 1999), are central to the PRC's vision of a new mainland Chinese modernity. Socialist narratives fix Guangdong in time and place as a point of rooting for overseas Chinese loyal to the memories of their native places. And while overseas Chinese involvement in mainland China may be read in both official and popular discourses as patriotism to the nation as a whole, such connections are seen as derived from those affective ties to the soil, water, and genealogy that bond overseas Chinese to their ancestral places. Chinese nationalist discourse developed in the early twentieth century explained these physical and emotional connections between people and territory in terms of race: Chinese (even those abroad), as descendants from a common mythical ancestor, shared a collective culture and biological heritage that tied them to the (local and national) soil.

But while in some ways the connections between various generations of Chinese Americans and China may appear to signify the continuous maintenance of patriotic Chinese identities rooted in native places in China, it is possible to read the connections in yet a different way. While identities based on shared territory and genealogical origins may appear to result only in the reinforcement of static, "traditional" identities, these same relationships form the basis for the construction of new and often contrapuntal forms of Chinese identity. As my examination of the Roots program shows, contrary to the expectations of the Chinese government, Chinese American attachments to native places in China may occur at both local and transnational levels but still not necessarily translate into nationalistic attachments to the motherland. Thus, Chinese Americans who visit China to search for ancestral roots may come to identify in new ways as Chinese Americans with roots both in the United States and in their ancestral villages in China. They may also identify with the same transnational popular culture flows as their mainland Chinese compatriots. However, they do so selectively and not necessarily in ways consistent with government narratives describing their attachment to the homeland. In this sense, territorial and genealogical connections may form the basis for new forms of identity that play out on both local and transnational dimensions, while at the same time possibly producing alternatives to state constructions.

The genealogies that are the focus of the Roots program are an apt metaphor for these connections. In an anthropological sense, genealogies are the products of imagined kinship relations that connect people over time and across space, including national boundaries. At the same time we can make a distinction between genealogy as a technical exercise of tracing kinship relations (and including or excluding of kin) over time and across space, versus how these relations are made meaningful in social practice. We can also distinguish between genealogy as concept and as practice. Thus, the idea of genealogy is inherently flexible, extending far beyond the shared point of origin to encompass varied relationships among those it encompasses.

In this sense, the genealogical relationships that are central to the roots searching that takes place in this book are also the basis for a number of transnational connections that can take varied forms. As social productions and constructions, they draw on the same conflation of race, culture, and territorial origins that both the U.S. and Chinese governments use to define Chinese identities. In the process of searching out genealogies, Chinese

Americans are at the same time re-creating and conferring new meanings on them. As I discuss below, these processes are not significantly different from the ways that genealogies are reproduced and made meaningful in other contexts.

The transnational flexibility of genealogical connections is well exemplified in the longitudinal study by James Watson (1975, 2002) of the Man lineage based in the New Territories of Hong Kong. In this work Watson has demonstrated the durability of lineage social structure and its associated economic, social, and political benefits. The Man lineage has drawn on genealogical connections to establish relations with "kin" all over the world, even bringing together members in mainland China with those in Great Britain who have never met and who do not share a common language. In this case, the idea of a genealogical connection, rather than a preexisting relationship, produced a new social relationship across national borders. On an even broader scale, Louisa Schein's (1998) research with Hmong/Miao shows how the mythology of common origins can produce a form of "forged transnationality" between Hmong refugees in the United States and their purported coethnics in China. As she demonstrates, this relationship is sometimes a complicated and somewhat unequal one, and is mediated through orientalist thinking, the sometimes uncritical romanticization of the "homeland," and the economic differentials between the two groups.

As will be seen, although the Roots program focuses on the recovery of genealogy books and the writing of family histories, its Chinese American participants do not passively record this information. Rather, they use this information in combination with their experiences traveling in China and of growing up Chinese American to craft genealogical tales and family stories that represent negotiations of identity that are in dialogue with both U.S. and Chinese government projects intended to shape them. Thus, the transnational identities that they produce result from the interplay of state and popular nationalisms emerging out of both state attempts to define cultural citizenship and popular attempts to create meanings out of these experiences based on connections at various levels and their interpretations at "local" levels.

So What? The Broader Implications

In this book I reexamine the relationship between processes of globalization and the continued importance of place as a location for identities, emphasizing not only the new connections facilitated by transnational flows but also the forms of difference that come to the fore under globalization. Transnational processes facilitate new opportunities for interactions between overseas Chinese and their native places at the same time these very flows are rapidly altering the places that have become statically fixed in the imaginations of those who wish to return there. Thus, what is perhaps most interesting about contemporary formations of Chinese identities is what is produced when multiple formations come together. Despite their heavy investment in them, state projects are limited in shaping Chinese identities, while at the same time they may indirectly result in alternative productions of Chineseness. These alternative productions include transnational flows of popular youth culture that link Chinese people in China and the United States and elsewhere. As will be seen, these popular culture flows become localized as they intersect with "local" Asian American/Chinese American/Cantonese American family productions of culture. Thus, Roots interns create their own subculture out of their experiences with both U.S. and Chinese state attempts to construct Chinese identities for them. This subculture is at the same time transnational, as it connects to villages in China and Asian popular culture forms, and localized, as it references particular Chinese American and familial concerns. For example, in the process of recovering genealogies and writing family histories, interns insert their own agendas into these productions by regendering genealogies to include both men and women, by selectively adopting and incorporating Chinese traditions, and by remaking Chinese American spaces to connect ancestral villages in China and their own family's place in the United States.

At the same time, the Guangdong Chinese are recasting the space of Guangdong as a result of these interactions with people and ideas from other parts of China and abroad. In the late socialist landscape of mainland China, the Guangdong Chinese are at the forefront of negotiations of modern Chinese identities. But their position on this leading edge may result in alternative possibilities for the construction of Chinese identity, as their exposure to ideas and people from abroad may cause them to reflect back on themselves as Chinese people in new ways. These productions of identity may not be Chinese as much as specific to Guangdong. Thus, the space of coastal Guangdong as a territorial entity may be reinscribed in interesting ways as Guangdong residents increasingly differentiate themselves both from the Chinese abroad and from Chinese from inland China. This would not be the first time that a form of popular nationalism has arisen in Guangdong that differs from official state nationalisms.

In the next chapter I discuss the ways that mainland China has historically been the symbolic center for Chinese identities and how it remains an important (but not the only) nexus for their renegotiation. I highlight the

Chinese state's involvement in creating a sense of Chineseness based on the ancestral roots of Chinese Americans in China. The relevance of ancestral places in China has changed over the years both for Chinese in mainland China and Chinese outside of China, as have concepts of nation and of what it means to be a Chinese person itself. However, historically rooted discourses continue to tie the Chinese abroad to their ancestral places in China through connections equating race, nation, and culture. At the same time, over the past fifty years mainland China has engaged in a socialist revolution and has emerged as a hybrid form of socialist-capitalist modernity, while Chinese Americans have become involved in their own form of politics as part of their emerging consciousness as racial minorities in U.S. society. These changes have raised issues from both perspectives about what it means to be Chinese that have been further complicated by China's opening up over the past twenty years. It is within this context that the formation of PRC's Summer Camps, of which the Roots program is a part, and its Youth Festival must be understood.

In chapter 2 I focus on the experiences of the In Search of Roots group in China during their village visits. In particular, I discuss how Chinese American participants build on both the structured and unstructured parts of the program to create impressions of China that differ from those intended by the program's organizers. I argue that Chinese American participants reference conceptions of geography, identity politics, and popular culture derived from Chinese, Asian, Chinese American, or Asian American culture that they bring with them from the United States to craft identities that go beyond the village as a fixed space for Chinese and Chinese American authenticity. The experience in China becomes the basis for Cantonese, Chinese American centered identities, as expressed in narratives and displays produced at the end of the year-long Roots internship.

In chapter 3 I provide a context for understanding the meanings that Chineseness has come to take within the contexts of U.S. politics of race, ethnicity, and cultural citizenship. While much attention has been focused on immigrant generations, Chinese Americans face different sets of issues and concerns that result in feelings of displacement from mainstream American culture. American-born Chinese are influenced by images and information about China originating not as much in their own direct experiences as in sources mediated through the racial politics of U.S. society and transnational media flows. Chinese American identity narratives show a departure from an orientation to China, while at the same time they reflect the fact that they are still seen as "others" or as perpetual foreigners in U.S. society.

This background provides a broader context for my ethnographic interviews with participants and leaders that focus on their views toward Chinese and Chinese American culture. I make special note of ideas of tradition and the authenticity (or lack) of Chinese American culture as expressed by my informants, and of how Chinese Americans conceptualize Chinese spaces in the U.S., China, and elsewhere. The political, social, and cultural activities in which participants engage in their daily lives reflect their varying degrees of politicization as Chinese Americans, Asian Americans, women of color, people from working-class origins, etc. These activities represent efforts at reethnicization but, importantly, they do not replicate the practices of "traditional" Chinese culture. While the "In Search of Roots" program encourages the bridging of Chinese and Chinese American spaces through the research and writing of family histories, participants to varying degrees draw connections between their daily political concerns as Chinese Americans and issues of family heritage. For many, their concerns with issues of Chinese cultural authenticity (or their relative lack of cultural authenticity) emerge and are to some extent addressed through the writing of these histories. These identities do not necessarily correspond with the spaces for Asian American identity laid out in conceptions of U.S. multiculturalism. In this sense, they are a response to the lack of expressive space that Chinese Americans of these particular generations and backgrounds have within the politics of U.S. cultural citizenship.

In chapter 4 I shift back to contemporary China to discuss changing views of Chineseness in China that are resulting in alternative discourses of Chineseness that counter official government narratives. The Pearl River Delta region of Guangdong—the area of ancestral origin for the Chinese Americans in the study—has been undergoing rapid changes under economic reform in the past two decades. I focus on ethnographic descriptions of perceptions of villagers and urban residents toward Chinese abroad in light of increased information about life "outside" that has become available through the media, as well as stories of returning migrants and interactions with others from abroad. Through these flows, the Guangdong Chinese are forming their own geographies of the "outside" world that reflect not only a new type of transnational imagination but also new relationships to Chinese from less properous parts of China. Their attitudes toward the privileged place given to the Chinese abroad are changing in relation to their own reevaluations of the potential that life abroad holds for them and their families.

In chapter 5 my focus is on the PRC-sponsored Youth Festival as a forum within which contradictions and inconsistencies in mainland Chinese and

Chinese Americans conceptions of Chineseness emerge. I provide an ethnographic description of the Youth Festival and of the ways that the correlation between Chineseness as a racial, cultural, and national identity are called into question for both sides throughout these activities. Discussions of economic growth due to overseas connections along with "cultural" events that are aimed to renew the latent pride that Chinese are supposed to feel in their motherland provide the central content of the Youth Festival, but often have an unpredictable impact on overseas Chinese youth. As part of this discussion, I incorporate interviews with various participants in the Youth Festival and related activities, including Chinese government officials and participants. I discuss these themes within the broader context of the role that the PRC sees for overseas Chinese in its new model of modernity. This ethnographic evidence points to the possibility that the PRC may need to rethink its conceptions of overseas Chinese identity as new generations renew their relationship with China in different ways. At the same time, the Guangdong Chinese may be reworking their relationships both to the Chinese abroad and to those from other parts of China.

In the final chapter I discuss how for Roots interns creating a sense of home is a multilocal and processual endeavor that relies simultaneously on their transnational mobility and their continued ties to place(s). Although continuities from the past, represented in family histories and genealogies, play a central role in interns' identity narratives, more important are the ways in which the rewriting of these histories legitimizes their identities as contemporary Chinese American youths. Roots interns have created their own subculture that draws both on their experiences in China and on broader connections to a transnational Asian youth popular culture. At the same time, this subculture is distinguished by a focus on their incomplete and often inauthentic understandings of China and Chinese culture that come to signify their Chinese Americanness. Issues relating to the future of the Roots program can encourage us to think about transnational theories in new ways that examine both the connections and disjunctures produced through these highly mediated transnational encounters. Roots searching is characterized not only by the deterritorialization that often accompanies transnational mobility, but also by processes of reterritorialization in relation to both the United States and China that enable interns to rework ideas of family, genealogy, gender, and history.

He cradled the aged box in his lap as his tanned fingers leafed through the tattered brown papers, dipping and searching for a memory lost through the sea of years. I, too, held my breath, as he peered through one envelope, only to set it aside for another. At last, he removed a jumble of cardboard stubs and yellowed photographs from its housing. Adjusting his bifocals, he unfolded a thin paper, scrawled in English and Chinese, and handed it to me.

"Is this what you are looking for?" he asked, as I stared at the names, the numbers, and especially at the face of a man my age, new to a country he'd soon call home.

"Yes, this is it. This is it."

China had always been foreign to me. Removed from the land of my ancestors for five generations, I only saw China through the eyes of others. Kung-fu fighting commie red laundrymen drowning their baby daughters as the tanks rolled on! And on top of that, No Toilets! No way! I was told to be proud of my American status, and to fear the foreign and unknown. Yet, as China opened her doors, my grandparents offered to take the family back to the homeland, I chose to stay, safe in the cool comfort of home. I listened passively to the wondrous stories they brought home, and again remained safe in the cradle of the Gold Mountain as the extended family once again ventured a few years later into the Orient that was not a mystery to them, but only to me.

Yet, as the years passed, I slowly began my own exploration. Chinese and

Asian American classes at the university helped show me Asian roles in America. I began to take pride in my grandparents, who persevered through the hardships of the times, particularly American racism, and gained strength to venture out into the Asian American community, working for the rights of fellow Asian Americans. But China, China was still foreign.

I don't speak their language, I don't know their customs, I don't dress like them, I DON'T LOOK LIKE THEM, I said. But it was only fear speaking. Fear of feeling lost, fear of feeling stupid, fear of feeling alone. The same fear, if it's in the eyes of the photograph of Gung Gung, I don't see it, even though I know it must be there. Yet he made it from there to here. And I can make it from here to there.

—J.O., 1991

A Toyota Coaster minibus bumps along a narrow road through the Chinese countryside, dodging potholes and bicyclists. Inside the bus is a group of ten Chinese Americans, some peering out at the rice fields and water buffaloes, some napping, others listening to music or chatting. Although they are of Chinese ancestry like those they pass in the hot July sun outside their air-conditioned bus, they do not fit easily into this landscape. They wear shorts and T-shirts, hold cameras and tape recorders, and move around as a collective unit. These behaviors, and the newness and excitement with which they appear to experience their surroundings, would tell an observer that they are not locals, even if they could not be heard chatting with one another in English.

The bus constitutes a self-contained, mobile world—a comfort zone in an unfamiliar place for the Chinese American visitors, most of whom are setting foot in China for the first time. They have come to tour their ancestral villages and to attend a festival for Chinese youth from overseas sponsored by the PRC government. Accompanying the group is a Chinese American trip leader who is fluent in Mandarin, Cantonese, and a number of village dialects. He is there to negotiate the logistics of their trip, and he also serves as a cultural broker of sorts who helps interpret for them what they see and hear in the villages. He coaches them in proper etiquette for official banquets, makes sure no one loses his or her passport, teaches them how to *bai san* (pay respects at one's ancestors' graves),[1] and helps them ask relatives and other local villages about their family history and genealogy. Also on the bus are two guides and a driver whom the group respectfully addresses as *sifu* (md. *shifu*) (master) because he is a master of driving and vehicle repair, the leader tells them. One Chinese guide, who accompanies

Pearl River Delta village scene.

the group throughout their two-week journey around the Pearl River Delta area, is from the Guangdong Provincial Office of Overseas Chinese Affairs (Qiao Ban), the office that is sponsoring the China portion of the trip. The other guide (a different person in every region) is from the China Travel Service, China's official travel agency, and is there to coordinate food, lodging, and other local logistics. The group's two weeks in China are spent participating in a seemingly endless series of briefings by local officials, tours to local parks and temples, banquets, shopping trips, and bus rides. Village visits, however, are the highlights of the trip. Although similar in format in each village, they are emotionally intense as participants meet relatives or friends of the family, see ancestral homes, find genealogy books, and become the center of attention for local officials welcoming them "home."[2]

The group's anticipation builds as each participant's turn arrives to visit their ancestral village. Will they be able to locate it? Will any relatives or people who remember the family be present? Will the ancestral house still be standing? Like tourists, they spend little time in the villages and must be introduced to the people and places there, experiencing them through the mediation of their Chinese and Chinese American guides. They record their experiences through photographs to share with family and friends and to commemorate their presence in these places. For most, their visit to China is brief but highly significant. Although the village experience may remain an important moment in their lives, it will be more as a symbolic connection to ancestral heritage, reformulated through recollections, than as a place in which they will continue to participate over time.

In one sense, these Chinese Americans are closely linked to their origins in the Pearl River Delta region of Guangdong through ties of history and genealogy. Indeed, until a generation or two ago, some members of their extended families likely had very intimate ties to the village, either having lived there themselves or having had close connections to someone there. However, the connections of these Chinese Americans are significantly different from those that characterize the relations of first-generation immigrants with their homelands. The ties of immigrant generations are based on affective sentiments, obligations derived from social relationships and memories developed from firsthand experience in these places. Those of Chinese Americans born and raised in the United States are based on images of China and ancestral villages constructed from afar. They have not participated in the continuous back-and-forth movement between China and the United States characteristic of earlier generations. They are also different from contemporary Hong Kong elites who easily and regularly cross the Pacific on jet planes (Ong 1999; Mitchell 1996). Unlike return migrants, they do not visit China to see familiar people and places. Their reasons for traveling to China are quite specific—they hope to (re)connect to the rural China of the past that their parents, grandparents, or great-grandparents left, a place to which they never have been but are attached to through historical and genealogical connections.

The relationship between Chinese Americans and China over the past fifty years has transformed from one that fit many of the characteristics of a transnational community to the less cohesive and perhaps more complex one we see here. A relationship that was once marked by continuous back-and-forth travel and communication or, more important, shared social interests and a sense of community, has evolved into one in which a shared past may be the only common denominator.[3] The summer culture camps that will be introduced in this chapter (and the Youth Festival that brings these camps together that will be discussed in chapter 5) represent intentional efforts from both sides to bring together two parts of a population that once were intimately linked through transnational ties. These events take place in the wake of the Open Policy and economic reform of the early 1980s, during which China reopened to the outside world after decades of socialist experimentation. The camps and festivals are significant in that they are based on the Chinese government's assumptions that Chinese identities, and indeed ties to the land of China itself, are derived from racial and historical origins in China. The myth of common origins provides raw material for a politics of cultural citizenship, Chineseness, and place in both the United States and China. An examination of these camps provides a basis for a question that is central to this book: How are these assumptions about Chineseness challenged by both Chinese and Chinese American participants within forums such as the Youth Festival that were originally based on these very ideas of common origins? How do these differing interpretations of and efforts to shape Chineseness emerge from within the broader context of the Open Policy, economic reforms in China, and the changing transnational relations between Chinese Americans and China? My fieldwork in China in 1993 and 1995 shows that ideas of roots and nativeness are also changing in complex ways in the wake of the Open Policy. Mainland Chinese, especially in the coastal south, increasingly have opportunities to move within China and to have contact with overseas Chinese coming to invest in or visit China. Official PRC government rhetoric, which has a long historical precedent, calls on overseas Chinese to return to build the nation (*jianshi zuguo*) out of patriotism and love for their hometowns. At the same time, sentimental ties to native places that are assumed on behalf of the Chinese abroad are rapidly changing for both Chinese Americans and mainland Chinese.

I begin here by discussing Guangdong as a historically transnational area from which emigrant Chinese communities in the United States originated. Relations between Chinese communities abroad and mainland China have focused on native place, or hometown, as the point of attachment to China. The centrality of native-place identities to Chinese both in China and abroad provides a background to Chinese government policies that link the love of overseas Chinese for their hometowns to love of the nation. These connections were key to turn-of-the-century nationalist activities in which Chinese overseas played a key role. However, the relationship between overseas Chinese and China has changed over time. And while in the wake of the Open Policy and economic reform the Chinese government has invoked a "politics of native roots" to once again call on the Chinese abroad to invest in China, the sentiments of the Chinese abroad toward these places have changed. American-born Chinese Americans may be interested in finding out about their ancestral villages in China, but their involvement in them, and in Chinese nation-building, contrasts with that of previous generations. At the same time, mainland Chinese are beginning to distinguish between ways that various types of overseas Chinese (from Taiwanese investors to Chinese Americans) relate to their hometowns, while their own views toward their places of origin are changing.

Whereas native-place connections previously were a building block for all social relations in China and a focus for sentiments of rootedness and familial linkages, such connections are becoming increasingly abstract for mainland Chinese. Yet at a basic level, finding roots in one's ancestral village in China is understood by mainland Chinese, both officials and folk alike, as a goal that all Chinese abroad must certainly yearn to fulfill. The Chinese abroad are expected to hold steadfast to these linkages, which represent perhaps their only remaining connection to China. The Summer Camps and Youth Festival represent collaborative efforts between the mainland Chinese government and organizations abroad to facilitate Chinese American visits to their ancestral villages in the wake of the Open Policy. While they are the end product of historical connections between Chinese Americans and Guangdong Province, they are also the basis for the negotiation of a new "relationship" built on fleeting interactions with one another.

Guangdong as Transnational

Located on China's southern coast, Guangdong Province has historically been a transnational space, defining itself in relation to both the rest of China and the outside world. The history of overseas emigration from China has been marked not by a one-way flow of migrants from China to places abroad, but by patterns of back-and-forth movement and exchange. Emigrant regions in Guangdong and destinations abroad have been linked in numerous ways, from specific ties based on familial relationships to more abstract identifications of overseas Chinese with their ancestral regions or the Chinese nation. A number of original and detailed ethnographic and historical studies on overseas Chinese emigration have focused on how the continued involvement of overseas Chinese in their native places and in nation-building efforts created communities that were transnational in scope and orientation (see Chen 2000; Glick Schiller 1999; Hsu 2000; Kuah 2000; Watson 1975). As these scholars have shown, transnational perspectives on Chinese emigration and immigration are central to understanding processes of community formation and change. These linkages shaped migrants' social worlds, which extended beyond everyday face-to-face interactions.

The majority of emigrants to the United States from the mid-1800s until the 1960s originated from the Pearl River Delta area of Guangdong Province. This region, marked roughly by a triangle between the former British colony of Hong Kong, Guangzhou (Canton), and Macao, is dotted with *qiao xiang*, hometowns of Chinese who have gone abroad. Most U.S. Chinatowns have historically been dominated by groups from areas of the Pearl

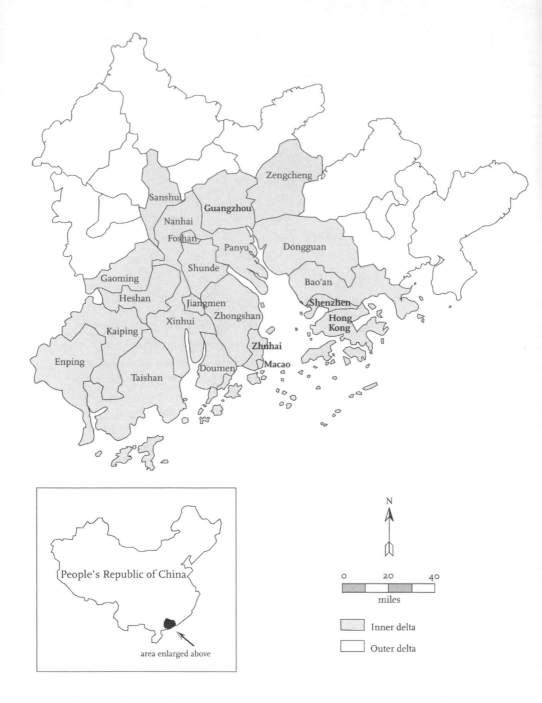

The Pearl River Delta area, showing Guangdong Province, Hong Kong, and Macao.

River Delta, including Sei Yup (Si Yi), Sam Yup (San Yi), and Jungsan (Zhongshan). Emigrants (the majority male) from China maintained ties and loyalties to their native villages in a number of ways. They made return visits to marry and father children, sent remittances, engaged in village affairs from afar, and maintained an orientation to China during their absences. In part because their options abroad were limited, emigrants endeavored to return "home" to retire and to eventually be buried in their native soil. They read local gazetteers (*qiaokan*) published by their native districts in China, which kept them updated on events at home, and they included the population abroad as part of their social world (Hsu 2000). They measured their status and success by how much they were able to earn in the United States and bring back to China to provide for their families. Legends of the United States as the Gold Mountain were fostered by returning immigrants laden with money and gifts. Unbeknownst to their relatives and friends in China, however, they had labored intensely and sacrificed greatly for these things.

But while these early immigrants maintained ties to China, they also constructed new relationships in the United States. Native place (*tongxiang hui*) and surname associations (*huiguan*) provided a means both for maintaining connections to China and for organizing social, cultural, and political life where Chinese emigrants resided. These interests were intimately linked—the Chinese abroad viewed their futures as tied to the national strength of China, which would determine their ability to make money and live well in America and to eventually return to their native regions to retire. Affective and political ties to native places formed the basis for connections that turn-of-the-century Chinese nationalists constructed between love for the native place and love of the nation. Building on native-place ties, reformers and revolutionaries at the turn of the twentieth century appealed to overseas Chinese on the basis of their concern for issues affecting their hometown and kin. They tapped ties to ancestral villages as symbols for nationalist construction that elevated the emigrants' affective sentiments for people and places to signifiers of racial and cultural ties to the nation. Love for the native place formed the building blocks for nationalism on the mainland.

The example of the Chinese Hand Laundry Association (CHLA) in New York illustrates the emergence of Chinese American identities that remained tied to the fate of the motherland. The CHLA was a Chinese American grass-roots organization founded in 1933 that grew out of traditional "district/ clan/family institutions, as well as clannish perceptions and ideas," and it used "traditional" clan, town/village, and *gongsifang* (corporate) connections to solicit participants (Yu 1992: 41).[4] Its leaders rallied members to become involved in a "new form of overseas Chinese nationalism" that was both a product of the laundryowners' experiences in the United States and of the complex and changing relations between China and the United States. These activities signified the members' emerging consciousness as Chinese Americans whose fate in the United States remained tied to activities in China. The organization's activities centered on the struggle for a better life in America, connecting China's weak position internationally and its undemocratic politics internally to the powerless situation of the Chinese abroad. Their campaign to support China in the war against Japan was named "To save China, to save ourselves" (*Jiu Guo, Zi Jiu*), an indication of how closely connected they saw their own fate abroad and that of the motherland. Their politics also addressed the power monopoly of the Chinese Consolidated Benevolent Association in Chinatown, supported by the KMT (Guomindang),[5] by drawing on events in China to support their struggle. The political involvement of Chinese laundryowners in the CHLA represents both a new form of overseas Chinese nationalism and a new consciousness as Chinese Americans.[6]

Native Place in China:
Transformation of a Transnational Relationship

Native-place ties, which transcended national boundaries to become central to the organization of emigrant communities, have historically been at the root of social organization within China. Native place[7] has traditionally referred to the particular village or region where one's ancestors originated. It signifies not only the physical place itself but also the deep attachments to the land, customs, and people from that place that are forged through generations of shared ancestry and history. It is through these bonds and sentiments, signified by genealogical connections to the ancestors buried there as well as contact with the soil and water, that space is turned into place.[8] Ties to native place are inherited, so that even immigrants to other parts of China would still claim their grandfather's native place as their own place of origin, even if they had never been there. As James Watson observes in the context of the New Territories area of Hong Kong, "Native place" (*heung ha*) holds great significance as "an individual's home district or village somewhere in China. . . . The term has very strong psychological connotations relative to security and kinship" (1975: 129).[9] Local customs, cooking styles, and local products become markers of identity and ethnicity for both those who have left their native place and those who continue to live there.[10]

Although native, or ancestral, places have historically been a central part of Chinese identities, both within mainland China and abroad, what do native places in China mean to people who have never lived in them and who do not possess the affective ties that come from having spent time in them? What is their significance for those who may no longer feel that these places are especially relevant or familiar to them? How can relationships to these places be crafted and taught? Furthermore, why do Chinese Americans want to learn about them and how does the state encourage this?

As children or grandchildren of immigrants, most Chinese Americans are a generation or more removed from villages in the Guangdong countryside, their families having taken often circuitous routes through Hong Kong, Southeast Asia, or Latin America before arriving in the United States. Demographic changes have occurred in the Chinese American community, as it has transitioned from one shaped by the limitations of legal exclusion,[11] to one composed of families with second-generation children, and to the third generation and beyond. At the same time, new immigration after 1965 has greatly diversified the Chinese population in America in terms of class background and region of origin (Hing 1993), bringing in immigrants from different parts of the mainland, Taiwan, Hong Kong, and other parts of the diaspora. As the second and third generations of primarily Cantonese origin gained middle-class economic stability, they moved out of Chinatown into other parts of the city and into the suburbs. Thus, many American-born Chinese Americans have learned about China only second hand through family stories or media and popular culture images. For them, China is at the same time a distant and foreign place and a place to which they have a connection. In this sense, ideas about China that come across in a highly mediated fashion are of central importance to the ways that Chinese Americans perceive their Chineseness. For most interns in the In Search of Roots program, the media, in the form of news reports about events in China, U.S. government policy toward China, and movies portraying China have shaped their knowledge, however incomplete, about China.

Huayi (descendants of overseas Chinese) are increasingly "able to distinguish between Chinese culture and the Chinese state and may identify with the culture and not the Chinese regime" (Wang 1991: 154). Many overseas Chinese identify with China's glorious history and their hometowns rather than dealing with political issues. For many young overseas Chinese, ties to China carry little emotional or practical importance, and personal identity may only partly involve identification as Chinese (Siu 1993: 33). They distinguish between "cultural roots and citizenship" (34). Many Chinese overseas, removed from mainland China by time and cultural distance visit China without a desire to find their ancestral villages

(Tien 1958: 53). For many Chinese Americans, Beijing (or sometimes Taiwan) represents the essence of Chinese civilization. They may identify more with the Great Wall than with their native villages. Images of China come in packaged representations through the media, history books, and documentaries. This phenomenon is represented in overseas Chinese tourism, which combines an interest in general Chinese history with a tenuous connection to home villages. Most visits to the mainland, organized by foreign travel agencies within Chinese communities abroad, involve a tour of the major historical sites and famous cities in China, most often followed by a trip to the native village.

Therefore, although visits by Chinese Americans to their ancestral villages are the focus of this book, it is not because Chinese Americans must go there to find out who they really are. Rather, it is through their experiences in China that Chinese Americans reevaluate and reframe their ideas about Chineseness in relation to their identities as Chinese Americans. As I will discuss later, it is through interaction with their places of ancestral origin in China that Chinese Americans remake these places into transnational spaces connecting the United States and China (and other locations). These experiences become reference points for Chinese American identities based on U.S. soil.[12] Chinese American roots-searching trips to China must be viewed within a multilayered political and historical context, and as more of a reterritorialization than a return to a territory. As Liisa Malkki has observed: "Notions of nativeness and native places become very complex as more and more people identify themselves or are categorized in reference to deterritorialized 'homelands,' 'cultures,' and 'origins'" (1997: 52). Relationships to places in China do not necessarily have to emerge from having lived in them. Ideas of place can be transformed from afar from concrete notions of villages to abstract notions of nation (Bisharat 1997), or they can be overlaid as geographies to tame an unfamiliar and hostile environment (Leonard 1997). Even from a distance, China remains relevant to Chinese Americans in numerous ways as a powerful influence shaping their identities.

The Open Policy and the Politics of Native Roots

The genesis of the Summer Camp programs reflects the mutual, but at times conflicting, interests of Chinese Americans and the mainland Chinese government in providing Chinese Americans with an opportunity to visit China. These programs must be understood within the context of the Open Policy and economic reform, the "politics of native roots," and historical and familial transnational connections between Chinese Americans and China. For the Chinese Americans who participate in the In Search of Roots program through the Chinese Culture Center in San Francisco, these programs represent an opportunity to explore family history and genealogy, to visit their ancestral homeland, and to engage in identity exploration along with other Chinese Americans. For the Chinese government, the programs and the Youth Festival that brings them together are an opportunity to reconnect with generations of Chinese people born outside of China. The importance of this connection stems in part from a longstanding belief that people of Chinese descent desire to remain connected to China, and in part from the government's hope that these sentiments can fuel nation-building projects in the near future.

Guangdong Province has spearheaded the economic reforms that have made China one of the fastest-growing economies in the world. Since Deng Xiaoping's implementation of economic reforms and the Open Policy in 1978, the province has undergone dramatic changes in all sectors. Guangdong became known as the *nandamen*, the southern door to China, open to new ideas and welcoming capital from overseas investors, especially from overseas Chinese. Its physical proximity and cultural ties to nearby Hong Kong led to the government's decision to open three Special Economic Zones (SEZ) in the province, in Shenzhen and Zhuhai in 1978 and in Shantou in 1980. These SEZs have been the centers of market reforms, infrastructure building, and foreign investment (stimulated through an incentive system) (Yeung and Chu 1994).[13]

The Open Policy once again put Guangdong, the ancestral region of most pre-1965 Chinese emigrants, at the center of China's transnational relations with the outside world. As China's modernist vision shifts from the center of the nation to the coastal areas, Guangdong resumed its historical status as "a diverse, rich, open, and vibrant region" (Siu 1993: 23). In recent years the Maoist nationalist narrative privileging the Han north has given way to the recognition of multiple centers and alternative histories. The Maoist project is now seen as flawed in its insularity and lack of openness to the outside world (Friedman 1994: 69).[14] Guangdong has become the model for a new national culture, replacing the northern Maoist nationalist narrative with a future-looking, south-centered vision (Friedman 1994: 85; White and Cheng 1993). Southern (Guangdong) Chinese are seen as having fled poverty and settled abroad, creating connections to a Chinese diaspora throughout the world. They are therefore viewed as outward-looking and open to the world, adept at negotiating capitalist market forces and with a non-Chinese world.

A central focus of China's economic reform is encouraging investment from the Chinese abroad to build a new nation. The opening of China's doors has created fertile ground for what Helen Siu calls the "politics of native roots" (1993: 32) in which the Chinese government appeals to the patriotic and nostalgic sentiments of overseas Chinese to help build their motherland through investment in their home regions. These politics involve the Chinese government's expectation that the cultural and racial identities of overseas Chinese will manifest themselves through "political commitment" and "patriotism." Their commitment, in the minds of mainland Chinese officials, should be "based on primordial sentiments and in the name of national unity, territorial bond, and family pride" (Siu 1993: 32) and demonstrated through their investment in China. The Chinese government's Office of Overseas Chinese Affairs (Huaqiao Shiwu Ban) concentrates its efforts on building propaganda that draws on the hometown sentiments (*xiang qing*) of the overseas Chinese who they assume certainly must miss their hometowns. These politics are based on assumptions that Chinese outside of China remain essentially Chinese (*huaren*) and that they retain ties to the Chinese nation and their native soil. Such views have been shaped through PRC policy toward overseas Chinese that has historically been intertwined with Chinese nationalist (Fitzgerald 1972) and racial (Dikotter 1992) discourse, foreign policy, and economic development.

These activities must be contextualized within the tumultuous history of overseas Chinese affairs in China, a politics that has never fully reflected a sophisticated understanding of the diversity of Chinese populations outside of China and that has viewed national consciousness as arising naturally out of Chinese racial heritage. As China emerged from its socialist isolation in the early 1980s, it was faced with the challenge of reaching out once more to an overseas population that had good reason to mistrust the PRC government. The government's policy toward overseas Chinese throughout its years of Communist rule had been far from consistent. At times, overseas Chinese and their relatives had been brutally persecuted (during the land reform campaign and the Cultural Revolution), but at other times overseas remittances and other forms of aid were quietly welcomed and accepted by the government and relatives. Following the end of the Cultural Revolution, overseas connections (including Hong Kong) were once again allowed by the government and cherished by families as potential escape routes from China and as channels for access to foreign consumer goods. The best way for the PRC to resolve the contradictions between its past and present economic policy and its past and present treatment of the overseas Chinese was to emphasize cultural and racial heritage over political belief.[15]

Chineseness as Race

Ideas about Chineseness as a racial form of identification extending beyond the boundaries of the nation-state (in fact, predating it) have allowed for the existence of a category of people of Chinese descent who no longer live on Chinese soil but who are still considered to be racially Chinese (*hua*). Dikotter (1992) describes a clear evolution of the discourse of race in China from the fifteenth century to the present, culminating in the ideology of race as nation. Race and national identity were the products of intellectual and political ideologies constructed in opposition to the foreign "other." The ideology of race developed in multiple stages, involving the creation of categories of purity symbolized through connections based on shared heritage (lineage [*zu*]) and blood. The color yellow was used to represent a "racial" (biological) cohesiveness that would subsume regional alliances in the face of foreign aggression. The equation of "race" and nation came with China's transformation from empire to nation (1911), and encompassed both hereditary and territorial components as the nation was imagined as descended from a common ancestor and living in a shared territory. Han Chinese, the majority race (*da minzu zhuyi*), were descendants of the Yellow Emperor Huang di, a mythical ancestor who was supposed to have existed between 2697 and 2597 B.C., and nationalism was reframed as a question of national preservation because love for one's country was equated with love for one's race (*ai zhong ai guo*).

Through these processes of racialization, black eyes and yellow skin became the racial markers of Han Chinese, whether on the mainland or abroad. This racial discourse has permeated all levels of Chinese society, from government propaganda to folk views of Chineseness. In the numerous fieldwork interviews that I conducted with mainland Chinese regarding their attitudes toward the Chinese abroad, these two physical characteristics were used time and time again in both official and informal discussions to explain why overseas Chinese would wish to return to China, and what, if nothing else, remained essentially Chinese about them. Derived from these physical characteristics were patriotic sentiments, attachment to one's native place (even if one had never been there, one should wish to go), and respect for Confucian values.

For example, having black hair and yellow skin was cited as a reason that tennis player Michael Chang was thought to love China, and it was often the reason that people who felt he did not love China thought he should. I was often reminded that I myself possessed these characteristics, as a way for others to assure themselves (and perhaps me) that I was indeed Chinese, even though I came from America. One student, asked to draw a picture of me on the chalkboard as part of a game, drew a rough stick figure with yellow chalk, explaining "You see, Andrea is Chinese, so she has yellow skin and black hair."

The Chinese Abroad and China

The emergence of the Summer Camps programs, and later, the Youth Festival, which represents a ritualized celebration of overseas Chinese youth visiting China, mark an effort by the Chinese government to reconnect with younger generations of Chinese descent that is in many ways an extension of other programs geared toward overseas Chinese investors. These programs work from the underlying assumption that visitors of Chinese descent would feel pride in China's recent economic growth and a responsibility to help further that growth in their "home" regions. So while the Chinese Americans who participate in the Summer Camps and Youth Festival are not necessarily considered representative of the capitalist classes of overseas Chinese who invest heavily in China, the PRC assumes that Chinese youth abroad are willing to participate in the building of their motherland. The PRC no longer refers to people of Chinese descent living outside of China as "overseas Chinese" (*huaqiao*) a term that in the past has caused trouble for Chinese populations abroad because of the implications it carries about political loyalty to China. But the PRC still presumes that the racial and cultural heritage of overseas Chinese links them to China in certain irrevocable ways.[16] These ways after often discussed in Chinese government rhetoric in terms of affective ties and yearning for home territories expressed in metaphors tying physical properties of the land—its soil and water—to characteristics that are somehow both physically and emotionally ingrained in the migrant and in their descendents. Chinese government officials believe that Chinese loyalty to native place, and therefore to the Chinese motherland/nation, is embodied in Chinese Americans through their "racial" heritage, but in a latent form that must be extracted through exposure to the traditional culture and land of their ancestors.

Newspaper and television reports construct overseas Chinese as returning sons to a newly strengthened mother, resuming age-old links of blood, history, and territory. But in appealing to native roots, the government is walking a fine line by claiming the loyalties of Chinese abroad who are no longer citizens of China. The political changes that have occurred in China, especially since 1949, have politicized the concept of "Chineseness" so that Chinese identity is no longer only a question of the inheritance or the preservation of tradition but also of political ideology and self-definition. The participation by overseas Chinese in the social, political, and economic affairs of their motherland is seen by the mainland government as a demonstration of nationalistic feelings. However, overseas Chinese nationalism is multifaceted and must be distinguished from and compared to other forms of identification as Chinese, both concrete and abstract, to be fully understood. Current overseas Chinese involvement in Chinese politics and the economy must be examined as more than a straightforward expression of nationalistic loyalty or hometown feelings. Although rhetoric used by the PRC may appeal to the overseas Chinese on this basis, it is necessary to make a distinction between ethnic and nationalistic sentiments. As the Chinese government has relaxed its extraterritorial rule, it is now possible to identify in a cultural sense as Chinese outside of China without having to take a stand on politics. Many overseas connections with China are rooted in localized, kin-based connections that have more to do with kinship relations, often fictive, than nationalism. And for some Chinese populations abroad, the desire for profit or the exploration of personal identities often outweighs any "patriotic sentiments or grand political schemes" (Siu 1993: 32).

At the same time, the native-place organizations of Chinese abroad continue to work to maintain ties between overseas Chinese and their hometowns (*gu xiang*) on the mainland, in both concrete and more emotional senses. Elizabeth Sinn's study of hometown organizations in Hong Kong finds this sentiment to be a strong factor for motivating overseas contributions. Organizations work on the basis of family ties, land ownership, business connections, "sentimental attachments," and "native-place consciousness" when sponsoring disaster relief and repatriation efforts, or to facilitate the communication of information (1992: 8). In addition to fostering the continuity of these links, these societies also play important roles in maintaining the solidarity of hometown mates (*tongxiangren*) outside of China. These organizations have undergone a revival with China's Open Policy and the subsequent renewed activity of the Qiao Ban and local overseas Chinese organizations at the hometown level. Old propaganda slogans have been revived and modified overseas, such as "*Ai xiang, ai guo; jian xiang, jian guo*" (Love the hometown, love the country; build the hometown, build the country) and "*Zhigen xiang gong, xinxi guxiang*" (Plant roots in Hong Kong, tie the heart to the home region) (Sinn 1992: 17; see also Kuah 2000).

The Open Policy marked not only the loosening of economic policy and the development of local industries but also the revival of lineage ties that had been attenuated during the years of Communist rule. Overseas Chinese have returned to renew these ties and also to claim property returned to them by the government to rectify its unjust removal during the land reform campaign. According to Yuen-Fong Woon in her study of the Guan lineage of Kaiping County, Guangdong Province, policy reforms also allowed for the revival of traditions that had been castigated as feudal during the Cultural Revolution of the recent past, as long as they lead toward economic growth and do not challenge governmental controls (1989). The partial revival of lineage institutions was an unintended consequence of economic reforms and modernization campaigns initiated by the Chinese Communist Party (CCP). In their attempts to revive the pre-Communist glory of the complex lineage system that had organized the Guan since the seventeenth century, the overseas Guan contributed to the building of schools, renovations, and a Guan lineage library. In its present revived form, the lineage organization is nonlocalized and without the hierarchy that marked its older forms.

Changing Attitudes toward Native Place in China

Contemporary comments by mainland Chinese about the importance of native place to overseas Chinese continue to reflect ideas about roots as heredity. Overseas attachments to native places are viewed as deriving from a combination of territorial, racial, and national loyalties. As a Chinese American doing research in China on mainland Chinese folk attitudes toward the Chinese abroad, I experienced many of these ideas firsthand and I repeatedly saw these concepts at work through my fieldwork. While the ways in which overseas Chinese are viewed in relation to their native places have undoubtedly been shaped by official discourses on overseas Chinese patriotism, they also represent a historical formation built on the long tradition of emigration as a way of life in south China. The pattern of return migration that characterized emigrant life was based on the idea that migration abroad was a temporary venture done to earn foreign capital. The ultimate goal of these migrants was to return to their families wealthy, and to live out the rest of their lives in China. Mainland Chinese understand Chinese American visits to China according to these historical precedents. Even overseas Chinese who had never before set foot in China were asked if this was the first time they had "returned" to China (c. *daihyat chi fanlaih*; md. *diyici huilai*). People in China would ask me (and other Chinese Americans) the name of my "hometown" (c. *heung ha*; md. *xiangxia*), referring to the ancestral village in China from which my grandparents had emigrated in the 1920s. Folk sayings, such as *xungen* (c. *chahm gan*), literally "searching for roots," and *luo ye gui gen* (c. *lok yip gwai gan*) "the falling leaf returns to its roots," were common ways for mainland Chinese to explain why

Chinese American visitors were in China. Some Chinese villages seemed to view personhood itself as being derived from knowing one's native place. In one emigrant village in the Zhongshan region of the Pearl River Delta, the family I interviewed used the saying "The first generation is a man, the second generation is a ghost" (c. *Dai yat doi haih yahn, daihyih doi haih gwai*; md. *Diyi dai shi ren, dier dai shi guei*).

However, at a time when government narratives are further crystallizing the concept of native place for patriotic overseas Chinese to identify with mainland China, in mainland China concepts of native place, and the places themselves, are rapidly changing. In the past, the expression of hometown sentiment (*xiang qing*) was a natural, almost obligatory expression of where one's identity was rooted. Nostalgia for one's native place represented a longing for familiar customs, foods, and of course, family. Research in Shenzhen, a Special Economic Zone of immigrants from all parts of China, indicates that people's sense of rootedness and locality are changing as they become more mobile. Interviews I conducted during fieldwork in 1995 show that many urban-born internal migrants living in the southern area of Guangdong Province (Shenzhen and Guangzhou) had never been to their native villages where their parents or grandparents had been born and raised. Many people expressed little interest in visiting these villages, which they saw as poor and backward (*luo hou*). And although Chinese identity cards list native place (*zuji*) and it remains a factor in determining legal residence, increasing internal immigration in China to cities and coastal areas is changing the relationship between people and their native places. In contrast I learned of other immigrants who had more recently moved from inland China, and they indicated a desire to maintain ties with their home villages. These processes were facilitated by advances in telephone service that allowed them to stay in touch with their home villages from a distance. They were able to gain new perspectives on their regions of origin from seeing them discussed in various media, especially on Hong Kong television.[17]

The definitions and differentiations made by many younger Chinese, especially urban dwellers, between the terms for native place and village of origin (*zuji, jiguan, jiaxiang, guxiang*) lack rigor. Today, *jiguan* continues to carry bureaucratic connotations and is used when filling out official forms. It can be conceptually distinguished from *jiaxiang* and *guxiang*, which imply a more immediate sense of connection to the place where one's father or grandfather was born and, often, raised. However, a high school teacher in Shenzhen told me that his students, most of whom had parents who were born and raised outside the Special Economic Zone, were usually confused about the location of their *jiguan*. He found that he usually had to check their previous records to make sure they were consistent with what had been written down. Many adult informants, when questioned about the differences between the four terms, gave answers that conflicted with those given by other informants, or they consulted others in the group because they were not sure of the answer.

In spoken conversation, one's *jiaxiang* or *guxiang* is often used as a way of identifying and contextualizing another Chinese individual. These more informal terms are most often used in such situations over the more formal *jiguan*. But although differentiated in usage, they are less clearly differentiated as concepts. While most informants can name a *jiaxiang*, the place they name may be determined by a different criteria than that of another person. Some people may refer to their birthplace, others to where they grew up, and still others to their father's birthplace. Depending on the context, they may cite places that vary in size from village to county to province. At the same time, there seems to be a double standard at work. While it is reasonable for mainland Chinese to no longer seek feudal attachments to ancestral places in China, it is understandable, and perhaps expected, for overseas Chinese to need to search for their roots in this way. However, as will be seen later, even these conceptions are becoming more complex.

Summer Camps

In the past, the sentiments of overseas Chinese toward their hometowns in China have been elevated to an almost mythical level within mainland Chinese discourses, both folk and political. An overseas Chinese visiting his or her ancestral village must certainly be searching for ancestral roots (*xungen*). Sending money to relatives or making charitable contributions to the native village were acts of national construction, demonstrating strong conceptions of nation and hometown. However, the views of mainland Chinese toward roots searching on the part of the Chinese abroad deserves further exploration. This context is necessary to understand how the politics of native roots is manifested in the beliefs and actions of mainland Chinese, both officials and nonofficials. It is also important to provide a perspective on how mainland Chinese understand the Summer Camps. As my fieldwork in China demonstrates, the changing attitudes of mainland Chinese toward overseas Chinese and their native places in China form the context for some of the contradictions that emerge within the Summer Camps and the Youth Festival. The fieldwork interviews that I conducted in 1995 show that mainland Chinese were beginning to distinguish in new ways between different types of overseas Chinese and the variety of ways that they identify with China. In the wake of the Open Policy, both those mainland Chinese involved in overseas Chinese affairs and those who have had informal contact with Chinese visiting from abroad have gained insight into the motivations of Chinese overseas for investing or donating (if at all) to their ancestral villages. They have increasingly come into contact with generations of overseas Chinese descent who become involved in China out of convenience rather than sentiment. Preexisting ideas about patriotic overseas Chinese increasingly were unfolding to reveal new types of relationships between overseas Chinese and their native places. In sum, the phrase "searching for roots," which appears to be universally understood by most mainland Chinese as a general concept, is quite ambiguous when it comes to describing the actual process.

Certainly, in recent years, Chinese from abroad have resumed historically rooted practices of making contributions to their hometowns that have drastically altered the lifestyles of these places. Villagers in Zhongshan County of the Pearl River Delta saw these acts as selfless and patriotic because they did not benefit the contributors directly, as far as villagers could see. They repeatedly emphasized how much they respected the overseas Chinese, who provided most of the charity in the area. In the past, donations (c. *fuk leih*) from Chinese abroad for such projects as building schools and installing running water had drastically changed the way of life in the villages. In recent years, one village built a center for the elderly with money contributed by fellow villagers living in Japan and Hong Kong. In Zhongshan, the People's Hospital and the Sun Zhongshan Memorial were both donated by overseas Chinese without apparent profit motives and for the benefit of the whole community not just their own families. To the villagers I interviewed, these public donations, for which they receive nothing in return, demonstrated that their greatest devotion was to their country.

However, there are now other types of overseas Chinese. Mr. Lau (pseudonym), a villager who has many relatives overseas, distinguished between the older generations of overseas Chinese (*lao huaqiao*) and the new overseas Chinese who left after the start of the Open Policy. The old overseas Chinese went abroad to earn money but returned to their hometowns, while the new overseas Chinese, who are mainly workers (c. *da gong jai*), place primary emphasis on making a living for their own families abroad (*sihai wei jia*). Still another type of overseas Chinese, often from Taiwan and Hong Kong, returns to invest in China primarily for profit, without any charitable motivations. Such a person may invest in a particular region for reasons more out of convenience than sentiment. Mr. Lau estimates that 70 percent of overseas money comes in the form of donations while 30 percent is for profit, thus benefiting both investors and villagers.

After the Open Policy, Mr. Lau encountered still another type of overseas Chinese—the descendants of old overseas Chinese whose ancestors left generations ago but have not had the opportunity to return. These generations of overseas Chinese understandably may not know much about their ancestral villages, but he believes they would certainly be glad to reconnect with them. He comments: "It's the advantage of the Chinese that they have Chinese tradition. The tradition of searching for roots [xungen] is psychologically rooted. Even if someone goes out for a few generations, he may have this type of thinking and can teach his children. But for many it may be unclear. Their ancestors may have gone out, but they may have not had the opportunity to return. But maybe if their children have an opportunity, they'll be happy to know where their family is."[18]

The shifts observed by Mr. Lau have also caught the interest of Chinese academics. Zhang Ying Long is a researcher affiliated with the Overseas Chinese Research Institute (Huaqiao Yanjiu Suo) at Jinan University in Guangzhou. He is particularly interested in the relationship between third- and fourth-generation overseas Chinese, such as those mentioned by Mr. Lau, and their ancestral villages. He has conducted research in emigrant villages (qiaoxiang) to try to understand how the conditions in these villages have changed over time. In the past, qiaoxiang were backward and people were forced to go abroad to make a living, yet they made contributions and sent remittances (qiaohui) back to their villages. However, newer generations of Chinese abroad are different from the old ones. Now they don't necessarily invest in their hometowns. It is not uncommon for overseas Chinese to open factories outside of their hometowns and use the profits to open schools in their hometowns. In the jiaxiang there are too many relatives who will ask you for favors, and if they work for you they won't be diligent (nuli). Of course, the main point in building a factory is to make money, but part of the reason may also be love for the hometown and love for the nation (ai xiang ai guo). After all, investors could go to other countries to open factories, but in China the culture is the same, and the language is the same.

When I mentioned to Zhang Ying Long that my great-uncle, Yi Suk Gung, wanted the family to build a home in the village, he said that perhaps the uncle was hoping to build a base to retain the family's roots and status in the village (bao liu nide jai xiangde diwei). Now, however, few overseas Chinese build houses. Some of those who continue to invest in their villages are those who went abroad after the Open Policy and economic reform. These people still have attachments to friends and family there. To him it is under-standable that these generations might retain their attachments, while the descendants of previous generations might forget their hometowns. These changes are natural because people have attachments to where they live and work.

While the older generations of overseas Chinese (*lao yibei*) maintain feelings for their hometown, younger generations such as their children and grandchildren think that these places are backward and dirty. The for-mer come back to pay respects to ancestors (*bai zu xian*), build temples, or construct genealogies (*zupu*), although they often do so because they believe that flattering their ancestors will help them become rich. Younger genera-tions only return to travel or do business. Zhang Ying Long and other Chinese researchers are trying to find out what differences exist between emigrant and later generations. The third and fourth generations have for-eign education, and the American culture has influenced their behavior. If they haven't been to China, it is just an abstract concept to them. They see themselves as Americans and believe that occurrences in China don't affect them. They're more concerned with the problems in America that imme-diately affect them such as unemployment and the economy.

To address this issue, the Chinese government has created the Summer Camp programs (*xia ling ning*) to introduce Chinese youth to their home-towns. These programs came into existence because for various reasons the parents of these youths are not able to take them back to China themselves. Their purpose is to help foster a feeling for the hometown and an under-standing of Chinese culture. While Zhang Ying Long understands that some people may view the camps as a form of propaganda, he emphasizes that it is also traditional Chinese thinking that one should not forget one's *jia xiang*.

Mr. Xin, a city-level Qiao Ban official in Shenzhen, contextualized the Summer Camps within the broader history of overseas Chinese affairs. Policies toward overseas Chinese have changed over the years. At first the goal of the Qiao Ban was to help the Chinese abroad organize themselves, as well as to aid those who wanted to return to China to make donations or build schools—however, these activities stopped during the Cultural Revolu-tion. Now the bureau's goal is to promote investment. The Summer Camp programs are related to this goal, but only as part of a broader, more long-term plan. According to Mr. Xin, the purpose of the Summer Camps is "to organize the third and fourth generation to search for roots and learn na-tional culture . . . so young overseas Chinese can know about their home country, about their motherland, and to strengthen their feelings for their country. When they grow up they can help Chinese construction as their parents did."[19] I asked whether their parents' generation actually helped with national construction, or did they only send money to their own relatives. Mr. Xin replied that sending money to one's relatives is a way of helping. If they had more money they would give it to the country. The two main purposes of the camps are to strengthen links with associations of Chinese abroad (such as *tongxiang hui*) and to strengthen the feelings of young overseas Chinese toward China to "help us absorb the overseas Chinese strength to build the country." Mr. Xin views this as a part of a long-term plan to cultivate overseas Chinese youth, citing an expression "a little stream flows long" (*xiao he chang liu*). He hopes that the visits by overseas youths to China will leave a deep impression on them, and they will keep it in their minds and come back again and again. Perhaps then eventually they will invest. Economic links are stronger than links based on feelings alone. Thus, although Mr. Xin does not expect immediate returns, he feels that eventually economic investment will result as an extension of feelings toward the hometowns. These connections only need to be fostered.

Rebecca Guan, a young mainland Chinese woman who works with a group of overseas Chinese youth attending Summer Camps, provided more insight into what the youths get out of the Summer Camp experience. She has worked with camps hosted by the Overseas Chinese School (Hua Qiao Bu Xiao) affiliated with Jinan University. The camps are organized into three periods. The summer camp runs from March to August and is attended by Chinese youth from Southeast Asia (Philippines, Thailand, Malaysia). The winter camp runs from November to January and is attended by youth from Reunion, Australia, New Zealand, Peru, Mauritius, and Tahiti. In July and August the camp hosts mainly youths from Europe and America. The camps' goal is to study Chinese culture and to visit one's hometown. Chinese youth have yellow skin and black hair, they should see how the ancestral country is. They may have heard propaganda about China and want to see if perhaps China isn't as bad as they thought. At the camps, they don't talk about politics. Rather, they talk about the ancestral village and their feelings toward it (*xiangqing*), as well as about history and how things have changed. Participants come to learn Chinese language, history and geography, kung fu, and Chinese songs. They go sightseeing to the Seventy-Two Martyrs Monument and the Sun Yat Sen Memorial. And although the summer camps can't encourage every Chinese American to go to China, perhaps the visiting youths will talk with their friends and family about their experiences there.

The Summer Camps and the annual Youth Festival are built on a somewhat contradictory blend of historically rooted PRC government assumptions about the sentiments that Chinese overseas hold toward their hometowns, and its recognition that these attitudes are changing. Traditionally in China, the Chinese abroad were thought to possess deeply engrained feelings toward their native places that under proper circumstances would translate into donations and investments to help better these places. Many emigrant communities have in the past been dependent on overseas remittances and have benefited from public donations that Chinese abroad have provided for them. Such actions on the part of the Chinese abroad have been viewed by both Chinese officials and lay people alike as proof of the devotion of overseas Chinese to their villages and nation. And while these feelings may be latent in some Chinese abroad who have not returned to their ancestral villages, they can certainly be fostered through education and exposure to Chinese culture and history.

The very existence of the Summer Camps and the Youth Festival signifies an awareness on the part of Chinese government officials that it has become necessary to reach out to the Chinese overseas in new ways. With increased contact with Chinese abroad after the Open Policy, officials have begun to recognize that the attitudes of the Chinese outside of China toward their ancestral villages, and therefore China as a whole, are changing. They have acknowledged that in order to reach out to generations of Chinese abroad who have had little previous exposure to China, it is necessary to implement specific policies and programs to cultivate these ties. While economic incentives and official welcomes may be sufficient to encourage some Chinese abroad to invest in building a modern China, it is necessary to start at a more basic level for *huayi*, those generations of Chinese with foreign citizenship who were born and raised abroad.

Numerous Summer Camp programs have been formed in the United States and other countries around the world since the early 1980s, focusing around activities sponsored by the mainland Chinese government.[20] They have often been compared to and no doubt have been inspired by motivations similar to those behind the Taiwanese government's programs for overseas Chinese. Taiwan has made concerted efforts to entrench itself politically in Chinese communities abroad, for which they have developed an extensive bureau of overseas Chinese affairs with massive propaganda capabilities. Part of these efforts involved the development of Summer Camps for Overseas Chinese Youth (Hai Wai Qing Nian Shu Ji Fan Guo Yan Xi Tuan), beginning in the 1970s. These camps have grown to accommodate one thousand overseas Chinese youth on three campuses.[21] The program is commonly known among Chinese Americans as the "Love Boat" program, because of the relationships that form among participants on their arrival in Taiwan (by plane, not ship) and continue throughout the six-week period. Although this program was not the central focus of my research, some of my informants had attended the Taiwan program. For many, the propaganda aspect of the program seemed overt to the point where it was not taken seriously. One individual said that it seemed odd that they were being welcomed back to Taiwan, when their ancestors had come from mainland China.

The organization of the Summer Camps in mainland China relies on various Chinese community organizations abroad to bring together groups of Chinese youth to attend activities in mainland China. In the United States and Canada these groups are most often arranged by travel agencies, performance groups, or district associations. Each group is then sponsored at a local level by units in mainland China, which host the group during its time in the country. While they vary in their agendas, most programs involve a two- to four-week summer residential stay in China, usually at a middle school or university. Participants, who range in age from the teens to the mid-twenties, learn traditional Chinese arts such as dance, calligraphy, kung fu, language, and history, and they are taken on tours of historic sights and other local attractions. Many programs now involve optional "roots" visits to ancestral villages or regions during which students are grouped by native district and are accompanied by local guides who bring them to be received by local overseas Chinese office officials.

While these programs vary in terms of background of the organizers, the focus of the activities, the selection of members, and sponsorship, they are all designed to educate Chinese Americans about "Chinese culture" outside the home. Chinese culture is represented and taught in terms of generalized and essentialized "traditions," "festivals," "art," and language. As far as Chinese government officials are concerned, the celebration of these practices, deemed "feudal" during most of the Communist era, are now encouraged on the part of Chinese from abroad. The prohibition of these ritual practices and festivals has been lifted in the climate of economic liberalization (Siu 1990; Woon 1989; Watson 1993) in an effort to lure overseas Chinese back to the mainland. In fact, this content is essential to reestablishing the connection between Chinese born and raised outside of China to their ancestral homeland. Most of these programs involve the implicit idea that visiting China, through a some sort of mystical communion with the homeland, will somehow be a step toward the completion of one's identity as an individual of Chinese descent. In other words, the camps are designed to reintroduce them to their lost heritage through exposure to "traditional" Chinese culture and arts while on Chinese soil. For example, the pamphlet advertising the 1994 Zhongshan City Chinese American Youth Language and Cultural program reads:

> This study tour is a summer program for students interested in studying Chinese language (Mandarin) and observing and experiencing present day social and economic conditions in the fast-growing Guangdong Province of the People's Republic of China.
>
> Sponsors: Overseas Chinese Affairs of Zhongshan City; Overseas Chinese Affairs Office of Guangzhou; Overseas Chinese Affairs Office of Jiangmen City; New China Education Foundation, USA.
>
> Open to Chinese American students in the United States and Canada, 18–28, limited to 100 students.
>
> Curriculum: Mandarin language classes five days a weeks and lecture series on China (culture, arts, history, etc.). In addition there will be day field trips to nearby sites and weekend field trips to other areas in the Province (i.e. Guangzhou, Zhuhai). Optional "Roots" visits to ancestral villages in or near Zhongshan City at the student's own expense—pending on study schedule.[22]

As will be seen later, while the In Search of Roots program fits this general format, it also departs from it in significant ways.

• • •

Relations between Chinese Americans and their ancestral homeland have been renewed within the context of a changed world economy and the globalization of capital. Pacific Rim economic growth, a new southern-centered nationalist narrative (Friedman 1994), increased flows of migrant workers and the possibilities of flexible citizenship (Ong 1993) have redefined the space of Guangdong. This newly defined space stretches beyond the boundaries of the province to encompass not only changing relations with the Chinese abroad, but also shifting relations between Guangdong's residents on the mainland and migrant laborers from the north. Thus, multiple ironies emerge within this space as visiting overseas Chinese, with their capital and mobility, are able to easily recover their ancestral places, as Guangdong residents become increasingly less interested in them, and as poor rural migrants from inland China are forced to leave their hometowns to come to Guangdong and other large cities in China. This "floating population" (Solinger 1999; Zhang 2001) represents a new type of migrant that is a casualty of China's most recent engagement with capitalism. Thus, in some ways they parallel the experiences of turn-of-the-twentieth-century emigrations whose journeys abroad were facilitated by an earlier form of global capitalism, yet they also differ dramatically from today's emigrants.

Earlier generations found themselves caught between legalized racial discrimination in the United States and extraterritorial rule of the Chinese nation from afar (L. Wang 1995). Today's Chinese emigrants go abroad with an increased understanding of the conditions they face in the United States. They enter a situation of anti-immigration sentiment in the context of a changing Chinese American community crosscut by differences in gender, class, country, and region of origin, and characterized by a complex and politicized racial and ethnic politics. These emigrants are also part of a revitalization of popular culture brought over by recent immigrants from Taiwan, Hong Kong, and other countries that have influenced Chinese and Asian Americans of other generations. Transnational information flows collapse space and time, allowing Chinese language channels to be broadcast in Chinese American homes. But while the emigration of many Chinese is marked by the exercise of flexible citizenship, most multigenerational Chinese Americans are staying put. They lack the connections, language skills, and incentives to participate in these back-and-forth travels, and their ability to participate in this new transnational space is therefore limited. There is increasing differentiation between these generations and others of Chinese origin in terms of divisions of class, geographic origins, generation; and between Cantonese, Taiwanese, mainlanders, FOBS (fresh off the boat), and ABCS (American-born Chinese). But multigenerational Chinese Americans are nevertheless affected by this resurgent Chinese identity. As Gupta and Ferguson (1997) observe, even people who stay in place are affected by global flows. In the case of Chinese Americans, Hong Kong popular culture, hype of "illegal" immigrants, and increasing attention paid to the East affect how they view being Chinese American.

As I discuss later, the participation of the In Search of Roots group in the Youth Festival hosted by the PRC government represents a collaborative effort on the part of both Chinese Americans and Chinese to bring Chinese Americans to China. Such events represent a type of forged transnationality (Schein 1998) through which changing relationships between Chinese Americans and China, and mainland Chinese and overseas Chinese, become evident. The Summer Camps represent forums for renegotiating meanings of Chineseness and attachments to China. However, the question remains to what extent the Summer Camps and Youth Festival are able to achieve the goals of rebuilding a relationship between mainland China and Chinese youth abroad. As I discuss in chapter 5, in its effort to focus on traditional Chinese culture (as opposed to post-Liberation China and politics) the Youth Festival format remains fixed on historically and politically entrenched ideas about Chineseness as tied to race, culture, and nation. At the same time, the China that the youth experience and are asked to support is one that on the surface no longer embodies the aspects of traditional Chinese culture with which the youth are expected to identify. In the following chapters, I discuss in further depth the contexts that shape Chinese Americans' views toward China (chapter 3) and mainland Chinese views toward overseas Chinese (chapter 4).

roots narrative)

One year ago, I never imagined I would know so much about my family history. Searching for my roots not only taught me a lot about my ancestry but enabled me to better understand myself as well. I think there exists a point in everyone's life where questions about family roots arise. Contrary to what some might argue, I don't think this experience took away from my being American. Learning about my family history was a mind-opening experience that allowed me to appreciate my heritage, which is an integral part of my Chinese American experience. Because I searched for my roots in China, I have a better understanding and appreciation for being Chinese American. . . .

Being Chinese American now means more than shopping in Chinatown and eating dim sum. It means having a better grasp of my Chinese heritage, without losing the American that will always be an integral part of me. I now know that I am not only from Fremont, California, but also from Kai Gok village, Longdu district, Zhongshan and Boloo [Buolo] district, Kaiping in the Pearl River Delta region of southern China. I have decided not to turn my back on my Chinese past but instead to learn more about it. I have decided to stop taking things for face value and to start asking questions.

—P.Y., 1995

The In Search of Roots program and the Chinese government's Summer Camps and Youth Festival appear to conceive of connections to native places in different but overlapping ways, neither of which fully takes into account the ways that relationships to native places change over time. The formation of the Summer Camp programs was in part an attempt to address what PRC officials had observed to be a lack of connection toward China on the part of generations born abroad. However, these programs are still based on the idea that Chinese loyalty to native place, and therefore to the Chinese mother-land/nation, is embodied in Chinese Americans through their "racial" heritage, in a latent form that must be extracted through exposure to the traditional culture and land of their ancestors. But, as I discuss later, it is unclear what exactly Summer Camp and Youth Festival programs accomplish in bringing Chinese Americans to visit their ancestral villages in China, or whether their effects are those desired by their Chinese organizers. At the same time, the significance of visiting China for most Chinese American participants appears to also differ from the sole emphasis on genealogy of previous Chinese American generations. As I show in this chapter, Chinese American experiences in China can only be understood in relation to how they are made meaningful within contemporary Chinese American contexts.

I interviewed Roots intern Fred Chang soon after he returned from his visit to mainland China as part of the program. He commented on what he perceived to be condescending remarks from acquaintances who discovered that he had visited China to do a family history project. "They just say, 'Oh, good,' or 'Why did you do that?' [or] 'Oh, family history, that's good.' I hate the insinuation, it's like, you've got this great epiphany now about being Chinese or something, or 'you didn't know yourself but now you do' kind of attitude. It seems a very condescending remark, because it's almost like them saying, 'I always knew who I was, but you didn't; and now you do, that's great.'"

The idea that Fred needs to search for roots implies that his cultural citizenship in the United States is questionable. It infers that he lacks a certain mooring or basis for identification until he can trace his heritage to a stable, fixed place (other than the United States) within which his identity can be recaptured. In his view, the people Fred spoke to insinuated that until he had gone to China to visit his ancestral village he could not know what it "truly" meant to be Chinese. They were also implying that one derives Chinese cultural authenticity from China, and that being able to trace his origins back to China will somehow make him a better Chinese American.

This incident, drawn from my field notes, highlights the ways Chinese American identities remain tied to notions of authenticity that are based on associations with "places of origin" in China. The perception that one needs to search for roots appears to arise out of particular social positions—those of refugee, minority, and immigrant—indicating that one is not truly at home in the place where one resides. Historically, U.S immigration laws tied to labor interests have cast Asian Americans as perpetual foreigners whose cultural roots lie outside the United States. And such ideas persist despite activism based on the idea of "claiming America," a form of Asian American cultural nationalism that emphasizes the central roles that Asian immigrants have played throughout U.S. history (Wong and Chan 1998). It is naive, however, to think that comfortable homes can be easily found in places to which one is connected through ancestral ties, but where one has never resided and has few current links. Such notions of identity place Chinese Americans in difficult positions, because they are involuntarily tied to their "places of origin" in China through exclusion from U.S. cultural citizenship, yet they are also excluded from "authentic" Chinese identities because of their cultural, physical, and temporal distance from their ancestral homes in China. This tension informs the experiences of Chinese American participants in government-sponsored roots-searching programs.

Such views of roots searching remain dependent on a return to particular, static, and cohesive places and conceptions of identity, restricting contemporary identities to particular places and times and connecting them to naturalized ideas of culture and place. They do not account for the ways people fashion relationships to the places they live, and how their conceptions of these places are continually reconfigured over time. At the same time, U.S. multicultural discourses focusing on cultural diversity and "tolerance" mask the fact that Asian Americans are still viewed as perpetual foreigners in the United States.

For the Guangdong Chinese, the Chinese Americans, and the representatives of the Chinese government on whose interactions I focus in this chapter, ancestral villages in the Pearl River Delta region symbolize a shared point of origin. These native places become a physical and symbolic nexus for present-day interactions that reference the past. At the same time they are rapidly changing due to these very interactions and the broader context of globalization that produces these interactions focused around them. Guangdong Chinese and Chinese Americans are brought together through government-sponsored cultural heritage programs for overseas Chinese youth that are built upon government ideas about the role that overseas Chinese will play in the creation of a Chinese modernity. However, it becomes evident that Chinese Americans create meanings out of their experiences in China that differ from those that the Chinese government intends to create and also depart from previous generations' understandings of genealogical and roots-searching practices. How, then, do they rework their identities through visits to their ancestral villages in mainland China, to create meaningful relationships to China in ways that ultimately refer back to their experiences in the United States.

Transnational flows of cultural and national representation, arising out of contemporary China and late capitalist global economic restructuring have expanded and linked the various places in the world that are significant to the creation of Chinese identities. These representations have affected both how Chinese Americans and mainland Chinese view themselves and the Chinese or Chinese American "other." American-born Chinese Americans exercise their privileges of mobility and travel to create notions of place that are both transnational and localized in scope, even as they participate in Chinese government-sponsored programs that attempt to fix their identities to their ancestral villages in China.[1] These Chinese Americans bring meaning to their visits to ancestral villages based on their experiences in the United States and through the exercise of their historical imaginations. They craft relationships to their ancestral roots during their visits to China that incorporate both their ancestral ties to Chinese villages and their continually changing identities as Chinese Americans.[2]

On closer inspection, roots searching both as concept and as practice requires interactions with places in China that can only be made fixed and stable if experienced in a selective, mediated way, which perhaps is most easily done from afar. Increased possibilities for travel may in fact result in the undoing of myths on which some Chinese American identities are formed, at the same time that travel and broader processes of change may alter the places to which one wishes to "return." Diaspora is a space of hybridity that cannot reference the homeland as a place of unmediated identification or easy return. Rather than being reclaimed through a permanent return, the ancestral homeland is a place that must be recovered through the work of the imagination—through the re-creation of histories and processes of reterritorialization (Hall 1990).

The Next Step? Transnationalism Past, Present, and Future

The influence of both the Chinese and U.S. states in shaping the roots-searching efforts of American-born Chinese is evidence that the nation-state remains a strong presence in this era of globalization. And while early efforts to theorize transnational processes may have hinted at its premature demise, more recent studies of transnational relations have refocused on the relationships between transnational projects and states as a corrective to assertions that the nation-state is weakening in the face of transnational movements (Glick Schiller 1999a; Schein 1998; Smith and Guarnizo 1998). In the context of this attention to the nation-state, there has been a renewed focus in academia on the meanings of place and territory within transnational contexts (Dirlik 1999b). What happens to places undergoing globalization? What types of relationships do people maintain or rework with their places of origin and how do these relationships change over time? What is the significance of place within transnational and diasporic identities?

In analyzing transnational relations, it is important to consider that people can identify with a place in a number of possible ways that do not necessarily imply allegiance to the nation-state within which these particular places are located. Connections take a variety of forms: people maintain social obligations and emotional ties to family, village, or clan members; they feel loyalty to their villages as remembered places; they identify with a particular region and local culture; and they retain nationalist sentiments. Connections can also exist on more abstract levels, as (often romanticized) identifications with a homeland, or as a place to search for one's family roots and to recover a sense of history. In this chapter, I reevaluate this place making within the context of transnationalism and state efforts to shape it, through the analysis of my research on the relationships crafted by Roots interns to their ancestral villages in mainland China. The identities of these Chinese Americans are tied to places in China through multiple processes.[3]

As previously discussed, both U.S. society and the PRC, as well as Chinese folk culture, conceive of Chineseness as a racial essence connecting people through their blood to the Chinese nation. However, as becomes evident through my analysis of the In Search of Roots cultural heritage program, the ways second generation (and later-generation) Chinese Americans experience China as a place are qualitatively different from that of first-generation transmigrants. A central part of this inquiry into the changing significance of places undergoing globalization requires the investigation of how not only the places themselves but also the relations between them form the basis for identities within contexts of unequal power. In this chapter I highlight historically and culturally specific ways that places become important to Chinese identities in global contexts by examining the multiple images of China (China as imagined, as family/clan, as village, as past and as present) and how the tensions between them are resolved by Chinese American visitors into an understanding of place. I reevaluate globalized place making as a transnational project enabled by various forms of transnational mobility (such travel and media flows) and as highly mediated by the Chinese state, by folk conceptions of Chineseness in mainland China, and by U.S. discourses of Asian Americans as perpetual foreigners.[4]

The Trip to China through a Chinese American Lens

Although heritage trips such as the In Search of Roots program involve voluntary participation by Chinese Americans through Chinatown organizations, the visit to China is a highly mediated affair. Chinese government agencies such as the China Travel Service and the Office of Overseas Chinese Affairs (Qiao Ban), which are part of the PRC's Foreign Affairs Department, choreograph the experiences of the Chinese American visitors by arranging hotel accommodations and transportation, organizing village visits, and communicating with local officials. Representatives of the Qiao Ban act as guides who accompany the group on its ancestral village tours, arrange logistics, communicate with local officials and guides from local branches of the China Travel Service and the Qiao Ban, and act as general resources for the group.

Although the anthropological literature on tourism may be relevant here because the China visits in many ways take the form of tours, I want to emphasize the historically and culturally rooted nature of the multiple discourses that are brought together through these encounters.[5] I argue that the case presented here represents more than a tourist activity because of the direct connection between the ancestral villages and the interns visiting them, and because of the particular ways that visits are mediated through both PRC and Chinese American discourses. I choose here to view the village as different from other commodified tourist destinations because of the multiple ways that Chinese American identities have been attached to it, both in the past and present.[6]

Roots participants' experiences of "return" are not wholly shaped by the choreographed ways that Chinese Americans are received in China, or by the ways in which identities are fixed in place through political discourses from both Chinese and American sides. These Chinese Americans build their own conceptions of China as a place that frames their process of return. The U.S. society in which they live shapes how they see, regionalize, and experience Chinese and Chinese American spaces. These spaces are crafted in relation to distinctions of class and generation and are tied to ideas about the degree of removal from China and "authentic" Chinese culture. Distinctions of class, generation, and cultural authenticity situate them in relation to various Chinese communities in the United States and shape how participants create expectations for their visits to their ancestral villages before they are even exposed to Chinese government discourses. They begin with visions of the ancestral village as a space of authenticity through which they can reconnect with the China of their ancestors, supported by the foundational knowledge of their family histories and genealogical connections.

Although many Roots participants discussed village visits in retrospect as the culmination of the In Search of Roots internship, these visits are framed by and must be understood within the broader social and political contexts that have been laid out in this book. The village visits are an exercise in the forging (Schein 1998) of a transnational relationship, where the often competing interests of the Chinese government, the Chinese American organizers, and the program participants converge over efforts to reterritorialize Chinese American identities in China. As I show in chapter 5, although on one level village visits provide a contrast point for Roots participants to the structure of the Youth Festival, they also reflect the Chinese government's goals that are encapsulated by the Youth Festival. It is during the village visits that multiple meanings of Chineseness, territorial roots, ancestral origins, and the significance of ancestral villages as places, come together. The ideal of a homecoming in its most romanticized form involves a natural, unmediated interchange between Chinese American visitors and the people and places in their ancestral villages, but this ideal is not played out. In what follows I discuss the village visits in further depth based on the perspective of the Roots participants.

The Village Visit

For most Roots interns the village visit is their first trip to China. With a send-off from friends and relatives, the group boards a plane from San Francisco to Hong Kong, arriving early in the morning after a fourteen-hour flight. Within a few hours, they board a nonstop train to Guangzhou, catching their first glimpses of mainland China as the train passes fields, construction sites, factories, and squatter camps on the two-and-a-half hour ride to Guangzhou. The arrival in Guangzhou is an eye-opening experience as the participants emerge into the middle of a bustling city of six million people. They laugh at ads for Oil of Ulan, which looked suspiciously like Oil of Olay, and dodge the throngs of people rushing to their trains as they recover their luggage, go through customs, and make their way to the Toyota Coaster minibus awaiting them. A local guide, a representative of the Qiao Ban, greets them on board and in polished English welcomes them to the city.[7] The group is then taken to their hotel, where they rest up for the activities to come in the following two weeks. During those weeks they will visit between ten and twenty villages[8] in counties scattered throughout the Pearl River Delta region.[9] They will stay in at least five different hotels and attend an average of two banquets per day, put on in their honor by local officials. All of these activities take place prior to their return to Guangzhou, when they will take part in the Youth Festival.

On the first evening in Guangzhou, as the group exchanges their U.S. dollars for Chinese currency and browses in the gift shop at the Overseas Chinese Hotel, Kevin, a seventeen-year-old high school senior, comments that if he didn't know this was China he'd think it was a slum in the United States.[10] Some of his Chinese American friends talk about going to live in China—they imagine that the cities are modern, like Hong Kong, and that the rural areas are green and lush. None of them have been in China, nor do they speak the language. He would like to take pictures to show them that China is not as great as they think. He adds that he, himself, could never live in China: "Physically, I'm Chinese, but I was nurtured in America." And he concludes that moving to China would not be a good escape from the problems his friends are facing in the United States.

The village visits, referred to as "rootings" by the Chinese American leader who accompanies the group,[11] follow a general pattern that has developed based on the experiences of previous trips. They are ritualized affairs in which each intern in turn visits his or her ancestral village under the guidance of local officials. Over their two-week period in China, in the heat of July, the group, accompanied by representatives from the Office of Over-

The Shunde City Federation of Returned Overseas Chinese (and Office of Overseas Chinese Affairs).

Roots interns meeting with local officials in Longdu, in Zhongshan County.

seas Chinese Affairs and the China Travel Service, visits ancestral villages scattered throughout an area similar in size to the San Francisco Bay area. The night prior to a visit to a particular village, the Chinese American leader sits down with the intern for a briefing session. He makes sure that all pertinent information, gathered over the past few months, is reviewed, and interrogation transcripts from INS files are reread. Who was the last one in the family to leave the village? What was the "real" versus the "paper" name of that person? This process is considered important and is taken quite seriously, although not without some levity. In one case, to vary the routine, the transcripts were read aloud to the leader by a helpful intern using an "Indian" accent similar to that of Apu on the *Simpsons* television show.[12]

The visits usually last less than two hours and are framed by meetings and banquets with local officials as well as travel from location to location through the Pearl River Delta countryside. While local officials arrange for local relatives to meet visiting Chinese Americans, these visits are usually brief but emotional occasions in which many photos are taken and details of family history are filled in, often with the help of translators. The group visits standard destinations: the ancestral house, schools or other buildings donated by overseas relatives, and sometimes gravesites, usually located away from the village in a spot with good feng shui. The youth look for physical signs connecting themselves to the village, locating pictures of themselves on the walls of ancestral homes, pointing out their family branch in recovered genealogy books, or matching features of the village to the sketches drawn by someone who had lived there.

Interns take interest not only in historically significant sites within the village but also in the everyday aspects of village life. They gaze at, and often photograph, the villagers, the open sewers, the pigs, and the chickens. The village map and the life stories that interns collect as part of the research process form a rough template on which village experiences are to be laid. Certain individuals, gravesites, ancestral homes, and other places that have become prominent in geographies created from afar through the research process come to signify the village even before interns lay eyes on it. In its focus on China as an ancestral space, the program moves both in time and space from the Chinese American present to the Chinese past. The program also works the other way along this continuum: the participants' research into their ancestral roots is meant to give them a stronger sense of who they are in the present. However, due to the program's focus on family history, the curriculum deemphasizes China's contemporary political and economic situation.

Although seldom formally stated, the goals of the village visit are consis-

Roots interns exploring an alley in a rural village.

tent: meeting any surviving relatives or friends who knew the family, visiting the ancestral home, seeing graves of ancestors, visiting schools built with donations from the family, and locating the family's genealogy book.[13] The latter goal fits in with the family history theme of the program, but it also coincides with renewed interest in tracing genealogy on the part of many local villagers with overseas Chinese connections. This interest stems partially from government relaxation of restrictions on such practices, which were outlawed during the Cultural Revolution when genealogy books and other vestiges of feudalism were supposed to be destroyed. Many villages find it profitable to reaffirm genealogical connections with the Chinese abroad, who had begun coming back to look for these books as well as possibly to invest or donate. The Zhongshan region village of one Chinese American intern employs a full-time historian and scholar. His job is to research the histories of the three surnames in the village because of the many overseas Chinese interested in tracing their roots through these lineages. In another village in the San Yi (c. Sam Yup) region, villagers had used overseas Chinese money to build a temple for a local deity. Yuen Fong Woon observes that post–Open Policy reforms have allowed the rebuilding of lineage ties among the Guan in Kaiping County.[14] Other studies have documented the revival or reemergence of traditions, as temples have been rebuilt and festivals revived in the post–Mao era, sometimes independently of overseas Chinese involvement (Potter and Potter 1990; Siu 1990; Watson 1993). At the same time, many Pearl River Delta Chinese that the group met, both villagers and urban folk, had never seen a genealogy book nor did they appear to be particularly interested in such matters.

In many ways, the focus of village visits to the ancestral home and of genealogy and family history reinforced static, essentialized notions of place. At the same time, however, the physical experiences and mediation of the interns' travel by local officials and guides altered the ways that they experienced and understood their ancestral places. As the Roots group traveled through the Pearl River Delta region, it was impossible for them to ignore the rapid and dramatic processes of change that the villages were undergoing (and had undergone). The interns' ideas of a village preserved in time were quickly revised when they saw electric wires running through the village and noticed that the walls of ancestral homes were papered with glossy posters and advertisements for consumer goods. Some ancestral homes were occupied by northern migrants because the original owners had moved into a modern, three-story buiding nearby. The group was frequently entertained by local officials with multicourse banquets in rooms equipped for karaoke. In fact, the message relayed to them in meetings with

Getting the interview on film.

local officials emphasized these themes of change—how much China had developed and modernized in recent years due in large part to overseas Chinese investing in their home regions.

Despite the dynamic and changing context of the China visit, however, interns remained primarily concerned with finding meaning in the village through its connections with the past. At the same time, it is the contemporary context and orchestration of their visit that shapes its powerful meaning. One intern remarked that what made the trip interesting was the process of traveling to a variety of villages. She recalled the emotional intensity and chaos characteristic of the experience: "The village scene was a little harrying; all of these things and then you have them recorded in three or four ways. That was kind of overwhelming. . . . You're so caught up in it, you don't really see anything."

Thus, the experiences of the Roots interns may have been so powerful precisely because of the ways the events surrounding the village visit were so carefully planned. The mediation of the visits by Qiao Ban officials and the Chinese American leader of the Roots group facilitated a fairly smooth journey from village to village throughout the Pearl River Delta countryside. Although on some levels the events are choreographed, the Qiao Ban officials are not able (and do not desire) to plan and interpret all events and experiences for the Chinese American visitors. The openness of this choreography leaves the Chinese American visitors the flexibility to map their own reference points and geographies onto their experiences in China.

Thus, in one sense it appears that static notions of place are reinforced as interns record and memorialize their village experiences in video and audio during these fleeting, chaotic visits in order to reflect on and experience them again at a later time. But as the group journeys from village to village, these visits become linked together into a series of dynamic, transitory moments, grounded primarily in the shared experiences of the group and framed by its construction and interpretations of place. This mobile, multiply positioned mode of viewing the villages, of traveling through the rapidly changing postsocialist landscape in a Toyota Coaster minibus, contrasts with the sometimes static renderings of native place carried by some Roots interns. The mode of travel also contrasts with how the Chinese government has conceived of overseas Chinese attachments to native place in their official discourses.

In contrast to the ideas of the Chinese government about village visits as a form of nostalgic return that reinforces the Chinese American's sense of Chinese cultural and national pride, these visits instead reshape the interns' ideas of what it means to be Chinese *American*. The Chinese American participants in the program rely on the multiple perspectives provided by their mobile, ever-changing view of China to create significance out of their experiences there. Indeed, the Chinese countryside and villages only have meaning in relation to people and things back in the United States connected to their family history and to a broader understanding of Chinese American history rooted in the Guangdong countryside. In this sense their mobility is also temporal, as interns are able to combine their collective experiences in the villages with their collective understandings of Chinese American history to contextualize what they see on their daily village visits. Thus, while their individual village visits were of central significance to their experiences in China, it was the aggregate of the shared experiences of visiting ancestral villages that created a context for these individual visits. The combination of various interns' interactions (although limited) with local relatives and the new information that they learned about their family histories during these visits created an atmosphere within which Roots participants could frame their own personal experiences within broader historical and political meanings of what it means to be Chinese American. Thus, many interns felt strong emotions while visiting others interns' ancestral villages, in part because the group had bonded on the trip and in part because they could often identify with their experiences. Fellow interns helped to shape these very experiences. For example one intern, Connie,

Intern wearing
Asian American
pride T-shirt.

Roots intern and group leader speaking with a relative in an ancestral village.

recalled later the great emotion she felt when, on arriving at her village, fellow intern Tom said "welcome home." At the same time, her visit to her ancestral village ultimately made her realize how "whitewashed" she had been growing up, and it encouraged her after she returned to the United States to express pride in her Chinese heritage to both her Chinese and non-Chinese friends.

The very effectiveness of the village visits for the Chinese American visitors, then, was related to the inability of Chinese government discourses (as expressed through the formal structure of the village visits) to fully capture or connect with what the Chinese American visitors expected, experienced, and interpreted during their visits to China. The referents invoked by Chinese government discourses were often interpreted by Chinese American visitors in ways that differed from their intended meanings. For example, while PRC government discourses saw overseas Chinese connections to their ancestral villages as based on a longing and nostalgia for "home," most Chinese Americans had never before been to their ancestral villages. While government discourses viewed Chinese culture, as represented in dance, art, *wushu* (a Chinese martial art), and song, as the basis of commonality between the mainland Chinese and the Chinese abroad, many Chinese Americans felt insecure about their knowledge of what they considered to be "high" Chinese culture, especially language. For most of the participants in the Roots program, the connections that were most compelling were those that directly related to their own personal experiences or to those of their friends and family. These connections were found in Cantonese food and language (even if interns did not speak Cantonese well) and in connections to physical features in the village. Popular culture provided the most familiar cultural references.

Throughout their group travel, the Roots interns were able to reference Chinese American spaces brought with them from America. The Taishan (c. Toisan) region of the Pearl River Delta, for example, was known to many interns through its significance in Chinese American history. Those interns who had taken Asian American studies courses recalled that most of the early emigrants to America originated from Taishan, which boasts of having a greater population living outside of China than in the region itself. Many interns themselves had ancestral roots in Taishan or knew of people from the area, and one intern collected Taishan postcards to bring back to his activist friends who had ancestral connections there.

Other contemporary references served as the basis for connections that the interns made to China as they visited various cities, towns, and villages during their trip. Rather than to ancestral connections, these references—

Taking pictures of village children after asking their permission.

Inside a village home.

Mr. Lau's (pseudonym) daughter and her grandmother in their kitchen in rural Zhongshan County. The house was built in the mid-1980s.

Hong Kong and Japanese pop culture, for example—were to contemporary cultural flows that had become part of Asian American popular culture. Many interns listened to Cantonese pop music (Canto-pop) and were familiar with the various stars whose (most likely unofficial) merchandise could be found for sale at various shops and open-air markets. Other interns were excited to find Japanese comic books (referred to as *manga*), such as *Ranma 1/2*, available for sale (in Chinese translation that most could not read) in a bookstore.[15] Other popular culture references included various Hong Kong movie and kung fu stars, who were also quite popular in southern China where Hong Kong television could be viewed. In many ways, these more mobile aspects of Chinese American culture provided points of identification and connection that were more familiar than the villages themselves. The villagers, most of whom did not directly interact with the interns, became little more than part of the scenery in the photographs that they took.

While it is difficult to describe fully the varied and dynamic ways in which the Roots group experienced its trip through the Pearl River Delta, it is important to emphasize that throughout the journey they were able to merge numerous cultural and historical references. Through their travels, the Chinese American visitors developed relationships to China and to their ancestral villages that were built through multiple images of China, past and present, that originated in the United States and Asia. These multiple referents are nicely illustrated in a four-minute video produced by intern Fred Chang for the Chinese New Year presentation of the interns' family history projects. I describe here the production of this video through the field notes I took as I kept Fred company partway through an all-night editing session where he chose and assembled scenes and music for the video:

> The video is a montage, set to the driving, dramatic opening music of the *Once Upon a Time in China* kung fu series.[16] The opening scene shows Fred looking out the tour bus window at scenes of Guangzhou, followed by glimpses of the Five Rams statue, the Seventy-two Martyrs monument, and other street scenes of Guangzhou. He shows each of the interns, then shifts to Carrie, telling us she is Carrie Lo, from San Francisco, and that she is here in China to find her roots. He cuts to a few scenes of interns in the villages. Then he shifts to Sharon on the bus, who is saying that she is on the way to see her father's village in Toisan. The next few scenes show Sharon being welcomed by relatives in the village, looking at pictures and artifacts, touching the water in the village well, giving a red envelope to her relative, and hugging.[17] Fred selects scenes for their emotional impact (a great smile, the hug, the relative refusing the money but holding it in the next scene). The section following consists of scenes in other ancestral villages: Tom looking at his genealogy in Tong Ga Wan village and worshipping ancestors with incense; Anne next to the village well, looking through letters sent by her mother back to her grandmother in the village (in U.S. air mail envelopes) and taking a photo with relatives; Pam posing with a relative in the Long Du district; Fred posing with his newly found uncle. For these scenes Fred uses the hip hop group Arrested Development's song "Tennessee," with its lyrics about "going back to where I'm from," and a song by Hong Kong pop star Jackie Cheung (although Fred didn't know what the Cantonese words meant, he thought it was a nice song). He also uses "Because I Love You" ("Yin-wei Wo Ai Ni"), a mainland Chinese pop tune and a reference to the Roots group leader's karaoke performance in Fatsan (md. Foshan) at a banquet hosted by local officials. With the credits rolling, Fred thanks the participants, and the piece ends with video profiles that treat each of the interns as Hollywood or Hong Kong movie stars.

Intern getting a vial of water from the well of her ancestral village.

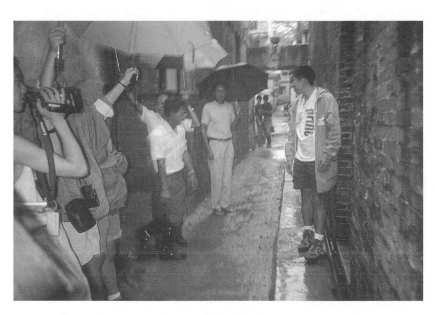

Intern in front of his ancestral home. The key had been lost, so he could not enter.

• • •

It is possible for practices such as returning to visit the ancestral homeland to be similar in form to the transmigrant practices of previous generations, but not similar in their content or meaning. While on some level Chinese American visits to China may represent renewals of ties to family or ancestral place, it is limiting not to look at the possibility that they represent a different type of transnationalism, transformed by cold war politics, U.S. exclusion and racialization, PRC extraterritoriality, and contemporary media and popular culture flows. For many of the Chinese Americans involved in the Roots program, the visit to China did produce a strong connection with mainland China—the mainland China of the past that derives its significance from connections to their family histories and to the Chinese American experience more broadly. Participants in the program translated this connection into actions that differed from the ways that previous generations of transmigrants who had engaged in back-and-forth travel expressed their attachments to China (whether as a place of origin to which one still had linkages or as a place to which one felt nationalist loyalties).

While a small number of former interns have returned to China to teach English, study Chinese, or work for short periods of time, the majority of program participants graduated from college and pursued professional positions in business and finance, medicine, computer engineering, education, law, social services, or nonprofit agency work. Although some interns have stayed involved with the program through its alumni association or involvement in the Chinese Culture Center or Chinese Historical Society, most do not work in China-related affairs or in the Chinese American community as a central part of their occupations. The majority of interns who become involved in activities related to their Chinese cultural heritage do so through activities and organizations that are primarily oriented to the American-born Chinese American population, which is in most respects disconnected from mainland China. They concern themselves with issues of social justice in the Asian American community and with promoting identity exploration through family history and genealogical research. Thus, while the program renews older transnational linkages, its participants build on these linkages primarily through involvement in U.S.-based activities that are removed from direct ties to China. In this sense, the forms of Chinese identities expressed by former participants are in essence Chinese *American* ones that reference preemigration rural Guangdong China as part of Chinese American history.

In light of this fact we must ask whether we need to reconceptualize the

A typical banquet of local delicacies.

idea of place to encompass new formations created out of these short-term visits that represent a new form of transnational practice.[18] Indeed, Nina Glick Schiller makes a distinction between sentimental attachments to home and transnational relations, noting that these sentimental attachments do not necessarily translate into transnational practices marked by participation in boundary-crossing networks. Portes, Guarnizo, and Landolt (1999) also make distinctions between these short-term visits and transnational practices. Given these distinctions, it becomes clear that Chinese American ties to China are crafted and mediated through relationships made possible by transnational connections, both historical and contemporary. Although their connections to China are based in the historical ties of family and kinship of the past, they are also informed by a broader sense of China as a symbol of heritage and as part of a broader Asian-Pacific popular culture that is as much about being Asian American as it is about being transnational. Although on the surface the "return" of Chinese Americans to China may coincide with Chinese government reconceptualizations of overseas Chinese as returning patriots, we must consider the context and significance of their return as it is mediated through a number of power structures that shape how China is experienced by Chinese Americans as a political, historical, social, and cultural place.

Chinese Americans come to know China as a place as much through their (usually brief) lived experiences in China as through secondhand, mediated forms. The significance of their attachments to place, clan, family, and kinship is transformed through their participation in the In Search of Roots program. Unlike traditional genealogies based on patrilineal kinship, interns trace either or both mother's and father's sides of their family trees. Although traditionally excluded from genealogies, women comprise half of the interns, many of whom actively discuss how they are changing the custom of excluding women from genealogies. The family trees are presented in fashionably designed displays incorporating photos and documents from both the past and present. Written narratives chronicle the trip to China, often incorporating reflections on personal identity, and family history, usually in more straightfoward historical narratives.[19]

As they rewrite their family histories, Chinese American participants in the Roots program flexibly employ meanings of history and place. They view their contemporary relations with China and their identities as Chinese Americans through a lens shaped by their family history research and their contemporary experiences as Chinese racial minorities in the United States. In this sense, Chinese American history becomes not only a historical legacy of past events shaping the present, but also a form of remembered history produced through Chinese American narratives. The Roots interns create their own meanings of place by reviving connections between Guangdong and San Francisco through their contemporary renderings of historical memory, which they combine with flows of popular and political culture originating in China, the United States, and other locations around the globe. These locations have been historically important as sites central to Cantonese immigration, but now they are important to the Roots participants in ways different from previous generations.

China, specifically Guangdong and its Pearl River Delta region, is important to Chinese Americans primarily because it provides a historically charged template on which Chinese American visitors imprint their own reference points. Thus, the space that the Roots interns craft between Guangdong and San Francisco represents something different for them than for their immigrant ancestors or for contemporary immigrants. Because the visits to China for most interns represent a first experience in their ancestral homeland, the connections between the United States and China that they create out of their journey represent a type of remembering that contrasts with the nostalgic memories of transmigrants who have at one time lived in the village. Far from representing a fixed and static relationship with place as conceived by the Chinese government, or evoking buried memories, the transnational relationship between the Chinese American interns and China is highly mediated, loose, and expansive, drawing on a broad time span that reaches back across generations and connects up to the present. The Roots participants identify with China not so much as contemporary nation-state as a historical and cultural entity that is part of a mix of other images that circulate as part of transnational flows of media, migrants, and capital. It is these media and popular culture images that allow the Roots interns to view China in ways that extend beyond its national borders and its significance as a political entity. Their experiences in their ancestral villages become one of many reference points, some anchored in their families' experiences in the United States, some based on deterritorialized conceptions of China and Chinese culture, and some rooted in contemporary issues of concern to Asian Americans. They incorporate these various influences as part of a flexible and multisited conception of Chinese American identity that is rooted in both American urban hip hop culture and Japanese *manga*; in Hong Kong kung fu movies and in Asian American activism. Thus, Chinese places are made accessible and understandable only through the mobility of these Chinese Americans going to and from them, a mobility that allows the Chinese Americans to connect the places back to their experiences in the United States.[20]

It is by way of the ancestral village, conceived as a container of tradition, Chineseness, and a representation of home, that Chinese Americans initially wish to (re)connect with China. But as these connections are played out, Chinese Americans decouple Chinese identities from static notions of tradition and bounded place, and reshape relations with their ancestral villages as mobile, dynamic places defined through ties to other places. Amid these multiple attempts by Chinese government officials to fix place and identity, the mobile sense of place assembled by Chinese Americans opens up possibilities for alternative forms of transnational identification with China.

roots narrative)

I, like many Asian Americans, grew up in two seemingly different worlds. In elementary school I was the little, pudgy Chinese boy with slanted eyes and bad English. At home I was the youngest of three sons with a strong craving for McDonalds and the television. And with bad Cantonese. . . . Not until I moved to the Bay Area of northern California did I realize that I did not have to choose between my "two cultures." That a strong desire for rice and for McDonalds is quite acceptable, and indeed common. I realize that it is acceptable to have limited skills in Chinese, and acceptable to have limited skills in English. I realize that names like "Jook Sing" and "Banana" are insults only if I take offense to them. I realized how to be proud of being a Chinese American.

And I also realized that I knew nothing about my Chinese heritage. ["Chinese" was] nothing more than the seven-lettered prefix for American. All along, China has been a mythical and legendary place, touched upon briefly and distantly in high school history. Yet history is not merely a subject students study in a classroom. Rather, history is roots. History can be a personal exploration of one's heritage. To the children of immigrant families, we especially must make an attempt to understand the Something when we call ourselves Something American. This is the beginning of my attempt.

—T.T., 1994

CRAFTING CHINESE AMERICAN IDENTITIES:

ROOTS NARRATIVES IN THE CONTEXT OF

U.S. MULTICULTURALISM

Each chapter in this book thus far has begun with a vignette by participants in the In Search of Roots program taken from the narratives produced for the Chinese New Year presentation of their family history projects. These narratives are written almost a year after they begin the program, and approximately six months after they travel to China. Thus, they have a coherence that most likely did not exist during the moment described in the narrative. When examined more closely, their stories describe an evolutionary process through which the writers feel they have come to a more complete understanding of what it means to be Chinese American. Each excerpt begins with a portrayal of the writer's initial fear or ignorance of China and also of their uncertain status both as Chinese and as Americans. And each ends with a statement about how the author has been able to negotiate a hyphenated Chinese American identity after their experiences in the Roots program. Although I selected these narratives because they reflect the themes of the chapters they preface, together they also demonstrate the processes of identity formation that I discuss in chapter 2. Chinese Americans negotiate changing relationships to people and places in both China and the United States, taking advantage of their mobility and global flows to draw on multiple resources. They create identities that reference multiple sources, both near and far, past and present.

In another sense, however, the stories presented in the narratives are almost too neat and do not clearly reflect the processes of negotiation that characterize identity production. Thus, it is significant that while the process itself is uneven and messy, participants in hindsight portray it as a progressive route toward self-discovery. Such identity narratives are characteristic of the identity politics of U.S. multiculturalism, in which identity is viewed as something out there waiting to be discovered. As I point out in chapter 2, such portrayals of identity are disturbing in the sense that they imply that one cannot form a complete identity without going to China, and that the identity that one has discovered through going there is somehow final. Thus, in some respects these identity narratives illustrate the ways that Chinese Americans are able to move beyond these limitations to craft identities that are attached to China yet are not derived solely from their ties to China. In other respects, however, the narratives also show how these productions require the negotiation of identity politics on multiple levels. American-born Chinese Americans in the Roots program find themselves caught within a politics of U.S. multiculturalism that both excludes them from cultural citizenship in the United States and associates them, willingly or not, with their ancestral homeland. Their relationship to China and their understandings of Chinese culture in the context of the United States are therefore complex and often somewhat ambivalent. China is simultaneously an unknown entity filtered through an orientalist lens and a place to which Chinese Americans are involuntarily and inextricably attached.

However, it is through the construction of alternative genealogies and family narratives that are localized in Chinese American experiences, that participants in the Roots program are able to begin to negotiate viable identities within these constraints. In constructing family histories and personal narratives, they carve out a "place" for American-born Chinese Americans such as themselves within a politics of cultural citizenship focusing on newer, more mobile immigrants. As I discuss in chapter 2, the "places" that they create draw simultaneously on historical connections to ancestral villages in China, contemporary relations with friends and relatives, and transnational popular culture flows originating in Asia. Their production, though, relies on the transnational mobility of Chinese Americans, which ironically is facilitated by the very states that are trying to shape their identities in restrictive ways. Thus, the Chinese state's sponsorship of their roots-searching activities and the ability to travel afforded them by their U.S. citizenship creates the road map for their mobility.

At first glance it may appear that by traveling to China, Chinese Americans have recovered their ancestral roots in the traditional romanticized sense. Most become more conscious and proud of their Chinese heritage, and some even become involved in the Chinese American community or travel to China to study or do business. Later in this chapter I discuss the process of reethnicization in which Chinese Americans selectively adopt parts of their Chinese heritage and consciously incorporate them into their lives. However, it is important to acknowledge the flexibility with which they create these meanings. Reethnicization involves more than adopting the "traditional" practices of previous generations. So, while some exercises such as tracing genealogies, making traditional foods, or learning to speak Chinese may appear to replicate those of older generations, the meanings assigned to the practices may differ greatly. Recognition of these differences is essential, because one of the controlling processes (Nader 1997) that disempowers American-born generations within the politics of U.S. multiculturalism is its emphasis on traditional cultural knowledge as a marker of cultural authenticity and legitimation. Multiculturalism in the United States, in its reliance on symbolic representations of diversity, only serves to oversimplify and essentialize the diversity of racial/ethnic groups in the United States. Distinctions of class, gender, and intraethnic/racial diversity are often glossed over within these superficial representations that often lump people together into broad, undifferentiated categories such as "Asian," "Chicano/Latino," "African American," or "Native American." As I discuss below, when cultural authenticity is measured in these terms, American-born Chinese Americans who know little about China are left with little to display. At the same time they may be unable to identify with these representations of their culture, and they may even begin to feel inadequate in comparison to them.

In a more specific sense, categories that encompass a range of identifications may also be inadequate to express the diversity within them. As Aihwa Ong (1999) notes in her analysis of cultural citizenship, it may be premature to suggest the formation of a shared Asian American panethnic identity. The Cambodian refugees and upper-class Hong Kong immigrants she studies, both of whom fall under the category of "Asian American," were inserted into U.S. racial politics on opposite ends of the black-white spectrum that defines U.S. racial politics. They share little in terms of class status and cultural practices. Similarly, the experiences of participants in the Roots program tell us that even pan-Chinese or pan-Chinese American forms of identification may not adequately represent the identities of those subsumed within them, particularly American-born Chinese generations. As I discuss below, although Roots participants gained knowledge about China and Chinese culture while visiting China, they often found these forms of Chinese identity inadequate to describe their own experiences. Instead, the identities expressed in Roots narratives were often formed in relation, or sometimes in contrast, to other ways of being Chinese. Thus the genericized forms of Chinese arts and "high culture" presented to the Chinese Americans in China actually served to make them feel less Chinese. Similarly, Roots participants continually made distinctions between themselves as American-born Cantonese Americans from peasant origins and newer, often wealthier immigrants from Hong Kong and Taiwan. Roots participants therefore selectively negotiated these categorizations. Ultimately, their identification as a person of Cantonese descent from a specific village or region, for example, may coexist with other levels of identification as Asian American, Chinese American, or just plain American. It also is accompanied by other forms of identification based on class, gender, or the specifics of their own family history in relation to broader Chinese American history, such as having emigrated through Southeast Asia or Latin America.

In the following sections I discuss these contexts and how Chinese Americans negotiate them. I begin with a discussion of the place of China in the Chinese American imagination and how this relationship is changing with increasing global flows. I then proceed to discuss the inadequacies of U.S. multiculturalism for creating a context within which American-born Chinese Americans can create places for themselves as people of color in the United States. Next, I describe the identity narratives as told by Roots participants during the interviews I conducted after the completion of the Roots program. These narratives reflect in greater depth the processes of identity construction and narration described above, because most begin with a discussion of the participant's lack of knowledge about China and end with statements about feeling more comfortable with their Chinese American identities. Finally, I end with an analysis of a roundtable group discussion by interns on the issues of Chinese cultural authenticity and their strategies for remaking these traditions in their own ways. In doing so I do not suggest that they have in any way settled on identities that are fixed and final. One participant in the roundtable discussion summed it up nicely:

> I think that for me I'm looking at it more as a Chinese American now, not necessarily as an ABC, or as a Chinese, but as a Chinese American. I'm very comfortable sort of knowing my personal family history, knowing [about] Exclusion Laws, knowing factual things, teaching, and researching on that . . . And that's my community, that's the stuff that I do, and definitely [the Roots program] is important, Asian American studies, my friends, family. All those things are definitely Chinese American. And I'm still trying to figure out exactly what does that mean. I don't want to make it that, well we pull some Chinese stuff, we pull some American stuff. It's a lot more complex, and I don't even know how to approach it, it's a much bigger thing and I think that's why . . . even though it's hard to describe what it is, I'm growing comfortable in saying I know what Chinese American culture is, but don't ask me to define it.

Chinese Americans and China: Redefining the Relationship

While American-born Chinese Americans may to differing degrees identify with China as an exotic tourist site, geopolitical identity, historical region, or place of origin, most have had little firsthand contact with China or mainland Chinese people. Most American-born Chinese have not been to China and do not speak Chinese fluently, if at all. Prior to their involvement in the Roots program many of the people I interviewed had little knowledge about China or their family history. During the era of the Exclusion Acts (1882–1943) and beyond, many Chinese families avoided talking about family history for fear that their "paper son" status would be discovered. In addition, during the Communist period the majority in the Chinese American community seldom acknowledged connections with mainland China, and the Taiwanese government gained a foothold in Chinatown politics. Even for the children of post-1965 immigrants, China remains at least a generation away. For these Chinese Americans, their family history frames their images of "Chinese culture" and of China as an ancestral home. At the same time, it becomes difficult to distinguish between what is particular to one's own family and friends and what is true of the larger context of Chinese and Chinese American culture and society. Because Chinese Americans live in a society where there are multiple and conflicting images about China and Chinese culture, it can become difficult for them to contextualize their own families' experiences and practices within a broad picture of Chinese and Chinese American culture. Family experiences and home culture thus must be resolved with what they learn outside the home about China and other Chinese from the media, school textbooks, and popular culture. As Dutch/Indonesian scholar of Chinese descent Ien Ang (1994) observed of her own situation, her preparation for her experience of visiting mainland China for the first time began long before she crossed the Hong Kong border into the Special Economic Zone of Shenzhen for a tour of China. After moving to Holland from Indonesia, she and her family became reethnicized as Chinese-Europeans, and in this context her parents eagerly assumed identities as Chinese and tried to learn as much as possible about China.

For American-born generations, "Chinese culture" is often learned outside the home and takes form and meaning as an entity that is consciously learned and explored. Chinese Americans grow up with preconceived notions of China, Chinese, and other Chinese Americans. Images of Chinese culture and authentic Chineseness are often media-inspired by sources outside the home. One twenty-two-year-old second-generation Chinese American said he grew up thinking he should know how to do kung fu because he was Chinese. Growing up in the Midwest, the only images he saw of Chinese were on TV, and in many ways he thinks these media images taught him how to be Chinese. For some Chinese Americans, these conceptions of their (lack of) Chineseness shape their images and attitudes toward China as a reservoir of an essentialized Chinese culture and source of family secrets that can be tapped to fill in the holes of their own incomplete and perhaps quirky understandings of their Chineseness.

Chinese Americans and the Asia-Pacific Region

The relationship between Chinese Americans and China emerges from historical processes that go far beyond the particulars of the individual stories of ancestors who emigrated. These broader processes shape how Chinese Americans conceive of their Chineseness. The creation of the Asia-Pacific region is a product of Eurocentric thinking and capitalist processes (Dirlik 1998). This region, then, exists not as an objective geographical entity but as a socio-historical construction. Through processes integral to its formation, the creation of the Asia-Pacific region has defined the relationships between Chinese Americans and China, and Chinese Americans and the United States. Arif Dirlik (1998) argues that Asian American history and identities have been shaped by the historical prominence of ideas of cultural difference in U.S. definitions of relations between East and West. From the beginning of U.S. history, the relationship between Asians and the United States has taken form around issues of labor and capital. However, the debates have always been framed in terms of cultural difference rather than political or economic tensions. The legal exclusion of Chinese immigrants between 1882 and 1943, then, was justified not in terms of the threat to labor competition posed by Chinese workers but in terms of irreconcilable differences between Eastern and Western cultures. Although the Chinese were integral to building the U.S. economy, they remained exotic and dangerous outsiders who needed to be controlled.

The problem faced by Asian Americans thus is one of the difficulty of comfortably claiming either Asian or American roots. Dirlik observes that "to the extent that trans-Pacific ties of Asian Americans have been recognized within the dominant culture, therefore, this recognition has served primarily to deny their 'Americanness'—and their history" (1998: 294). In light of recent attention focused on the Asia-Pacific region, a new emphasis is being put on the potential held in those connections (284). However, for the Chinese Americans in my research, this emphasis puts them in a double bind. Although lacking strong connections to Asia, they are at the same time still viewed through the prism of cultural difference that has historically defined relations between Asian immigrants and the United States. While black Americans are seen as lacking a cultural heritage, Chinese Americans are viewed as having too much culture (Ebron and Tsing 1995). But at the same time the "Asian" and "American" parts of Asian American represent two irreconcilable parts of a single identity within U.S. multiculturalism. Dirlik (1998) and others have referred to this problem as a dual or split personality, neither side of which can be recognized as whole. The idea that the Asian and American parts of Asian America cannot be integrated into a cohesive singular identity makes it very difficult to conceive of processes of cultural change that blend Asian and American elements.

When China Is Brought Closer

Ideas of relative Chineseness become even more salient as diasporic or historically transnational (Hsu 2000; Glick Schiller 1999a, 1999b) relationships between immigrant populations and their homelands are redefined under globalization. Processes of globalization are reshaping the borders of historical diasporas, multiplying the channels through which identities can be negotiated. In many ways, increased access to China has opened up new possibilities for the formation of identities within the context of a racist U.S. society that constructs Chineseness in restrictive ways. However, while Chinese Americans may control this information, in other respects they may be controlled by it.

The increasing contact between the United States and China through trade, immigration, and popular culture constantly reminds Chinese Americans of their "motherland." The prominent presence of the Pacific Rim in the media makes representations of Chinese culture available on a daily basis. These representations come attached to discussions of economics, international relations, illegal immigration, and campaign finance scandals. Through these transnational flows—of commodities, popular culture, and media—Chinese Americans are sometimes unwillingly reattached to their homeland. Media hype over transnational overseas Chinese business and social networks portray a Chinese diaspora driven by Confucian values and a culturally engrained business drive as a united world force to be reckoned with. China is discussed in the news media, it is found on product labels, in popular culture, and in many other dimensions of American life. Andrew Lam, a Pacific News Service commentator originally from Vietnam, satirizes the ease and extent to which Asian Americans are tied to Asia in the American imagination. He marvels at the power and influence he and his Asian

American friends must now have to influence politics. All they have to do, he quips, is to make "a few well-placed campaign contributions" to ruin the careers of politicians. After all, his transpacific web of connections is extensive—he has an uncle in Saigon, cousins in refugee camps in Hong Kong, and the ability to make a good Thai soup (1997).

As one participant in the Roots program remarked, images of China, although changing, still strongly affect his ideas of what it means to be Chinese in America:

> I think the idea of China always having an effect on your perception of Chineseness, I would tend to agree with that, because no matter what I think, I think the media plays a role in what I absorb and what I don't, whether I agree with it or not, it affects the way I think. Whatever is going on in China or about what Congress says about China, or what movies are out about China, it always has this effect. . . . Basically it seems to me like it's opening up a little more, and China is becoming more like any normal country. Whereas twenty years ago I thought it was this dark, Evil Empire II kind of thing.

This distance from China combined with the pressure to know and identify with China results in a complex and confusing relationship between Chinese Americans and their country of origin, a relationship that is mediated by the discourses of multiculturalism and race in the United States. While Hong Kong transnationals (Mitchell 1996; Ong 1999) use multiculturalism to their advantage, Chinese Americans are in many ways controlled by American multiculturalism without realizing the extent of its impact. The global flows of capital and culture created by and used to the advantage of Hong Kong transnationals reattach Chinese Americans to their places of origin, sometimes unwillingly. This both opens up new alternatives and raises new complications for rooting (and routing) identities. Although meant to be empowering, the identity politics of U.S. multiculturalism provide a distorted lens through which Chinese Americans view their "Chineseness," their "Americanness," and their relationship to China and America.

Roots in the Context of U.S. Identity Politics

The structure and focus of the In Search of Roots program arose out of Chinese American community-based politics. These politics originated in 1960s activism that claimed that American-rooted identities developed through a reinvolvement in community issues in Chinatown, Japantown, and Manilatown[1] on the part of second-generation Asian American college students. A corollary of these activities was involvement in Third World movements overseas. One group of Chinese Americans visited China in the 1970s to participate in Chairman Mao's Cultural Revolution, which in their eyes paralleled the revolutionary struggles of Third World people of color in the United States. Many of these individuals combined in interesting ways their revolutionary goals in China with roots-searching experiences, and they did so through a political lens that differed from current multicultural identity politics (see Louie, 2003). An important element of these early Asian American politics involved the development of a pan–Asian American identity that focused less on roots and origins, and more on the shared struggles of Asians as minorities in the United States. "Yellow Power" did little, however, to remove essentialized notions of ancestral roots in Asia as the basis for Asian American cultural and political legitimacy. The cultural politics of diversity that activists developed in the 1970s around Third World student activism had the unintended effect of perpetuating racialized categories by referencing Native Americans, Chicanos/Latinos, African Americans, and Asian Americans as the only legitimate and recognized minority groups.

The production of hypenated Americans created models of racial dynamics in the United States that worked against more nuanced understandings of processes of racialization. The hyphen linking Asian and American did not remove the ambiguity of how these racialized groups fit into U.S. society. The "Asian" part of Asian American has been produced through a broader set of discourses stemming from the history of U.S. involvement in Asia and its hegemonic definition of Asia as a region (Dirlik 1998). Asian Americans have been portrayed as perpetual foreigners who maintain deeply engrained, perpetual ties to Asia. These perceived ties have taken on new meanings in recent years as the transnational potential of connections between Asian Americans and Asia has received an increasing amount of attention. Asian Americans, especially those born in the United States who usually have fewer connections with Asia, are placed in awkward positions when they are cast in these popular and political discourses as bridge builders across the Pacific. While renewed pride in Asian roots and culture cultivated through these connections can be viewed as a basis for Asian American political empowerment, scholars such as Evelyn Hu Dehart have asked, "Can Asian Americans . . . claim . . . 'ethnic nationalism' without jeopardizing their cultural and political citizenship in the United States?" (1993: 3). In a similar vein, Dirlik notes that Asian American "groups have acquired a new significance in light of global economic developments, and the localized identities that they acquired in their settlements abroad have been overwhelmed in reassertions of cultural nationalism that stress their 'essential' unity across global spaces" (1999a: 40). These racialized, essential forms of cultural nationalism are dangerous because they emphasize cultural origins over the complex national contexts that shape the varied meanings of what it means to be Chinese in particular times and places.

U.S. Multicultural Politics: The Problem with Assimilation

Chinese American culture is defined within U.S. multicultural politics as a form of inherent and immutable difference from U.S. mainstream culture (whatever that might be). As mentioned previously, from the beginnings of Chinese emigration the class and labor tensions that the Chinese presence in the U.S. represented have been framed by opponents in terms of cultural difference. The Chinese have been portrayed as unassimilable and unable to live democratic, civilized lifestyles (Choy, Dong, and Hom 1995). They have thus been marginalized and excluded from mainstream American culture not only in political and economic realms but also culturally. The emphasis on the inherent difference of Chinese people within U.S. cultural politics is used as a basis to criticize Chinese Americans as less American, while at the same time forcing them to reference China and Chinese culture, about which they know little, as a basis for their identities. Although Chinese Americans are forced to define their differences in cultural terms, the hybrid blend that Chinese American culture has become is not recognized by mainstream U.S. society or by Chinese Americans themselves as legitimately "Chinese." Chinese Americans thus are forced to either form a relationship with mainland China or attempt to claim a wholly "American" identity, something that is difficult if not impossible to do in racialized U.S. society.

Conceptions of cultural change and adaptation to U.S. culture must be understood within the larger context of the social science, folk, and official models that have been used to describe minority experiences in the United States. Each of these models falls back on basic assumptions about culture and identity. Multicultural politics in the United States are based on implicit assumptions that one's true identity is "out there," waiting to be found through a process of self-reflection and of finding oneself. Within the consciousness-raising (Bondi 1993) identity politics of U.S. multiculturalism, assumptions about culture change, preservation, and authenticity constrain avenues for identity exploration and expression.

Assimilationist models originally used to understand minority experiences in the United States have inadequately dealt with processes of cultural change and with issues of race, yet at the same time they have provided a framework for folk understandings of cultural change. As Omi and Winant (1994) have observed, models of race relations for U.S. minorities have been shaped by the legacy of Robert Park's race relations cycle, which described a continual drive toward assimilation. Although it has become evident that racial minorities do not melt into a uniform blend, this model of assimilation remains influential despite the discourses of multiculturalism that have arisen in its place. This is due in large part to the inadequacies of these models in dealing effectively with the question of race. Within academic models, race has been relegated to the realm of biology, subsumed under class, or hidden by the idea of ethnicity (Omi and Winant 1994; Visweswaren 1998).

Both folk and academic discourses on Asian American adaptation to U.S. culture have been subsumed under the model of assimilation to American culture, according to Lisa Lowe (1991). Within this model, the differential abilities of immigrant versus American-born generations to adapt to American ways is the main source of intergenerational conflict. Lowe argues that this vertical, generational model of understanding both conflict and diversity within the Asian American community and family should be replaced by a horizontal model. A horizontal model would acknowledge the heterogeneity of the Asian American community, a first step toward strategic political action. A particular difficulty with generational models, Lowe observes, is the relationship that they construct between authenticity and assimilation, and therefore with China as a place of origin. The further one is removed from China, the more assimilated to U.S. culture one will be and therefore the less authentically Chinese. As an illustrative example, Lowe uses a fictional story about two Chinese American girls, each of whom assumes that the other is more "authentically" attached to China and more culturally Chinese. They come to find out that, contrary to their initial assumptions about one another, they are both American born and neither possesses the Chinese cultural authenticity assumed by the other.

The idea that one can be more or less authentically Chinese places Chinese Americans in an ambivalent relationship with people whom they view as being "more Chinese" (those who speak the language or have immigrated more recently). While on the one hand Chinese Americans, under assimilationist models, should identify strongly with their U.S. roots, the realities of racial politics cause them to remain perpetual foreigners. Chinese Americans have always been told that "home" is in the United States but that their "roots," and therefore a missing piece of their identity, is somewhere in China. Furthermore, U.S. multiculturalism conceives of some societies, such as the United States, as being composed of multiple cultures, and others of a single one. According to David Segal and Richard Handler: "Culture, in this view, is not itself 'multi'; rather, multiplicity and diversity arise from the aggregation of cultures. Cultures, in short, are figured as elemental. From this perspective, it is not that diversity is intrinsic to social formations, nor simply that the United States is diverse, but more specifically, that the United States consists of some unspecified number of cultural elements" (1995: 392). In addition, because there is a tendency in Western thinking to view "culture as a thing: a natural object or entity made up of objects and entities ('traits')" (Handler 1988) culture is often objectified and commodified within movements for cultural preservation.

In the Chinese American context, culture is objectified and then broken down into discrete practices, customs, and traditions, (using chopsticks, eating certain foods, celebrating certain holidays). These elements carry symbolic weight as features and traits that can be measured to indicate the authenticity of a culture. Within this context, Chineseness becomes a measurable and commodified form of cultural capital (Bourdieu 1984). Some people have more Chinese culture, while others (having lost it) have less. This sets up a situation where some lack culture and others have too much. For Chinese Americans this is a double-edged sword because they are thought of as having, in contrast to African Americans (Ebron and Tsing 1995), too much culture but at the same time they often worry about lacking culture (Lowe 1991).

Chinese American culture, when compared to authentic Chinese culture, becomes something that is impure, diluted, and devolved. Meanwhile, "Chinese tradition" and culture is rendered static; as something that has been left over or preserved. Thus, within folk Chinese American culture, Chinese Americans critically describe one another as "not being very Chinese" or "being too Chinesey." Some are accused of being *jook sing* (hollow bamboo); others are viewed as bananas (yellow on the outside, white on the inside). The term ABC (American-Born Chinese) carries a negative connotation, implying assimilation to the dominant American culture and the loss of Chinese culture.

Popular ideas about Chinese culture are comprised of often essentialized and static representations of "Chinese tradition" seen through an orientalized filter. These notions of tradition, customs, food, language, and history are viewed by the broader American public as being deeply historically rooted in a mainland Chinese past. At the same time, this is a past about which many American-born Chinese Americans feel they know little. Under U.S. multiculturalism, specific "racial" backgrounds become associated with packages of essentialized cultural traits, ranging from work ethic to superstitious beliefs. As "Chinese people," Chinese Americans are expected by the broader society to possess knowledge of Chinese language and cultural practices. The specifics of family history are disassociated from these more visible identity markers, so that Chinese Americans are expected to know something about China and Chinese culture despite the fact that many Chinese American families have been in the United States for generations.[2] Thus many view Chinese culture with ambivalence, as mysterious, foreign, and irrelevant to their everyday lives. In comparison to popularly accepted views of China and Chinese culture, they see their own Chinese American family practices as diluted or as inauthentic versions of "real" traditional Chinese culture.

The emphasis in mainstream American constructions of Chineseness on having knowledge of visible identity markers such as language and customs makes many Chinese Americans feel inadequately and inauthentically Chinese when judged according to these criteria. Yet at the same time they feel inescapably Chinese because processes of racialization in the United States mark them as inherently and immutably Chinese. Folk models of culture conceive of it as something natural, possessed, and innate (Jackson 1995). These attitudes form the basis of popular attitudes toward culture change. Popular conception holds that pure cultures can be neither created nor invented. People "have" or "possess" cultures "in a way that an animal species has fur or claws" (Jackson 1995: 18). Culture is acquired slowly through one's lifetime of personal development, and cultural change occurs gradually. Rapid cultural change is viewed as resulting in acculturation, in other words, the loss of culture (18). For Chinese Americans, these naturalized conceptions of culture and cultural change imply that consciously learned culture is a less authentic or an inauthentic type of culture. One fourth-generation Chinese American woman shared the following event in a discussion session with fellow American-born Chinese: "I was having a conversation with a friend of mine who was born in Hong Kong. He was saying that . . . I think this was fairly harsh term . . . but he was kind of disgusted how ABC I was. I think he used the wrong word. He was kind of joking to me . . . and was saying that I have no culture. And I was saying that I can't help the way I was born, I'm fourth or fifth generation, and whatever culture that I have is going to be learned culture, and then he said, and I think that this is controversial, he said that you can't learn culture, it's something that you're born with."

The idea expressed by the Hong Kong friend that culture cannot be learned but rather is "something that you're born with" is consistent with the earlier discussion of folk ideas about culture change. This type of thinking leaves no room for processes of reethnicization. Many Chinese Americans consciously research and adopt practices, material culture, and beliefs that signify "Chineseness" or "Chinese Americanness" to them. Or they may mark as ethnic certain values, traits, and customs that they view as being part of their family's core. Reethnicization often involves learning more about Chinese history and culture, or Chinese/Asian American history. It may involve becoming active in Asian American or Chinese American "community" issues, or going to China to learn to speak Chinese. Or it may consist of consciously associating with other Chinese or Asian Americans, or watching Chinese or Hong Kong movies. But in claiming Chinese culture, Chinese Americans must negotiate a politically charged atmosphere in which both the sources of this culture and the content of the parts to be "preserved" are contested by other Chinese people and by broader U.S. society. In this sense, reethnicization takes place within a context that is both in cooperation with and in resistance to state-sponsored identities.

Chinese American Identity Narratives

Although family histories are the routes through which Chinese Americans explore their identities, not all versions of history and means of exploring them are effective or relevant toward this goal. Histories are versions of the "past" created in the present within a context of power relations. The past carries heavy symbolic weight, and the creation of narratives of the past is necessary for the legitimization of interests, ranging from personal to national, in the present.[3] But the question of the past is problematic in the Chinese American case because of the way in which the symbolism of the Chinese American tradition remains in large part embedded within notions of traditions, customs, food, language, and histories rooted in a mainland Chinese past, a past that many view with ambivalence or as irrelevant and foreign. At the same time, this history is hard to escape because of the way that historical traditions and heritages, like cultures, are viewed as bounded entities that embody a group's cultural heritage (Segal and Handler 1995). This process of cultural innovation is driven largely through ritual exercises of solidarity that incorporate powerful symbols (Kertzer 1988). Symbols, whether of unity, protest, authority, or equality, are the language in which cultural battles are fought. The power of symbols and their ritual exercise lies in their ability to remain stable in form, yet flexible in content (the message they present). Symbols can be co-opted and reinterpreted, empowered and disempowered, through manipulation by social actors. David Kertzer argues that because of the existence of this symbolic diversity, symbols can play a role in fueling and legitimizing alternative viewpoints. In this case, the heritage of Chinese Americans is bound within a Chinese culture that in the context of U.S. multiculturalism represents a grouping or element that unproblematically merges Chinese and Chinese American cultures.

Chinese American identity narratives demonstrate this merging and the processes through which they try to negotiate meanings of Chineseness and Chinese Americanness as heritage, racial category, and political identity. They reflect the process of translating meanings of family history and heritage into a contemporary social and political framework that they create as Chinese or as Asian Americans. The formation of these identities is embedded in social experiences. For many of the people that I interviewed, coming to an understanding of their Chinese American identities involves developing an awareness of class and ethnic differences between themselves as descendants of Cantonese immigrants and Chinese from other parts of the world who emigrated under different circumstances. The development of this "Cantonese consciousness" encompasses an identification with the history, language, and food of the Pearl River Delta, with Chinatown, and with other Chinese Americans as they intersect with their own family experiences.

Throughout the interviews, interns often mentioned China as being something unknown or only partially understood. Political activity in the community of Chinese Americans, Asian Americans, or women of color also played a significant role to varying degrees in the interns' expression of their identities. But what these narratives most strongly bring out are the processes of sorting through what is particular to one's own and one's family's experiences and those of a larger Chinese American community; that is, the processes of developing a sense of a Chinese American community and one's place in it. For all of the interns mentioned, their experiences in the Roots program were a major factor in these processes.[4]

The Chinese American participants in the Roots program conceptualized China and Chinese culture in ways that were influenced by their class and positions within U.S. society. Most were born and raised in the United States, identified strongly with the Cantonese dialect (even if they did not speak fluently, if at all), and grew up primarily in middle-class areas outside of Chinatown. These factors defined their relationship to other "Chinese" groups in the Bay Area, such as Chinatown residents and newer immigrants from Taiwan.

Susan, a third-generation intern who grew up in a Bay Area suburb, said that until she arrived at the Bay Area private university (at the time of the interview she was a senior biology major), she did not have any consciousness about being of Cantonese descent: "I used to think that if you're Chinese, you're Chinese." Growing up, she did have Asian and Chinese classmates, "but it didn't seem like they were as 'culturally aware' as the ones here [at the university] do. We never talked about 'our Chinese pasts' as people here do. Here [at the university] it seems like it's more on people's minds." Susan believes that her growing awareness of her Cantonese identity comes from the heightened distinctions made among students of Chinese descent at the university and is reinforced by her participation in the Roots program and her visit to her ancestral village. During her China trip she related a story about how on her arrival at the university she found that others would ask her "what kind of Chinese" she was. She recalls knowing that she was not Taiwanese but not remembering whether she was Cantonese or "Mandarin," and having to go home to ask her mother what she was. She used to wonder why people seemed to make such big distinctions between various origins. But now she thinks that these differences are significant because they reflect how she was brought up in relation to Chinese from other backgrounds: "My grandparents' past, when I read [about] them in the archives,[5] [relative to] other people's parents when they emigrated here, I don't think had to go through as much interrogation and they weren't here when there weren't that many [other] Chinese . . . I think it affects how they were brought up and how I was brought up, so I think that's where I made the most distinctions, how we were raised."

A few of Susan's anecdotes are particularly indicative of issues faced by third-generation Chinese Americans, and of their understandings of community and of stereotypes of themselves and others as Chinese Americans. These issues involve a feeling of incompleteness, of not knowing about how one's own experiences fit in with those of other Chinese Americans, and of not having the context to differentiate "what is Chinese" and "what is American." When Susan's elementary school teacher assigned her class to make a family tree, Susan filled in her nuclear family's names, as well as those of her maternal grandparents, who had English names. She knew her maternal grandmother's name because the family would visit her, but she didn't know her paternal grandfather or any of her great-grandparents' names.

> So I was like, my teacher will never know, and I knew they were from China so that they would have Chinese names, so I kept that [last] name and then I went to look at Chang, or whatever in the phone book, and so I just chose some. I never thought much of it. I didn't

care that I didn't know my great-grandparents' names, though I knew that other people probably did. . . . It was mainly because I didn't want to turn it in blank because the teacher would probably ask me about it and I didn't want people to think, "she doesn't know." I didn't want it to be blank . . . it just looks bad if it's blank.

In elementary school, Susan thought that all Chinese Americans were like she was—they spoke English at home to their parents, and their parents spoke half English and half Chinese to their parents. But then she realized that some of her friends spoke half Chinese and half English to their parents, and in high school she came to the conclusion that half of the Chinese Americans were like her and the other half like her parents. "I always thought that if they were Chinese American, they were like me, but if they were Chinese from China, they would be more in touch with their Chinese background, like speaking to their parents in Chinese."

Susan recalls while growing up seeing public service announcements on KPIX, the local PBS station, portraying people from various "ethnic" backgrounds claiming "I'm proud to be [Chinese, Jewish, etc.]." One spot showed a Chinese American girl walking through the streets of Chinatown, proclaiming, "I'm proud to be Chinese American." To this, Susan states "And I was thinking, how could she be Chinese American if she was in Chinatown, because I always related Chinatown to Chinese from China, and I always thought that Chinese Americans were more like me. I never really thought that they were really different from anyone else, but from those public service clips, it made it look so different . . . like she was Chinese from China. I didn't really relate to them because it didn't seem like she had the same experiences that I did." She says she doesn't remember when she figured out that she was Chinese, but in junior high one classmate said to her, "I bet you eat Chinese hamburgers." She recalls just brushing off his comment, not knowing exactly how to respond because she didn't know whether or not there really was such a thing as Chinese hamburgers.[6]

Many of the Roots interns grew up with negative or ambivalent associations concerning mainland China. Few remembered learning much about China in school; even fewer knew much about Chinese American issues. In the images they were exposed to, China was either romanticized as an ancient and proud civilization or vilified as dark, evil, and communist in the orientalist discourses filtered through American education and the media. In essence, rather than representing a place that was familiar and comfortable to Chinese Americans, China was a foreign and unknown location to which they had an ancestral connections.

Roots participants were influenced by essentialized ideas about Chinese culture brought to them through portrayals of Chinese culture in the American media and through interactions with first-generation immigrants who (are thought to) have better command of the language and customs of Chinese culture. Most of the Chinese Americans that I interviewed felt that their lack of knowledge about Chinese culture, language, and customs made them less authentic as Chinese. This concept was relational, because even some interns who had a fluent command of spoken Cantonese felt inadequate in terms of their facility with the written language or felt that their vocabulary was limited to a child's household word stock. No matter how fluent they were in the spoken language, most felt inadequate with their level of proficiency, especially in the written language. Some entered school not speaking English, and this experience for them represented the first time they had to recognize themselves as Chinese. Before entering school, they never had a label for the kind of "Chinese" they were or the type of Chinese they spoke. One intern, Alexa, remembers coming home from school one day and asking her mother, in Chinese, whether she was Chinese; Tom said that he came home from school and told his parents that his classmates had asked him how to say "John" and other typical English names in Chinese, but he didn't know how.

Carl is fourth generation on one side of the family, and fifth generation on the other. He is a graduate of San Francisco State University and active in the Chinese Historical Society. He and his cousin completed an extensive family tree based on research at the National Archives, a project that he continued long after the assignment for the Roots program had been turned in. I asked him to what degree he was conscious of being of Chinese descent as he was growing up. He observed that at the school he attended in the Richmond district of San Francisco there was a "distinct difference between those who [had] just arrived here and those who [had] been here for a few generations." He sees this distinction as correlated with the ability to speak Chinese.

Carl was sent to the same Chinese school in San Francisco that his father attended as a child, but he lacked the Chinese-language background at home that many of his classmates had. "To me it was kind of awkward. I wasn't afraid and I didn't want to rebel, or block myself from being Chinese or anything, but the Chinese school I went to, now that I think of it, I should have gone to a 'CSL' (Chinese as a second language) program. . . . I was brought up with English and didn't know Chinese." He remembers going to friends' houses and being spoken to in Chinese by his friends' parents. He often felt embarrassed. He could comprehend the basic meanings and would tell them that he didn't know that much Chinese. He thinks his friends' parents found that odd. He adds "I'm willing to admit, the Roots program and the Taiwan Study Tour made me realize I accept my identity the way I am. I'm not one or the other. I'm not Chinese or Chinese American. I'm an American of Chinese descent."

In certain contexts, not only generational background but "Cantonese-ness" is a social marker that was closely tied to class distinctions. Interns viewed their Cantonese background and the family's history of emigration from Guangdong as one of struggle and a strong work ethic, paving the way in the United States for the success of later generations. While many families had risen to solid middle-class status, many interns still identified with the struggles of their immigrant ancestors. Thus, for many Roots participants, their rural Cantonese backgrounds reflected a class identity that distinguished them from the more prosperous immigrants from Hong Kong and Taiwan that they encountered at their universities.

One intern recalled that he did not identify with the Chinese culture that he learned about in a college course in Chinese history, because he could not see any connections to his own family background: "When I took History of China, which I just barely passed, I didn't find any connection to the history of Beijing or to the empires. It didn't mean anything. I could have studied the history of any other country and it would have been the same."

Another intern, Kim, is a graduate of Harvard's Kennedy School of Government, where she specialized in housing and urban development. As a child, she and her family occasionally went shopping and visited her grandmother in Chinatown. But for her, Chinatown seemed "sort of crowded and dirty . . . It was always a place to do errands rather than a destination." Growing up, she was "always that shy Chinese girl." She recalls a separation at school between recent immigrants and American-born Chinese, who did not associate with each other. She does not recall having what she terms a "Cantonese consciousness" until she participated in the Roots program. Like Susan, she became aware of class and cultural differences among different types of Chinese when she arrived at the prestigious private university. Her view of the Chinese American experience that she read about in class or heard about from her family differed from those of her classmates, many of whose parents emigrated from Taiwan after 1965: "I think when we would read all these books, like *Longtime Californ'* [and] . . . *Island*,[7] I would identify with them. I would think, 'Oh my grandfather went through that.' My grandfather picked fruit when he came over, and just from seeing Chinatown I knew that there were garment workers, they were poor . . . but then a lot of the Taiwanese had a really different experience. They were well educated . . . [and had] no sense of connection to the Chinatown . . . [This was] sort of the class difference that began to emerge." As a student, Kim fought to add classes in Cantonese to the university's curriculum, but both administrators and students would ask why she wanted to learn Cantonese, a peasant language: "I . . . feel like language is a key element of culture, especially for me . . . Well, my case is a little bit different since I was adopted, I mean I was like a day old, so for all intents and purposes my parents are my parents, and they're Cantonese, but biologically I'm half Cantonese and half Italian, so I don't look completely Chinese . . . For me language is a way of connecting with that culture that is very important, it's one thing that really separates the generations . . . you know, it separates sort of your identity." After I last interviewed her, Kim went to Hong Kong for a year to study Cantonese.

The family roots of intern Henry Jung extend through Latin America. Henry's mother is of Chinese descent but was born and raised in Peru, and his father's family is Chinese from Hawaii. He remembers as a youth going with his mother to shop in both the Mission district (the Chicano/Latino section of San Francisco) and in Chinatown, and he speaks Spanish at home with his grandparents. It wasn't until he entered school and was asked by other children about his ethnic background that he was forced to distinguish between the Peruvian and Chinese parts of his family.

I asked Henry what his impressions of China were while he was growing up. He says that he didn't think about China that much. He recalls seeing pictures of Chinese kids in Chinese school books. The stories of China he heard at school conjured up images of the countryside and of isolated farms. China was ancient, with a history thousands of years old. In contrast, images of Peru were more vivid for him; Peru and Hawaii were the "old country" for his family. Even though his grandfather listened to Chinese opera at home, he thinks that in the Richmond district where he grew up, "being Chinese" wasn't stressed, even though there was a large concentration of Chinese Americans there. He felt that he had trouble relating to Chinese Americans in Chinatown, because they seemed "more Chinesey" from having grown up in the Chinatown environment.

Henry became involved in Asian American studies while attending UC Berkeley. He studied for a year at the Chinese University of Hong Kong, and returned fluent in spoken and written Cantonese. He identifies strongly as a Chinese American of Cantonese descent (from the Zhongshan region) as well as with his Peruvian background. When I asked him what about himself he considers to be Chinese, he mentioned language, a group-oriented family attitude, the celebration of certain Chinese holidays and eating certain foods, deference to authority, and his physical characteristics.

Another example of the complex forms of identity created through secondary migration is Laura Lau's family. Laura was born in Burma, from where her family emigrated when she was a young child. Burma thus figures prominently in her interest in her ancestral roots. She knows that she spoke Burmese and some Toisanese (a dialect of Cantonese) at one time, but now she sees those languages as having been taken away from her in the process of her English-language education, which marginalized multicultural literature. When I first met Laura in 1992 as a coparticipant in the Roots program, she was a recent graduate of Lowell High School in San Francisco and was waiting to enter her first year at a private women's college in the Bay Area. When I interviewed her in 1995, she was in the process of packing for a study abroad semester in Thailand, after which she hoped to cross the border into Burma to contact relatives there. In recent years, she had become actively involved in Asian American feminist politics, and her views were marked by this perspective. I asked her how she identified prior to participating in the Roots program and becoming involved in politics in college. Although she attended Lowell High School, where Asian American students are the majority, on reflection she thinks that at the time she did not have the resources available to "inspire [her] to become more active." The first Asian American literature she read was in a college course and the only Asian teacher she'd had prior to that point was her Mandarin teacher in high school. She states: "[It was] almost a complete turnaround for me having teachers of color (in college) . . . I always felt that in English class I had to take myself out of myself and try to relate to the author, and when I write it seemed I had to take on this academic voice, something that wasn't real to me when I took an Asian American literature course [in college] it brought the two together, my love of writing, and my cultural history and family issues."

Laura hadn't heard the phrase "people of color" until she began filling out college applications. Her first year in college was the first time that she'd really learned about the Asian American movement. Despite her activist/political leanings, she sees her family background as consistent with her values. She thinks that her family has given her a "real grounding of my culture. . . . There isn't just one way of doing a movement, marching down the street with a sign, it's more than that, it's your daily acts of preserving your culture . . . I think I owe a lot to my parents for passing down the history and preserving traditions, teaching me where I'm from."

Roots Rap Session

On February 24, 1996, I recruited a group of Roots interns for an informal discussion session on the question of the "Chinese" in Chinese American.[8] The issue was framed by the following questions: To what extent should knowledge of specific cultural practices, traditions, customs, or rituals and histories be used as a basis for judging one's Chinese authenticity? To what extent should the rituals and traditions of mainland Chinese culture, past or present, be representative of contemporary Chinese American culture? What are the differences between being Chinese versus Chinese American? Why are these terms sometimes used interchangeably in the U.S. context?

I began the discussion with a number of quotes on the question of Chineseness, taken from various sources:

> As soon as my feet touched China, I became Chinese.—Amy Tan, *The Joy Luck Club*

> The Chinese have never had a concept of identity, only a concept of Chineseness, of being Chinese, and of becoming un-Chinese.—Wang Gung Wu, *China and the Overseas Chinese*

> The idea that I have an identity crisis is too simplistic and incorrect.—Roots intern

> The symbolic construction of "China" as the cultural/geographical core of "Chinese identity" forces "westernized" overseas Chinese to take up a humble position, even a position of shame and inadequacy over her own "impurity."—Ien Ang, "On Not Speaking Chinese"

After reading the quotes, I opened up the discussion. Many interns felt ambivalent about "Chinese" traditions, their knowledge of which was usually fuzzy, decontextualized, and often learned in bits and pieces and outside the home. In fact, their lack of knowledge about Chinese traditions and language made many interns feel inadequate and inauthentic. A number pointed out incidents in which they were accused of "having no culture" or "being too stupid to know their own culture." They felt judged as "incomplete" and were envious of others who could speak the language and had more immediate connections with mainland China. One intern remarked: "In some ways I think I have this internal jealousy of people who have closer connections, who can speak the language or know more traditions, so I think that it may be part of it, but I think there's also another part of it which is going around Chinatown and being like "oh, don't speak to me in Chinese." I mean, I can understand parts of what they're saying, but I don't respond. And like people of other ethnicities, it's always surprising that I don't speak Chinese. I'm third generation, what do you want?"[9]

But what finally emerged in the discussion was the interns' desire to flexibly adopt Chinese customs and practices that were meaningful and familiar to them, while at the same time modifying these practices for a Chinese American context. In this way, rather than feeling that irrelevant traditions were being imposed on them as a measure of their Chineseness, they were able to take ownership of them in new ways. Their experience of having visited a rapidly changing mainland China encouraged them in this process.

One of the coleaders of the Roots program, an educator of Chinese descent from the Philippines, made the following observation:

> There are certain traditions that we still practice like the Spring Festival, the New Year . . . those are traditions. Some people celebrate Ching Ming, Chong Yung . . . I [had] never celebrated Chinese New Year in my life until I came here [to the United States]. I have never celebrated Ching Ming in my life . . . in the Philippines we celebrate All Souls Day. All I remember is my nose would be all black when I came home from the candles, but it's not the Chinese tradition . . . [and] it's only when I came here when I celebrate that. My wife has more traditions than I do . . . but I know about it. We go [to] pay respects on the birthdays of our parents . . . that's how we do it. But I don't do Ching Ming. That doesn't make me not Chinese, or mean I don't have that Chinese culture.

He continued by saying that while he believes that there are certain things that are Chinese, these things are "meaningless unless the individual constructs something out of that." The intent of the Roots program is to teach interns about these customs, greetings, and other aspects of Chinese culture and for the trip to China to show them that "these are things that people do." But he emphasized that not everyone may necessarily want to construe what they've seen in China as definitive Chinese customs, such as spitting and smoking. Similarly, he observed that while karaoke and driving Mercedes Benz's are popular in China now, it is another thing to say that these should be part of Chinese or Chinese American culture.[10]

Many of the female interns whom I interviewed in this mixed-group (male and female) setting viewed the gendered practices associated with traditional Chinese culture, such as the exclusion of female names from written genealogies, as practices that they could change in their own rework-ings of Chinese culture in an American context. They found customs such as generational naming and not washing one's hair on New Year's Day to be practices that seemed no longer relevant in modern U.S. society. The original meanings and functions of these traditions were often not known by the interns, which usually made them seem even more irrelevant. Generational naming was viewed as part of a patriarchal system because only males received these formal names when they married. Similarly, the names of women were traditionally excluded from genealogies, and descent was traced through the male line. Many interns strongly objected to the gender bias of these traditions. But many still expressed a desire to perpetuate such customs, stressing that understanding them is an important part of remembering one's Chinese American history: "To me the [generational] name doesn't mean as much, but it could also be because I'm a woman, so most likely I won't have my own anyway. But I also think the most important thing is that we remember our history, so I think that if we just remember that and remember how the [paper] name got changed, then I think that it's sufficient for me."

In deemphasizing the importance of generational naming but reinforcing the importance of genealogy as an exercise in reclaiming family history, interns were recasting genealogical writing in a new light. Thus, tracing genealogies became important both as a way of symbolizing the linkages between China and the United States, past and present, and a way of reclaiming the family's rightful identity, which had been forcibly altered to skirt unfair immigration laws. At the same time, interns altered not only the function but also the form of the genealogies. Many traced both sides of the family and included both men and women.[11]

The custom of not washing one's hair on Chinese New Year, which symbolizes the avoidance of washing away prosperity,[12] is one that few interns practiced. And they did so only after weighing the relative implications of following what is known to be a cultural superstition versus the social connotations of walking around for a day with dirty hair. While they viewed their decisions to follow or not follow these customs as a conscious choice, they also saw them as having no real personal consequence. Many customs were deemed important not because they were necessarily consistent with the interns' own belief systems but because they retained meaning within the context of their own families. In many cases the meaning behind the custom was not known.

One intern remarked that he wanted to learn how to make *jin doi*, the meat-stuffed, fried triangular dumplings made for certain occasions. He says that his mother makes them every year, even though he knows making them has "no [practical] value." "I honestly want to know how to make them. I was eating them every year and I finally asked her, what's the meaning of making these, what do you do? [She said] the large ones and the small ones represent sort of families and having offspring and longevity. . . . Still, part of me wants to keep [the tradition] going because I sort of like it, but it has no value." Indeed, the traditional meanings of the custom are often secondary to the association with family:

> I don't think I do it because it doesn't have a real value, I think it may not be traditional, well actually I don't know what is traditional about it, but I see Chinese New Years as being a time to celebrate being around family, and so when [for example] . . . I bought oranges . . . it wasn't because oranges represented something, it was something that I thought my parents would enjoy having. For me, I could have bought them peanuts, and it would have represented the same thing, but for me it was being around family . . . making *jin doi*, and learning how to make *jung*[13] is important, but I think I do know certain marked holidays for a certain reason and I try to celebrate the spirit of the holiday more than the tradition of the holiday.

Many interns saw the following of certain practices and the emphasis on certain values as being Chinese American, even though they may differ from the practices and values in mainland China. And although they viewed not following some customs as a matter of having assimilated or developed beyond those irrational practices, they saw other behaviors as common and proper behavior etiquette—things that Chinese Americans should know not to do: "I was joking with a friend of mine, and I guess a lot of people don't eat meat on Chinese New Year . . . [I asked] did you eat meat today, and he said, yeah, in fact we're going out to dinner tonight. And I'm like, you don't have to eat meat, you're just assimilated. And he's like, no I'm just evolved. But how would you react if you saw someone like, *messing up*, like putting sugar in their tea and pouring soy sauce over white rice?"

• • •

The content of Chinese American culture consists of far more than the practice of traditions deemed "Chinese" based on their association with traditional mainland Chinese customs. As they construct their own versions of Chinese American culture, Chinese Americans employ a selection of symbols from the Chinese past that acknowledges the Chinese past yet falls outside the ritual constraints of traditional Chinese culture. They emphasize things that seem a unique part of the Chinese American experience, such as the history of railroad laborers and the common experiences of racial oppression with other minority groups. But in emphasizing that their Chinese heritage makes them different from other "Americans," Chinese Americans find themselves in the position of deciding how much of this past they wish to claim. And regardless of the degree to which Chinese Americans are adamant in claiming the "American" part of their identity, they continue to face judgment, by both Chinese and non-Chinese, as "Chinese."

At one point during my research I encountered an Internet chat-group discussion on Chinese culture and biculturality in North America. For one first-generation Chinese American in the group, the choice between Chinese and American culture was one of "tea and paintings" versus "electricity," where Chinese culture was conceived of as ancient high art and rituals while American culture was viewed as progressive and modern. As Richard Handler (1988) points out in his study of Quebecois nationalism, the objectification of cultures for the purpose of preservation often results in "high culture" being seen as embodying the whole culture. Thinking of culture as elite traditions and the fine arts increases the sense of cultural "lack" felt by Chinese Americans and devalues their everyday practices and family traditions. One intern remarked that the Chinese Culture Center, which sponsored the Roots program, should continue in such efforts, because "culture is passed through people, not institutions [and the] high culture" they embody. Indeed, the rewriting of genealogies by the Roots interns in many ways represented their spurning of "high culture." According to David Faure (1989) the construction of genealogies originated in the gentry classes and later spread to the common people. The altering of genealogical forms by Chinese Americans thus can be read as a rejection of this "high culture" and a celebration of new Chinese American forms of culture.

Although there was not consensus among the interns, some main themes ran throughout the discussion I held in 1996 and my other fieldwork interviews with the interns. Being Chinese American was ultimately a subjective concept, created variously through experiences with family, political activism, investigations of family history, being informed about the history and current situation of Asians in the United States, visiting ancestral villages, and placing value on family. The meaning of each of these issues is left to the individual to create. The Roots program was instrumental for many, both as a way to learn about Chinese and Chinese American history, family history, and ancestral places in China and a way to recontextualize personal experiences within a larger context through understanding the meanings behind many customs and traditions that were viewed only in a piecemeal fashion at home. For many this involved a process of relearning aspects of Chinese culture that they were introduced to through the program in the process of research, spending time with other interns, and visiting China. This creation of a Chinese American identity selectively wove elements of family, history, and personal experience, to which each individual assigned his or her own meanings. The Roots program was flexible in this respect because it did not focus on a single ideological way of being Chinese American but rather on learning about one's family and group history both in China and the United States as a basis for pride and a feeling of legitimate belonging in the United States.

Thus although the Roots program didn't focus explicitly on issues of power, its format allowed for reworking various hegemonic constructions of Chineseness and Chinese Americanness, of which the interns were aware to differing degrees. For example, rather than dwelling on the state of in-betweenness that many interns said they felt, the program provided a basis from which identities could be supported independently of the dichoto-mized categories they felt caught between.

I provide here three statements by interns to show how their ideas about being Chinese or Asian American are varied and changing in meaning according to the particular experience. These statements are, of course, not representative of the individual's entire viewpoint, but what the statements do emphasize is the limitation of categorical, prescriptive ideas of identity that are forced on the individual, as well as the subjective nature through which the meaning of individual identity is created. Although all of the interns had participated in the Roots program, and many had exposure to Asian American studies, it becomes evident from their statements that each has had to deal very specifically with images of China and Chinese cultural authenticity.

> I used to have a lot of ideas about what people had to know and what people had to do [to be Chinese] . . . I grew up in Chinatown and was in college in basically this really white background, and so basically I would say that anybody who knows that they're not white, then I would say, yeah, you're Chinese. . . . For me, personally, I think that Chinese American means all the things that my parents chose to pass on to me, and all the things that they chose not to pass down to me . . . All the stuff that I choose to learn, like all the traditions and stuff like that, and also this feeling of being in between, not really being able to be fluent in the white community, and also going back to China and not really being able to be fluent there, . . . and also being very self-

conscious.—*Twenty-one-year-old second-generation female who grew up in Chinatown.*

[What] it all basically boils down to is that the identity issue is basically subjective; the discussion has to start with how you're going to define being Chinese. Is it just this ethnic, biological thing, or is it a cultural thing, or language, or whether you follow the customs or not? Every person has a different standard that they're living, you know, if [when] you grow up . . . and all that being Chinese was is celebrating Chinese New Year every year, well for you, that's what being Chinese is, if you never had the language before, then that's not the main issue. I also [want] to point out that when we went to Hong Kong to study, a lot of us Chinese Americans were like, well you go to Hong Kong and you look like everyone else, end of this identity crisis [laughter], but it's identity crisis but all in reverse. You go there and you say you're Chinese, and they say, "you're not Chinese, you don't live here, you don't speak the language," things like that, "you're American." I had people there telling me I was American, I had people saying I was Chinese. Every time you talk to someone, there's a different reaction. So I'm like you can't go anywhere in the world and fit in completely.—*Twenty-five-year-old second-generation male who grew up in the Richmond district*

I'm questioning all this as we're talking, this question of what it means to be Chinese American. Because I realize that as you ask the question, a lot of how I view it is what I've been told by my parents or by the culture itself—it's more been defined by other people, but to leave that question open to myself, and for me to try to answer that, it seems that it's someone else's idea. I know that certain things that I do . . . like lion dancing, when I take the meaning for myself, it has meaning for me, sometimes I don't interpret that to be Chinese . . . It's how I express myself, in a way maybe that my ancestors did at one time.—*Twenty-seven-year-old third-generation male who grew up in Marin County*

One of the most vocal interns, Fred Chang, who has been actively involved in Asian American politics, wrote in his final report, "The idea that I have this identity crisis is too simplistic and incorrect." As mentioned earlier, he had observed that on finding out that he had gone to China to visit his ancestral village, others would make statements insinuating that it was great that he had finally found himself. His statement refutes common assumptions about identity searching within identity politics that see the individual as incomplete and not whole until a satisfactory identity is formed. This assumes that any one form of identity, as it has been broken down within identity politics (ethnic, gender, sexual, class, to name a few), is totalizing. While Roots participants are still to some extent constrained within politicized ethnic and racial politics, many have come to the conclusion that identity is ultimately personal and constantly changing.

What the Roots program does most effectively is to help participants begin to negotiate an understanding of themselves in relation to China and its traditions. The program does this through the experience of researching family histories and visiting ancestral villages, and through the involvement in a peer group concerned with similar issues. These experiences are instrumental to reworking the bounded categories of U.S. multiculturalism, particularly in the interns finding a way to counter the hegemony of the cultural authenticity of China in the Chinese American past through building their own cultural capital, writing their own histories, and creating their own family rituals based on their experiences in the United States. The hybridity of Asian American identity must be recognized as authentic and complete, an act of cultural construction and an acknowledgment of heterogeneity (Lowe 1991).

In chapter 5 I discuss the relationship between Chinese Americans and China more specifically through an examination of the interns' visits to China as part of the Summer Camp activities, and within the historical context of relations between the PRC and the Chinese abroad. In the following chapter I discuss how the views of the mainland Chinese are also changing.

roots narrative)

Like many of us in the web of CNN, I watched with horror as the Chinese national guards killed the student protestors in Tiananmen Square. I often wondered what those who were left behind felt. Did they know? Did they have access to the news footage that shocked the rest of the world?

In every region of the country, from Beijing to Guangzhou, the answers to my questions were the same. All of those whom I talked to had the same answer. Since they were not government officials and not directly in power, they concluded that earning money was the only worthwhile thing to consider.

Those among us who are more cynical might respond that this is no different anywhere else in the world. True, many have become disillusioned with the inability to affect government policy, and certainly I do not mean to suggest that I am not aware of the need to be cognizant of economic realities. I believe, however, that this sentiment has permeated into many facets of the land that has changed so dramatically from my previous visit [at age twelve]. The promise and the potential for danger in China's future is evident whether it be in the big cities such as Beijing or Guangzhou or even the small communities such as the villages around the Shendong Stream of the Yangtze River. In vast contrast to 1984, China now has many of the problems seen in the western world. Several times during my visit, I was asked, "Ni yao bu yao peng you?" or "Do you want a friend?" Our tour guide explained that many young women who are unable to find work in the big cities resort to prostitution. The highway underpasses of Guangzhou have become the "home" for

Chinese from the North who have unrealized dreams of the riches to be had in the South. Even tour guides from the government travel service company asked if we would allow presumably black market resellers to use our U.S. passports to buy duty free items meant only for those who would be exporting such purchases home. Instead of the Communist world I had left [visited] ten years ago, China had taken on a decidedly capitalist flavor.

—A.C., 1994

THE FENG SHUI HAS TAKEN A TURN (*FENG SHUI LUN LIU ZHUAN*): CHANGING VIEWS OF THE GUANGDONG CHINESE TOWARD LIFE ABROAD FOLLOWING THE OPEN POLICY

Massive social changes have accompanied China's reentry into the world economy in the wake of the Open Policy and economic reform in the early 1980s. Mainland Chinese conceptions of the outside world, and of power relations both within mainland China and in relation to diaspora Chinese, have shifted dramatically over the past twenty years. In this chapter I focus on interviews I conducted in the Pearl River Delta region of Guangdong Province in the mid-1990s.[1] Overall, the interviews indicate that many residents of this relatively prosperous region of China are reassessing their views toward permanent emigration. However, what is significant about these changing views toward the outside world is that they are obtained less through direct experiences with racial discrimination and lack of opportunity, and more through stories filtered through the media and popular culture, and gossip most often heard indirectly from friends or relatives both in China and abroad. In some ways, the mediated nature of this information makes it even more influential, as it leaves more to be embellished through the imaginations of the Guangdong Chinese hearing these stories. The conceptions of first-class, second-class, and third-class citizenship that Guangdong Chinese use to assess their current positions and future opportunities in China or abroad are abstract and relational. They are less measures of concrete achievements than they are statements about perceived opportunities for development.

These ideas are thus closely tied to a history of overseas Chinese relations that have been marked by mediated communications and inequalities in relation to relatives from abroad, who have in the past provided charitable aid to them. The Guangdong Chinese population's imagining of overseas relatives in positions that are now more equal, or even in some ways less privileged than they are, is part of this turning of the tide. The indirect nature through which these impressions of the overseas Chinese "other" are formed is significant; in this book I have emphasized how formations of contemporary Chineseness are increasingly created across national boundaries in highly mediated ways. Thus, while I began this book with a description of the back-and-forth movement of my own family, the mainland Chinese and Chinese American players presented here are in some ways increasingly disconnected and in other ways increasingly connected. In other words, while they are increasingly connected in their opportunities to form impressions of one another, this is accomplished indirectly through media and migrant flows. Ironically, as I show in chapter 5, when Chinese Americans are brought together with their mainland Chinese relatives in the context of searching for roots, they seldom discuss the issues described here. This is due in part to the format of the village visits and in part to language barriers, but I speculate that the greatest reason is that Guangdong Chinese already feel they know about these things.

In the previous two chapters I discuss how Chinese Americans form imagined attachments to China and to Chinese traditions not only through visiting China but also drawing on information relating to "Chinese" or "Asian" culture circulating more broadly. The relationships they craft to China are shaped within the context of the politics of identity searching in the United States. Similarly, contemporary Guangdong Chinese imaginings of identity take form within the context of Chinese state attempts to define a modern Chinese identity based on "socialism with Chinese characteristics." However, in contrast to Mao's socialist project, which aimed to put China on its own path of development separate from the outside capitalist world, flows of Chinese culture and capital extending beyond the Chinese nation-state now play a central role in reshaping mainland Chinese ideas of Chineseness, often in ways that contradict official narratives.

In this chapter I discuss in further depth how the Guangdong Chinese are renegotiating their ideas of what it means to be both Chinese and modern in postsocialist China. In doing so, I focus on how they are forming new opinions about Chinese Americans and other Chinese people living abroad, particularly in relation to their relative economic and social positionings. As I will show, these changing perceptions of the Chinese abroad by mainland Chinese are especially significant because of their implications for historically rooted ideas about the relationship between the Chinese abroad and China that also ironically form the basis of contemporary Chinese development and modernization schemes. In this sense, transnational flows connected to this development are challenging the ideals on which contemporary Chinese nationalism is being built.

As mentioned previously, the southern part of Guangdong Province has historically been an outward-looking region of China. Its proximity to the coast has shaped both its tradition of sending emigrants abroad and its historical role as a point of entry for foreign powers. Not surprisingly, the region has also served as a filter through which ideas, people, and products from the rest of the world have entered China. For centuries, returning migrants to Guangdong have brought with them capital, goods, and ideas from abroad that have in some cases inspired popular movements for revolution or reform, including the founding of the Chinese nation-state in 1911.

In the nineteenth century, imperialist powers attempted to impose their influence on a closed China through the city of Guangzhou, and although their success was limited, their victory in the Opium War gave them the colony of Hong Kong. As a British colony perched just over the border from the mainland, Hong Kong has for over one hundred years played a key role as an exchange point between mainland China and the outside world for capital, goods, people, and ideas. For the Guangdong Chinese, Hong Kong has served as a nearby reference point and a site through which much information about the outside world enters the region. At the same time, however, it has been a source through which many others have accessed China, including at least two generations of Chinese Americans seeking their roots (Louie 2003) and earlier generations of anthropologists studying Chinese societies. Even during the period when China isolated itself from most of the outside world (1949–1979), the Hong Kong–Guangdong connection remained somewhat porous. During these years, the Guangdong Chinese frequently attempted to cross the border to illegally enter Hong Kong, which at that time represented freedom and an opportunity for many to reunite with family members. In particular, the late 1970s was characterized by a period of *chu guo re*, or emigration fever, as people scrambled to go to Hong Kong or other places abroad.

Thus, in many respects Hong Kong has in the past represented a location of desire for the Guangdong Chinese. Indeed, Hong Kong is visible from certain points in mainland China, and vice versa, thus serving as a constant reminder of the mainland Chinese or Hong Kong "other." It was a place inhabited by Cantonese speakers like themselves, many of them relatives, who symbolized the potential for development that many on the mainland felt they could achieve if only given the opportunity. Hong Kong's influence in southern Guangdong extends beyond the affluence it symbolizes to ways to enjoy and display this prosperity. In this sense, it represents a Chinese version of the American dream, although it remains unclear whether Hong Kong as a former British colony represents the West or a form of alternative Chinese modernity. A hybrid form of culture that combines influences from its Chinese roots, other Pacific Rim nations, and the West has flourished there. In the past as well as the present, Hong Kong popular culture has played a key role in shaping Guangdong Chinese tastes in fashion, music, and movies, and the Guangdong Chinese have in turn shaped the tastes of other parts in China.[2] Items symbolizing prestige in Hong Kong, from good brands of cognac to expensive automobiles, also were desired in Guangdong because of the cachet they carried in Hong Kong high society and the proximity that allowed these products to flow, both legally and illegally, into China.

In a different way, Hong Kong has also occupied a place in the Chinese American imagination. Hong Kong–based popular culture has impacted Asian communities in all parts of the world, including the Chinese American participants of the In Search of Roots program. It is thus perhaps significant that the Chinese Americans in the Roots program entered and left China through Hong Kong. As mentioned previously, many Roots interns were familiar with music and film stars from Hong Kong, along with the popular culture icons such as Hello Kitty, kung fu movies, and Japanese *manga* that were favored there. Although it is difficult to say exactly how the interns came to know about these things, Asia chic, or the popularity of "Asian" things, became increasingly widespread in the 1990s, especially in the San Francisco Bay Area where the interns live. Thus, without even having traveled to Asia or having had direct contact with new immigrants from Hong Kong, they have been able to incorporate various images and icons as part of an Asian American popular culture.[3] As I discuss in chapter 3, these popular culture flows are important to understanding contemporary negotiations of Chinese American identity.

Most Guangdong Chinese form impressions of their own lives relative to those in the outside world less through direct contact with outside populations than through information obtained through the media and gossip. Significantly, while Hong Kong remains an important reference point and source of information for the formation of these ideas, the Guangdong Chinese are at the same time reimagining their position relative to their Hong Kong compatriots, based on information they receive primarily via Hong Kong. As mentioned earlier, the Guangdong Chinese have long been in a position in which they have had to reassess their identities as Chinese in relation to the outside world. They have often been the first to point out contradictions between China's path and alternatives offered by the West. Following the Cultural Revolution (1966–1976) and Mao's death, Deng Xiaoping's implementation of the Open Policy and economic reform (*gai ge kai fang*) reflected a new path for China's development and modernity that had implications for shaping Chinese identities in new ways. Mao's Cultural Revolution had aimed to reinvigorate a socialist revolution that had lost its momentum, in large part by attacking feudal superstitions and capitalist practices, including those of familial ties, ancestor worship, and connections to capitalist societies abroad. During this period, many families with overseas connections were persecuted and rituals reinforcing kinship ties ceased. Ironically, however, the Open Policy and economic reform, which began only a few years later, drew on these very attachments. Central to Deng's plan for economic development were his policies encouraging investment from the Chinese abroad, who he felt could lead China on a path of development that was progressive yet still could be called socialist. In implementing "socialism with Chinese characteristics," China would not be selling out to capitalism but rather finding its own path that was modern yet still Chinese.

However, socialism with Chinese characteristics has in many ways proven inadequate for providing a clear path for the development of a modern Chinese identity amidst massive social and economic change. Its obvious departure from the reforms of the previous decades are difficult to ignore, despite slogans and campaigns legitimizing the new plan, the most famous of which is Deng's "It doesn't matter whether the cat is black or white as long as it catches mice." While the successes of the Open Policy and economic reform are obvious, particularly in the South, there remains a mismatch between China's rapidly changing society and the foundational ideas on which these new policies have been built, especially in relation to the overseas Chinese. Specifically, Deng's plan cast the Chinese abroad in a central role for China's development by encouraging them to come "back" to build the motherland through capitalist investment. Their desire to return was thus explained as deriving not from the opportunities for investment but from the love of their homeland. Throughout the period of socialist reform many families had secretly kept genealogy books, and as Potter and Potter (1990) have argued, the family remained the basis for social organization. However, on an official level these renewed kinship connections to overseas Chinese were based on the presumed connections between race, culture, and nation that had not been used for decades. These were laid on the rootless, iconoclastic ideologies of the Cultural Revolution.

Perhaps because this plan for economic reform produced relative prosperity, most Chinese people have been slow to point out the contradictions. However, as I show later in this chapter, the differences between the mythical patriotic overseas Chinese and the actual behaviors and sentiments of Chinese visiting from abroad are beginning to emerge. What I argue here is that China's reopening to the outside world has created discourses of Chinese culture that are problematic because of their lack of fit both with recent societal changes and with the historically rooted assumptions that they are based on. They are thus easily complicated and often contradicted by other discourses of Chineseness increasingly available to mainland Chinese through transnational flows of media, migrants, and capital (Grewal, Gupta, and Ong 1999). The notions of Chineseness available through government discourses are limited in the sense that they do not allow for the diversity of ways of being Chinese in mainland China and abroad. In other words, they do not adequately take into account regional and class variation within China or abroad, or the acculturation of the Chinese to local cultures. Government discourses infer from Chinese "racial" origins certain cultural practices as well as nationalistic feelings toward China. At the same time, many Guangdong Chinese are increasingly being exposed to different ways of being Chinese through capital and media flows that are creating massive internal changes in China, including a large "floating population" (*liudong renkou*) of migrant workers who are forced to leave their hometowns to find employment yet are denied basic citizenship rights in the places where they live and work, and the creation of new boomtowns without histories such as Shenzhen. These massive changes are creating even bigger divides between rich and poor, and urban and rural dwellers. At the same time, alternative narratives of Chineseness from outside China include not only the idea that one can be both Chinese and capitalist, but also the idea that Chinese in other countries are victims of discrimination and are thus perhaps not as successful as previously thought. They crosscut the often outdated ideals on which the Chinese government has based many of its reforms, and which do not reflect China's changing relationship with the outside world or the changing identities of Chinese people within or outside China.

For many Guangdong Chinese, ideas about personal fulfillment and nationalist pride are increasingly tied to opportunities for mobility, whether through migration and travel, opportunities to earn money, or the availability of consumer goods. They increasingly believe that they can be "first-class citizens" in China, whereas in America they may only be "second-" or "third-class" citizens due to discrimination. They hear about such situations of racial discrimination and chances for upward mobility indirectly, through Hong Kong television as well as through gossip from friends and relatives who have been abroad. In many ways, the sometimes exaggerated tales they hear may produce in them images that are even more vivid and fearsome than expressed in the stories. So while most have had few opportunities to speak directly with visiting Chinese from abroad about their experiences of racial discrimination, this knowledge nevertheless frames their interactions.

Transnational fantasies of alternate lives take on a magnified significance when examined through the processes of interaction narrowed within what has been defined as a diaspora population. For Pearl River Delta residents, overseas Chinese are not just abstract conceptualizations fed to them through government propaganda. Throughout modern Chinese history, the state media has portrayed the overseas Chinese in various, often contradictory, ways—at times as traitors, at other times as capitalist roaders, and still others as patriotic sons whose obligation it is to help build the Chinese nation (Fitzgerald 1972). More recently, however, they are seen as friends, neighbors, and relatives like themselves who have had opportunities to go abroad and gamble at making a better living. The lives they lead represent the potential lives they imagine themselves as having. Still, many are thinking twice about whether they want to be in that position. Transnational flows of capital, information, technology, and people have been integral to the economic development, the more comfortable standard of living, and the increased access to outside information that have occurred in the years since the Open Policy. These changes have complicated the "fantasies of moving" (Appadurai 1991) of many Pearl River Delta residents.

Arjun Appadurai (1991) describes "the fabrication of social lives," enabled by the global reaches of the mass media and the increased role that fantasy as a "social practice" now plays in people's lives, which has allowed "more persons in more parts of the world [to] consider a wider set of lives than they ever did before" (1991: 198).[4] These "fantasies of moving" include migration within China or abroad. For Pearl River Delta residents, global economic changes are manifested on a microlevel as alterations in the imagining of "potential lives," informed by secondhand stories and media portrayals of the experiences of friends, neighbors, and relatives abroad, and contextualized in terms of perceptions of their own life choices. Within this context, conceptions of the Chinese abroad have also become more sophisticated. They frame the situation of the Chinese abroad in comparison to their own lives, which are no longer seen as "givens" but rather, in Appadurai's words, as an "ironic compromise between what they could imagine and what social life will permit" (198).[5] As understandings of the opportunities and limitations of the Chinese abroad become more realistic and detailed, and their sense of agency about their own opportunities increase, many

Guangdong Chinese find themselves in a position where they are renegotiating their relationships with their overseas Chinese friends and relatives.
They are beginning to question the relations of power, class, and privilege
within the Chinese state's construction of a Chinese diaspora that has in
past years ascribed greater symbolic and cultural capital to the overseas
Chinese by virtue of their mobility, foreign citizenship, access to information and goods, and economic position.[6] In the first part of this chapter I
focus on changing views toward the outside world and toward emigration in
recent years; in the second part I address the shifting relationship between
the mainland Chinese and their overseas relatives.

Changing Views toward the Outside World

Many Pearl River Delta residents describe the period prior to the Open Policy
as c. *bai sat* (md. *bi si*) or c. *mong sat* (md. *mang si*), meaning that they were
naively blind, ill-informed, and blocked to knowing conditions both within
and outside China. More than twenty years have passed since the Open
Policy began, and the Guangdong Chinese now view themselves as much
more sophisticated and better informed than even ten years ago. A shift has
occurred from previous views molded through government propaganda that
socialism is the best path for development, to the worship of a hybrid capitalist form of "socialism with Chinese characteristics." Mr. Yeung, a Hakka
native of Shenzhen in his fifties who works as a supply clerk at a local high
school, observed: "Before if you wore leather shoes you were considered a
capitalist. Socialism meant you had to be poor. Now it has reversed. Socialism
means to be *fu* [prosperous], to have everything [c. *mat yeh dou yauh*]."

The introduction of the Open Policy and economic reform in Guangdong
is viewed in retrospect by most residents as a liberation from previous feelings of blindness. Not only has it enabled the economic development that has
allowed Guangdong greater autonomy from the Chinese state, it has also
given many residents of the more prosperous Pearl River Delta region a
sense of being able to rely on their own abilities and on the information
available to them in negotiating the terrain of this capitalist landscape. In the
eyes of many residents, economic reform has both directly and indirectly
provided opportunities for individual economic development. The Open Policy has helped the Guangdong Chinese see themselves as more informed
through transnational sources channeled into Chinese popular culture via
the print media, television, books, returning migrants, and tourists, which
have helped them form comparisons between Guangdong and the rest of the
world. These changes in Guangdong people's images and understandings of

the outside in the years since the Open Policy have resulted in a rethinking of their place in China and the world. Economic reform has brought China as a player into the competition of global capitalism.

In many ways, as the Cantonese universe expands more toward the outside world, dreams of becoming richer become more tightly enmeshed with symbols of modernity and forms of foreign capital, both monetary and cultural. At the same time, Guangdong distinguishes itself even more from the rest of mainland China, not only because of its openness but because of the social relations that are becoming more and more distinct between the poor, rural immigrant laborers (the "floating population" as discussed by Solinger 1999) entering Guangdong from poorer regions of China and the local Guangdong residents. However, while understandings of what is vaguely referred to as the outside may form an implicit basis for comparison between Guangdong and places abroad, rather than serving to inculcate a belief in foreign superiority, these conceptions are increasingly being used critically in negative contrast to what is good about living in China.

Gazing Back on Oneself

When uncensored images of the outside world first appeared in the stories of returning overseas Chinese, in the newspapers, and on Hong Kong television, the mainland Chinese newly began to see themselves as poor and their country as backward and undeveloped in comparison. Of course, there had long been internal differentiation in wealth within mainland China, but for years many had been convinced that socialist struggle and reform, including the lean times that accompanied it, would rectify these feudal inequalities. But when Pearl River Delta residents gained access to Hong Kong television in the late 1970s (many on communal televisions rigged with fishbone antennas) the increased access to images of and information about the outside allowed them to view themselves and their nation through the eyes (of the camera) of the "other."[7] While socialist schemes of development had been promised as the most moral, proper, and effective path to China's advancement, in contrast to capitalist decadence, it became evident that in many ways China had fallen behind in terms of economic and technological development.[8] Mainland Chinese developed a self-consciousness about how the outside viewed China as backward and undeveloped, along with a new perspective on how China compared with other nations within this development scheme. However, many mainlanders responded to what they saw as unfair judgments of China's development. A seventy-year-old retired army officer in Guangzhou, my Yi Suk Gung, aware that many foreigners and overseas Chinese are afraid to come to China because the countryside is viewed as dirty, stated, "Of course it's dirty; they're running a farm!"

The vocabulary of socialist development that was once used by the government to describe traditional China as feudal (*feng jian*) and backward (*luo hou*) was now being used with renewed connotations of self-criticism and shame of China's position in relation to the outside, as the reality and severity of these conditions were reconfirmed by the condescending gaze of the West and beamed back to the Chinese on their television sets. Much attention has been paid to the six-part Chinese television serial *He Shang* (River elegy), shown in 1988, which focuses on the weight of Chinese tradition as the source of modern China's problems and looks toward the Pacific Ocean, as a symbol of the West, as the only viable way of rescuing China from her backward condition. This production used flashy advertising imagery from American television as part of its representation of the West.

I Saw It on (Hong Kong) TV

The following excerpt from my field notes describes a visit with Mr. Lau, a man in his forties who has lived all his life in rural Zhongshan County, a *qiao xiang* (hometown of overseas Chinese) not far from Macao.

> Pearl River Delta, Zhongshan, San Xiang, Bai Gong village
> We sat around the table after dinner in the spacious kitchen of the Lau family's two-story house, built in 1985. A Chang's younger brothers and sisters, grandmother, and *yi po* (visiting from Hong Kong) watched Hong Kong television on the 25-inch TV in the living room, sitting on wooden furniture built in her father's small factory. Mr. Lau leaned back in his chair and puffed on his cigarette. Before, he said, he wanted to go to Canada or Panama, but he doesn't regret it now because of *hoi fong* [open policy]. "Before one could only farm, and there was no goal [c. *muk biu*; md. *mu biao*] so one had to go outside. Now we can make money here. Twenty years ago in Guangdong people admired the life of overseas Chinese. Overseas Chinese could earn a lot of money. Now life here is getting better and better. No one admires them as much. The difference has been reduced. This new generation of immigrants are workers [*da gong jai*]." If he needs to choose between being a worker here or outside, he said, he would prefer to be a worker here.

With only an elementary school education Mr. Lau worked much of his life as a farmer, but after the Open Policy he opened a small furniture factory in the nearby market town. After returning from work, Mr. Lau usually watches Hong Kong television, especially the news and American shows such as *20/20* and *60 Minutes* on his large-screen Sony television. His daughter says that both her parents and her grandmother have learned a great deal from watching Hong Kong TV. She comments: "Their thinking is more open. They know about Hong Kong people's lives, and those of people in America and Canada [including Chinese in these countries] from movies. . . . They know more about [the] outside, but don't know much about inland China because they don't watch TV or read the newspapers. Most of the Pearl River Delta is like that."

Television is a "popular cultural medium" (Fiske 1987: 37), a form of mass communication geared toward a mass audience whose differences it tries to homogenize to capture the greatest market. Since the late 1970s televisions have been among the items most desired in Pearl River Delta households, represented in the folk memoirs of overseas Chinese by their mainland relatives' requests for improved and larger sets through the years.[9] Hong Kong television has become increasingly available to Pearl River Delta residents, with earlier restrictions and attempts to block its signal having been eased. By the early 1990s it could be received in some big cities through cable services such as Star TV, which transmits, and occasionally censors, the signal. Some of the aspects of Hong Kong television most appealing to Pearl River Delta residents are the quality of programming, the fact that the programming is in Cantonese, the information available through the news, and the opportunities to see how other people live (Lull 1989). The majority of my informants watched the Cantonese news, and even those originally from northern China who couldn't speak Cantonese said they could understand the news from having watched it regularly.[10] In addition to the news, variety shows, often featuring famous singers or actors; news magazine formats; foreign movies; Channel V (music videos); and TV dramas, often set in ancient China, are popular. The show *Bao Qing Tian*, which portrays the deeds of the legendary, highly moral-and-just Judge Bao from mythical Chinese history, was among the most popular shows during my fieldwork period.

Television advertising has a major impact, and brand-name shampoos, medicinal oils, clothing brands, detergents, and so forth are popularized through ads that often feature famous Hong Kong celebrities recognized by most Pearl River Delta viewers. One ad features Chinese American tennis player Michael Chang promoting a dandruff shampoo. Chang has become popular in Hong Kong and some parts of China as a *Chinese* tennis star, despite the fact that he is American born and speaks little Chinese. Hong

Kong television has not only influenced both the consumer values and the conceptions of the outside world of many Guangdong residents, it has also had an impact on their bodies through modeling new ways of speaking and acting that are deemed more modern and sophisticated. Ways of carrying oneself, of dressing, of using make up, and of speaking Cantonese are modeled through images in ads, movies, and TV shows. Susan Fang, a twenty-four-year-old junior college graduate whose family comes from Guangzhou demonstrated for me the difference between Hong Kong and Guangzhou Cantonese. Hong Kong Cantonese is softer and more refined (*si wen*): for example, while Hong Kong people would say, "it's very *hot*" (*hou "hot"*), using the English for "hot," Guangzhou people would exclaim loudly, "*yit sei ngoh*," or "I'm dying from the heat." Another woman bragged about her good Hong Kong accent (which she said she learned from watching Hong Kong television), noting that many people ask her whether she's from Hong Kong because of her refined accent.

James Lull, in his book *China Turned On: Television, Reform, Resistance* (1989), states that one role of television in China is to provide a reference point according to which mainland people can compare their lives with others. Lull argues that far from serving as a tool for state propaganda and thought control, television in mainland China was viewed critically by the urban Chinese residents he interviewed in Beijing, Shanghai, and Guangzhou. Because images, including those broadcast on television, are polysemic (Fiske 1987), they produce a "diversity of sentiments" (Lull 1989: 209) for viewers. The medium of television serves to "amplify contradictions" such as those between the socialist realism shown on the screen and the experiences of everyday life, and serves as a referent for the discussion of these issues in daily conversation. In Lull's interviews many people referred to it as "mind opening" (209). Many of my informants demonstrated their critical perspectives through observations made while the television was on. Mr. Lau said that from watching shows such as *60 Minutes* and *20/20* on Hong Kong TV (with Chinese subtitles) he can see how the style of news in China is biased (*pian jian*). He says that the American programs don't tell you directly what to think or what is right or wrong. Instead they try to present both sides and let you decide for yourself. Hong Kong news is somewhere in the middle, he said.

Hong Kong television sparks criticisms of a different nature than those directed toward the state-controlled media in China. While mainland productions are criticized as representing unrealistic state-sponsored visions of society, Hong Kong television provides a reference point representative of a Chinese society outside of China and of the outside world and the West, resulting in both positive and negative commentary. While televised images consist largely of what may seem to mainland Chinese as decontextualized generic visions of America and other Western countries, the way that these images are consumed and understood is indigenized when framed in reference to their own living styles and standards. Studies of popular culture describe the way in which images, such as those of television, produced by the culture industry, which may seem totalizing and hegemonic, are creatively reappropriated and reinterpreted on a local level by consumers. Television images are polysemic, structured discourses, which are intended to be read in specific ways by targeted audiences but can also be interpreted in different ways according to the social context of the viewer (Fiske 1987). Ien Ang, in her classic essay "Watching Dallas" (1985), describes how Dutch viewers see the show as representative of American values and lifestyles, while they interpret the events portrayed in terms of their own cultural values, sometimes watching it in parody. The references that many informants made to the Western world came from television—ranging from the size of houses and number of cars in America to what foreigners look and act like to conceptions of the lives of the Chinese abroad to knowledge of world political events. Moreover, these television images were often used to illustrate examples of what they disliked about Western Society, such as the instability of social relationships, lack of respect within kinship relations, street crime and danger, and the treatment of minorities.

For the mainland Chinese, portrayals of life overseas are contextualized further as representative of the conditions under which the Chinese overseas are living. While the Chinese community overseas has always been part of the conceptual universe of the majority of Guangdong Chinese from emigrant areas, access to the foreign media and television has allowed this community to be imagined in a different, much more vivid, and seemingly "real" way, by incorporating images of life abroad garnered from television news, movies, and documentaries. These images serve to illustrate stories read in the newspaper or told by returning friends and relatives.

In recent years, these images have been telling them new things, as they see and hear about the problems of unemployment, racial tensions, economic downswings, and violence that tell them that the United States is far from the paradise they thought it was.[11] Mainland Chinese people have long been aware that China is not at the bottom of the scale of development. Mao's Third World plan had positioned China in the role of aid-giver for the development of Third World places such as Cuba or in some nations in Africa. More recently, images in the Western media of world news events portraying starvation and poverty in places such as in some African nations and in India were especially effective in convincing Chinese people that "China isn't the poorest country"—resulting in a rethinking of the place of China on the scale of development. In addition, recent emigrants returning from abroad brought stories of hardship in their economic and social conditions such as not being able to find work or working long hours for little pay. These conditions result from shifts in the global economy, including the infusion of capital investment in Third World countries such as China to tap its massive labor force, and the accompanying restructuring of the economies of many destination countries such as the United States. Meanwhile, the economy of Guangdong has boomed, resulting in dramatic improvements in living standards and income, albeit at the cost of large-scale migrations and social problems.

Possibilities for Mobility

The post–Open Policy period has been marked by an increase in information, goods, and people flowing not only into but also out of China.[12] Beginning in the late 1970s, wealthy "patriotic" overseas Chinese began returning to China to invest, serving as living examples of the economic success that perpetuated notions of the wealth to be obtained abroad. On a smaller scale, relatives began returning from abroad after the Cultural Revolution, bringing aid to kin and making small donations and investments in their hometown areas. For many Guangdong Chinese, these notions of success overseas had historical roots in the stories brought back by previous migrants. Dreams of the gold mountain (America) and successes elsewhere abroad inspired numerous generations to send family members overseas. These fantasies hit the level of an emigration fever (*chu guo re*) at the end of the Cultural Revolution, as tens of thousands of Guangdong Chinese rushed overseas and to Hong Kong, most illegally, to fulfill fantasies refueled by reconnections to the outside.

Recently, growing numbers of Chinese have had a chance to travel, both within China to nearby Hong Kong and, increasingly, to other countries such as Thailand. The Chinese tourist is a new phenomenon, not only because of new freedoms to travel, but also as a result of the consumer-based mentality, luxury, and modernity that tourism represents. Starting in the mid-1990s it became possible for mainland Chinese to travel to Hong Kong for business, to visit relatives, or to take a tour (which cost about HK$3,000). Tour companies run charter buses from Guangzhou to Hong Kong, and numerous trains run daily to the border town of Shenzhen. Chinese citizens must go through special channels and paperwork procedures at the border, but once in Hong Kong they are free to visit relatives, shop, and go sightseeing. Many Hong Kong shops, especially jewelry stores selling gold, advertise that they accept *renminbi* [Chinese currency]. My aunt, a Hong Kong resident, said that she had taken some guests to the jewelry store that she usually patronizes. Their display cases were practically emptied of goods—a large group of mainlanders had just left and had bought up most of their stock of gold jewelry, paying in cash. Mainland consumers are viewed in Hong Kong as being savvy customers, willing to spend a lot of money in proportion to their income and knowing what they wish to buy. The same commercials on Hong Kong television that advertise items only affordable to the elite are seen by viewers on the mainland, thereby setting their standards of consumption and conceptions of status symbols. Gold jewelry, name-brand clothing, fine brandies, Japanese cameras, and leather purses are popular status items.

On one of my last days in Hong Kong at the end of my fieldwork, I decided to venture into Mong Kok's Fa Yuen Gai outlet district to do some last-minute shopping. Feeling quite anonymous among the throngs of pedestrians on this crowded street, I was surprised to hear my name called out in Chinese. I turned around to see Mr. Ruan, the Qiao Ban (Overseas Chinese Affairs) official who had, days earlier, accompanied me to my maternal grandmother's ancestral village in rural Duan Fen, Taishan—which was an approximately three-hour ferry trip plus a one-hour bus ride from Hong Kong. He said he was in Hong Kong for business and travel and that this was his second visit. He seemed not nearly as disconcerted as I was about making the transition from the small, poor, agricultural district in Taishan to this bustling city street in Kowloon. Indeed, his information about Hong Kong was not limited to those things he saw and experienced during his visits there. Hong Kong has been part of the imagination of Pearl River Delta residents since they began hearing stories of returning migrants and were able to receive Hong Kong programming on TV, a form of virtual travel similar to the way a large number of Americans (and others around the world) "experience" the United States without having moved much farther from their living-room easy chair than to their workplace, the shopping mall, and an occasional vacation.

Changing Views Toward Emigration

One of the major concerns relating to mainland Chinese discussions of the status of other Chinese abroad is the problem of racial discrimination (*zongzu qishi*). Among the questions asked of me in China those about racial discrimination toward the Chinese in America were among the most common. The position of the Chinese abroad has for centuries been linked with the strength of the motherland, and up until 1956 when China withdrew its extraterritorial rule over the overseas Chinese, the Chinese government took an active role in assuring the "protection" of her "subjects" (Fitzgerald 1972). Older Chinese, especially, with strong nationalist educations, are sure that when China becomes stronger, the Chinese abroad will no longer be bullied.

Ideas about the exact nature of discrimination abroad remain vague: How does it affect daily life and getting a job? Does it become less of an issue with later generations? But while reports about overseas Chinese in the news and print media have in the past concentrated on the lives of wealthy overseas philanthropists, information is increasingly becoming available about more common, less wealthy overseas Chinese. Broadcasts featuring the lives of the Chinese abroad appear on Chinese national television (CCTV), on some provincial stations, and on Hong Kong television. Programming on CCTV includes portraits of famous overseas Chinese who have contributed to their motherland, but it also includes shows such as *Window to the World* (*shijie zi chuang*) that focus on the lives of Chinese living in different parts of the world. There has been a spate of popular literature during the last few years about new Chinese emigrants, mostly exchange students (*liuxuesheng*) and the difficulties of adjusting to foreign life. The popular novel *Manhattan's Chinese Lady*, which was also made into a television miniseries, communicated a complex and somewhat ambivalent account of life abroad. The central character initially faces hardships and discrimination but in the end succeeds. But by far the most influential impressions of the conditions of Chinese abroad come from immigrants returning for visits or permanent stays.

Mr. Lau, a villager in Zhongshan County who has never been abroad himself, lamented that "Chinese people, wherever they go, are excluded (*pai chu*; c. *pai cheut*)." He's heard people recently returned from Canada who say that's the case: "Chinese invest, help you, why are they excluded? Wherever they go, it's like that. People come back and say so. Over there, they sell beautiful houses, but they don't sell them to Chinese."

These impressions of the status of Chinese abroad play a role in people's own views toward emigration. One twenty-four-year-old female junior college graduate, working for an American company in Shenzhen, indicated that she was not sure whether she would want to go abroad. In China she has a circle of friends and is familiar (*shu*; c. *suhk*) with the society, and she had the potential to be a "first-class citizen" (*diyi deng gong min*); overseas, however, Chinese are *di san deng gong min*, third-class citizens, because of discrimination. Similarly, a twenty-five-year-old female middle school graduate who works as a baggage clerk in the Guangzhou railway station commented: "People here know that there's discrimination outside. Chinese are second-class citizens [*daih yi deng gong min*]. This is true especially for new immigrants." In China, she observed, Chinese people, including herself, would also look down on foreigners here.

Among my informants the use of the "first-class," "second-class," and "third-class" citizen designation was a common way of identifying status levels, although the designations met no rigid criteria. These levels of citizenship referred to the degree to which one could live up to one's potential to fully participate in society through negotiating work and social life without having barriers of discrimination placed in the way. For this reason, many people said they wished to emigrate to an Asian country such as Japan, Hong Kong, or Singapore, under the perhaps false impression that in those countries their position would be stronger as part of a majority "yellow" race.

Relative Comparisons

China's development since the Open Policy has been far from a steady upswing, although it is often portrayed in popular memory as a series of dramatic, almost revolutionary improvements, both social and economic. Many informants boldly contrast the poverty and blindness before and in the beginning of the Open Policy with their current living conditions, with a sophisticated understanding of complex political and economic conditions, and with the present potential for future development. They express a sense of agency in making informed, realistic decisions and of being able to rely on one's own abilities to succeed in China, combined with a sense of cautiousness and relativism about thinking in relation to one's own situation and in light of one's information about the outside. This has resulted in changing attitudes toward emigration and the dreams that accompany it. They weigh the ideal of the American dream and all of its trappings with cautious assessments of the likelihood of their achieving it, and of their willingness to make the drastic and risky change of entering a foreign society. At the same time, they take a more relativistic stance in comparing the situations of mainland China and First-World countries whose lifestyles since the late 1800s have been marked by increased difference—differences that in recent years have diminished slightly.

Mr. Zhao, a Guangzhou city Qiao Lian (Overseas Chinese Union) official expressed the present conditions as a matter of thinking realistically, making comparisons, and thinking about "one's own reality": "You must ask yourself whether you can develop in the American society, or in China. You must be realistic. Before, if you mentioned the word 'immigrate,' people would immediately run [to emigrate]. Now people can compare the two places according to [their own] expectations; think clearly, according to one's own reality and conditions. Even common people can think so." This sense of thinking realistically is seen as a check for the pursuit of foolish dreams. Mr. Lau, for example, stated: "You can't make the whole world's money—this is only a dream, so many people choose to stay here." While many Pearl River Delta residents find the life portrayed in America to be attractive, they also question whether it would be suitable for themselves. They realize that not everyone can develop easily abroad, and they consider carefully the drawbacks of living in a non-Chinese society as second-class citizens.

For many informants, the issue boils down to where one will work to earn a living. While for previous generations of emigrants, going abroad was seen as a matter of earning a living (c. *wan sic*), for new emigrants it is viewed as a gamble for attaining a better quality of life. The Cantonese use the term *bok a bok* (md. *bo yi bo*)—to take a risk or gamble—when referring to taking one's chances at a better life abroad. However, many people take such risks cautiously, asking themselves what really would be different or better about life abroad. The following comments represent common expressions of this sentiment:

> Whether you are "inside" or "outside," the goal is the same: to earn money to eat. The difference is in the opportunities.—*Zhongshan villager who runs a small factory*

> Wherever you are, it's the same, you must rely on yourself.—*Twenty-nine-year-old female barber in Guangzhou*

> You must work hard to make a living, perhaps even harder in America.—*Overseas Chinese Affairs employee*

While earning American dollars is still seen as desirable, many say that there is more to compare between China and America than the amount of one's salary, type of dollars earned, the size of one's house, or kind of car owned. Many informants articulated the impossibility of comparing the history, economy, and society of China and other countries such as America. They say that it is unreasonable to compare the life one is leading now with an imagined, potential life abroad. Many people I spoke with engaged in an implicit dialogue against the judgments that a U.S. liberal democracy (Madsen 1995) places on China's state of democracy, human rights, and development, using China's weighty tradition as an explanation for its current situation. But this undertone did not override the form of China-centered relativism expressed.

Rebecca Guan, a young woman of about thirty, has worked with many groups of Chinese from abroad in her job with the Summer Camp programs. A native of Guangdong, she moved to Guangzhou from a small town in the north to attend the university. She says that she has had an opportunity to talk with many overseas Chinese through her work, and from this perspective she can compare China with other countries. She's decided that "every country has its different character" and that "not everybody can live a good life abroad." She tells her friends not to imagine that other countries are better. "Why do you definitely have to go? You don't definitely have to go out. At the beginning of the Open Policy, many people went out to settle permanently, blindly thinking that China was the only poor country. This was because of the abnormal psychology and thinking [bu zheng chang xinli] of the Cultural Revolution." But now she's happy here in China where she's familiar with the people and the place, and where she feels there is no racial discrimination. In China, she says, you don't need to *kan biede lian se* [watch the facial expressions of others]: "Here you can do anything, you are the hostess." She continues:

> You can't compare the United States and China in terms of democracy. China has had a long feudal history. The United States is young. It's like three generations of a family; their thinking is not the same. Chinese history is so long, the United States is so young. The population of China is so large, traditional. You can't compare it with America. It's easier to build a new building on the plains [in America]. The United States has new houses. People envy [xian mu] you. But for China to build new houses, it's more difficult. You must destroy the old house to build the new one. It's necessary to compare the history and the economic situation [of the two countries]; to compare with one's own past, future, and present. Don't compare with others.

She implies that it is not only difficult to build new physical structures such as houses and buildings, but that the weight of China's tradition may result in different political and social structures that cannot be compared with those in the West.

A similar sentiment was echoed by my aunt, Yi Suk Gung's daughter, a woman in her late twenties who has lived in Guangzhou since her early teens. She says she doesn't want to go to America because she doesn't like the government: "They're always trying to be like the policeman of the world" by involving themselves in the affairs of other countries. "America is not a democracy. If you have money, you can buy justice. America can't be compared with China. You can't necessarily say China is all good either, but it's different because of its four-thousand-year-old history." American society is not suitable for her, she said. She wouldn't feel safe (c. *mouh on chuyn gam*), and she's afraid of having to work too hard (c. *pa san fu*). She makes about four hundred renminbi per month (in 1995) at the university where she works as a classroom teacher, a salary that is low compared to that of many people outside of academia. But she also receives housing benefits, and she likes her job.

Many Pearl River Delta residents have close family relations—parents, siblings, children, and sometimes spouses—in nearby Hong Kong or Macao. For example, Mr. Feng, an administrator and former English teacher at a Shenzhen high school, is from Zhongshan County. However, his mother and father emigrated to Macao, and he has many other relatives in Hong Kong and elsewhere overseas. He states: "When China was closed, people saw everyone overseas as very rich but didn't know that many of them were working harder to make a living than they [in China] were. Now it's different; now Chinese people can get more information. They know the situation. Each family has its own business, each has its own troubles [c. *yat ga yat sih*]."

When he met my parents when they visited the school where I taught English, he thought it was interesting that they had returned to their hotel by bus not by taxi. "Not every [*sic*] people are rich and can use money freely. If they could use money freely, they wouldn't have needed to watch it" (by taking the bus). He realizes that "many overseas Chinese are richer [than my parents], but it's not easy to get money." For example, his classmate in Hong Kong is rich, he is the boss of a jewelry shop: "But [I'm sure] he's not as rich as I think. Every family has its own trouble. He must support his life, his shop, his family."

Before Kai Fang (the Open Policy), he said, he didn't think deeply. He only knew that "America, Canada, France were rich countries [with] good living." Now he knows that in the world "there are two hundred countries, but only twenty countries are rich. The other places are not easy. Even in those twenty countries, many people lead hard lives." After the Open Policy, he thought more about it. "America is the richest country, but there are still millions of homeless people there"; indeed, he had heard that a businessman was producing and marketing paper sleeping bags for them. He himself would like to spend time abroad traveling. But he does not wish to emigrate. He is happy in Shenzhen, in Guangdong Province, to which he returned after spending most of his young adulthood in Shanghai. He is after all, a Cantonese; his native place is in Zhongshan. "There's no place like home" (c. *ji gei ukkei haih ji gei ukkei*), he said.

Self-Reliance

Seeing oneself as able to make informed decisions, to compare, and to think about things clearly (c. *lam ching cho sin*) signifies a new sense of self-reliance, of having options, and of being able to think rationally about them and to exercise them. This sense of agency perhaps naively underestimates the biopolitical (Ong 1999) power of the Chinese state to control migration, emigration, housing, job allocation, etc., and feeds off the idea that there are always ways around this control. The level of corruption among officials has convinced many that money can buy anything. Nevertheless, many Guangdongese see decisions about whether or not to emigrate as being made within this context of rational choice, of exercising options, acknowledging of risks, and relying on one's own abilities. The following story demonstrates one future emigrant's assessment of these issues.

While in Shenzhen in 1992–1993, I became friends with the school's barber, A Liang, a young, single woman of about twenty-six, and a native of Guangzhou. She rented space from the school to run her shop, which was open to the public but provided special pricing for school staff members. We were about the same age, and I enjoyed visiting her in her shop to practice my Cantonese. She wanted to learn English and was very curious about American life. A very capable businesswoman, she worked long hours at the shop and supported herself with her income, as well as her hired workers. A portion of her earnings she chose to spend on personal beautification; she had her eyelids operated on to make them double, and her eyeliner and eyebrow makeup were tattooed permanently. She saw these modern markings as distinguishing her even more from the unsophisticated *heung ha mui/jai* (literally, boy or girl from the countryside, but here referring to people in general from the countryside),[13] who she (and other Cantonese) often put down as being crude, simple, and unfashionable. She seemed more oriented toward Hong Kong, having told me numerous times that people in Guangzhou and Shenzhen were much more well informed than those in the inner areas because they had contact with people from Hong Kong as well as access to Hong Kong television. She was intimately familiar with Hong Kong products and would often ask me to bring things back for her when I made trips over. Another friend said A Liang would often model a new outfit for her, asking her whether she looked like a Hong Kong person. It became evident early on that her goal was to emigrate to America, as she embarked on many letter-writing relationships with men her relatives introduced her to. A year later, when I returned for a visit, she introduced me to her boyfriend, a Vietnamese-Chinese who had lived in America for seven years and was just about to become a citizen. The following year, I stayed with her in her home in Guangzhou. She and her boyfriend had married that past fall, and the couple were now parents of a two-month-old baby boy. The father had returned to San Francisco and had yet to see the child. While I was visiting, she received a letter from her husband's sister, assuring her that her application for emigration to the United States would be processed before she knew it. The letter also included a check for u.s.$200, half of which was for my friend, and the other for her husband's sister, who was still living in Guangzhou. She said to the baby, "Look, Hou jai, your father sent you $100 American dollars to buy diapers." She said the baby smiled.

A Liang once told me that even homeless people in America eat better than the Chinese do. On my most recent visit I asked her what she thought about the many people who had told me they were less eager to emigrate now because they were comfortable with their lives here and they feared the difficulty of making a living abroad. She replied, "But the life in America is even better [than here] . . . It isn't stable here, Chinese laws are too strict, changeable. They don't even let you give birth to two babies." She said she has been influenced by the example of her godmother in the United States (c. *kai ma*) who emigrated many years previously. "The life there is more stable than here . . . There are certain things you *must do*. Whether here or in the United States, you must work. Wherever you live, it's the same; you must rely on yourself . . . But the 'brands' (c. *pai ji*) aren't the same; they have better brands there . . . The common life in America is better than here. For the same kind of work, you can enjoy yourself more in America. There is discrimination in America, but you yourself can be diligent. You can study English, and depend on your own intelligence." She said she wants to c. *bok hah*, gamble at having a better life. If there's work to do, she's not afraid of working hard; although she speaks little English, she plans to work in her sister-in-law's barber shop. "You can earn money gradually," she adds. "For example, some people in Guangzhou buy a motorcycle and use it like a taxi to earn the money back. They use time to slowly earn their money. In Shenzhen they say 'Time is money.'"

A Liang's story shows that the terms in which attitudes toward emigration are framed have shifted from a blind faith in the American dream to a more cautious view of emigration as a gamble. Changing views toward conditions outside, channeled through transnational flows that have also altered conditions at "home," have resulted in an increased sense of relativism and self-reliance. Perceptions of emigration for many have shifted from a strategy of survival to a calculated choice.

The Changing Relationship with Overseas Relatives: Gift Giving and qinqing

Aid to mainland Chinese relatives has been an essential defining point in the relationship between overseas Chinese and their mainland kin. This relationship has evolved through the years from the giving of necessities for daily living (food, clothing, oil, buckets, etc.) to basic household goods (electric fans) to luxury items (televisions and washing machines). Although these items are given as necessities that mainland relatives didn't have access to or couldn't afford, they can also be seen as gifts. The same ethical and moral obligations implied within kinship relations require one to both help relatives in need, and to express feelings (ganqing) through the proper conduct of giving and sharing. However, due to their lessened dependence on overseas help in recent years, many informants have described a shift in emphasis from gift giving as an ethical obligation to gift giving as a demonstration of qinqing (c. chanching), or feelings between relatives. However, as will be discussed later, the giving of such large amounts of money and goods has itself created an unequal power relationship, a debt of "symbolic capital" (Bourdieu 1977), between mainland Chinese and their overseas relatives.

Gift giving is an essential act of propriety within relationships between relatives and friends. While many informants said they no longer expected specific items from their relatives from abroad when they visit, most agreed that the giving of gifts was an important demonstration of qinqing. The issue was not as much whether, or how much, the gift was needed but rather the sentiment the giving of the gift represented. Nevertheless, all gifts, whether exchanged between mainland friends or relatives or overseas relatives and mainland residents, had to conform to certain standards of size, appearance, and cost depending on the relationship between sender and receiver.[14]

Mayfair Yang's (1994) analysis of ganqing and renqing as they relate to kinship and guanxi (building relationships) is useful in understanding the relationship between gift giving and the sentiment referred to in the idea of qinqing. The demonstration of qinqing is seen as important on the part of both mainland and overseas relatives. However, the building of these feel-

ings is not entirely an emotional issue but also comes through the fulfillment of an implied "ethical kinship conduct" (195). Relatives and friends
visiting from abroad, especially from First-World countries in North America and Europe, are expected to bring gifts because of their usually higher
economic standing and access to products not available in China. However,
many informants insisted that the gift itself wasn't as important as the
feelings its giving represented. This feeling was described as something less
tangible than the willingness to give gifts, but rather as an act of a moral,
ethical, and obligatory nature. Relationships, even between relatives, have to
be cultivated in part through this gift-giving behavior, which carries with it
the sentiments and feelings of obligation as described by Harumi Befu's
"expressive gifts," although "obligations need not be activated by giving
gifts" (cited in Yang 1994: 195). Nevertheless, as Yi Suk Gung said "you can't
expect to have *qinqing* without having spent time together."

A personal incident and its interpretation by my Chinese friends illumi-
nates this issue of gift giving by overseas relatives. I needed to retrieve
something from my aunt's house in Guangzhou and I had been having a
hard time trying to arrange to go there. Every time I called, she said she was
"very busy" (c. *hou mong*). I mentioned this problem to my friend A Liang,
who asked when the last time was that I had given my aunt a gift. A Liang
felt it was possible that my aunt was angry at me, particularly because I may
have committed a faux pas by not bringing gifts for her family when I
returned from a vacation to Beijing.[15] She added that "some Chinese expect
their overseas relatives to bring them things." Other Chinese people I spoke
with agreed. So, worried that I had committed a serious breach of etiquette
and ethics, I went gift shopping with A Liang at a Hong Kong supermarket
store in Guangzhou before my final visit with my relatives before leaving
town. A Liang selected a sixty-four ounce container of Tang beverage powder, packaged in a decorated glass container. I told her I wasn't sure if my
relatives liked Tang, but she replied "it doesn't matter if they like it; it looks
good and it's expensive." She explained further that it had to be something
foreign made. Most people expect their overseas relatives, especially if
they're returning from America, to bring such gifts. But really, she said, it's
because it's representative of *qinqing*.[16]

Overseas Chinese are often accused of having become selfish while
abroad, of having lost their sense of *qinqing*. They are seen as having been
affected by Western culture, which is viewed as lacking the affective sentiments of *ganqing*. These images of Westerners as not having *ganqing* or
renqing come from stories of people returned from abroad, as well as from
watching relationships portrayed in foreign films and television (Yang

1994). During my fieldwork I heard stories of children abandoning their elderly parents to nursing homes and friends splitting the bill at a restaurant, which were told as examples of the lack of sentiment and the selfishness in American relationships.

In the past, expensive gifts from overseas relatives were viewed as almost ethical obligations, of helping out less fortunate family members. Overseas Chinese were expected to bring large-ticket items such as washing machines, radios, and television sets to their mainland relatives when they returned for a visit. A system was set up through which overseas Chinese could bring in cash to purchase these items duty free in *mian sui* shops on the mainland or pay for them in Hong Kong through the China Travel Service and pick up the item on the mainland.

In the past, a leveling mechanism in Chinese society involved the sharing of wealth and good fortune within the family as demonstrated in the equal division of inherited land and property among sons in rural China. Gross inequalities in economic levels between close kin were viewed as almost unethical if resulting from the more prosperous having neglected the needs of the less fortunate. These moral obligations were used in combination with nationalist rhetoric to encourage overseas Chinese to fulfill their "duty" of donating to their home villages. In aiding their own kin, they were also helping the nation. Therefore, the giving of these "expressive gifts" by overseas Chinese demonstrated not only affective sentiments but also the fulfillment of the ethical responsibility of having helped less fortunate relatives and one's nation.

Renegotiating the Relationship with Overseas Chinese

Relations between the Chinese and overseas Chinese can be considered kinship in nature, in both literal and fictive senses, because of racial and kinship metaphors used to construct this relationship. As demonstrated in Yang's work, the ethical obligations of mutual aid are understood in kinship relations. The family strategy used by earlier immigrants of sending husbands and sons overseas to earn money for the family entailed that money should be sent from overseas to help family in China who were unable to support themselves. But great differences in status between kin are cause for some discomfort, because ideologies emphasizing the shared Chineseness of all people of Chinese descent, both in China and abroad, don't take into account these class differences.

Because Chinese and overseas Chinese are kin both through traced relations and in the sense that all Chinese are assumed to share a common ancestor, inequities between them are problematized in a magnified, complex way. The inequality between what has been given to mainland Chinese by their overseas relatives and what, if anything, has been given in return, has become the basis for an unequal relationship between them. Although these exchanges have been conducted under the propriety of traditional kinship obligations, perhaps with some manipulation on the part of mainland residents, mainland Chinese relatives have accrued a debt of sorts in the process of receiving these gifts.

The giving of what were essentially donations by overseas Chinese to their mainland relatives has been framed by the Chinese government in terms that on the one hand represent this aid as the natural outcome of feelings of kinship and patriotism, but on the other hand has glorified them as benefactors. This official praise, consistent with the Chinese concept of gaining glory by showing off to the hometown (returning to one's hometown wearing "golden clothes") has been the basis for this glorification. And their mobility and access to information, foreign capital, and other things from the outside additionally represent a form of what Bourdieu terms "cultural capital" (1977). However, the layers mystifying this capital have gradually been stripped away as mainland Chinese begin to perceive themselves as having increased access to these things and are no longer depending on overseas relatives.[17]

The Feng Shui Has Turned the Other Way

Reliance on contributions by overseas Chinese in past years has been a given in China. It is estimated that at least 80 percent of Chinese emigrants came from the Guangdong region (Vogel 1989). Overseas emigration, originally a strategy for bettering a family's position, made dependence on overseas relatives the accepted result of this strategy for survival. Overseas residence was initially considered only as a way to earn money abroad; and, with the ultimate goal being to return to China to settle, all earnings were pumped back into the home community. Relatives of overseas Chinese (qiao juan) have ridden out the unpredictable campaigns and policy changes since liberation and have suffered or benefited from the various consequences of having relatives abroad. In past years, especially during the Cultural Revolution, overseas Chinese and their dependents were viewed as subversives. Since the late 1970s and early 1980s overseas connections were prized. Now, it seems, overseas Chinese are no longer as special, although these connections are still valued by those who can take advantage of them to go abroad.

During the fieldwork interviews I conducted in the Pearl River Delta region in which I asked people about their relationships with their overseas Chinese relatives, the mainland Chinese I talked to in both rural and urban areas expressed changing attitudes toward these relations. An overseas Chinese union official said: "Before, when people heard the word 'huaqiao,' others would say, 'wow.' Now, there's not as much sensation [hong dong]. Before huaqiao created a big impression. Now, everyone has become richer, it doesn't matter." A middle school teacher in Shenzhen commented: "Before, when Guangzhou people mentioned the word "Hong Kong guest" [c. Heung Gong haak], people would exclaim 'Ai ya' in excitement. But by 1997, there won't be much difference between Shenzhen and Hong Kong. They expressed pride in no longer depending on overseas relatives for monetary donations. In some cases they were able to give presents back in return. Before, many Guangdong residents had to rely on their overseas relatives, many in Hong Kong, to bring money and items from abroad. It has only been recently that they have been able to earn a salary that has allowed them to buy the basic necessities, and even luxury items, that have become increasingly available with economic reform. Now, many are adamant about not relying on the support of overseas relatives: "Now we don't envy overseas Chinese so much. We ourselves have ability [c. jigei bunsan], and life conditions allow us to earn more money ourselves. It's not necessary for others to help. We can have everything we want" (Mr. Yeung, supply clerk).

While in the past, mainland relatives welcomed donations and gifts and their overseas connections helped raise their status in relation to those without outside connections, having had to rely on others for aid seems to have also been a central point shaping a status differential between themselves and their overseas relatives. This is a subject of some sensitivity because many people are now reluctant to be seen as begging from the overseas Chinese. There is a storehouse of folk stories about overseas Chinese who were afraid to come back for fear they would be asked for money or stripped of their possessions. A friend told me that her uncle, who had emigrated from Taiwan to America, wrote a letter to her mother in Guangzhou, asking if it were really true that the clothes would be taken off his back if he returned to China (a story that people said had occurred during the hardest times).

In 1995, many people emphasized that they feel they may be better off than their foreign relatives,[18] that many people are choosing to come back to China to take advantage of the opportunity to be first-class citizens, and that some are returning because they couldn't make it abroad. Many residents with average incomes (in 1995 about six hundred renminbi per month) now say that while they didn't like to ask for money from their relatives, they would accept it: "If they have money (to give), they can give it." They reflect back on how excited they would be when relatives brought bags of worn, unwanted clothes for them to wear. Now, one young Shenzhen worker said, she would be insulted if an overseas Chinese tried to give her their unwanted used items, which she terms "garbage" (c. *laat saap*). In fact, many people pointed out that the overseas Chinese now come to China to buy things such as clothing, medicine, and other goods to bring back to their homes abroad.

A few years ago the phrase *nanfeng chuang* (southern-breeze window) was a common saying referring to the window of opportunity and fresh feeling provided by having relatives abroad. Now this phrase is no longer in fashion. While in the past, having overseas Chinese connections would allow one to buy duty-free items such as televisions, washing machines, and later, motorcycles, these items are now readily available in Guangzhou. One overseas Chinese union official, a Guangzhou resident, said that previously a remittance of u.s.$100 would make a dramatic difference in a family's income, but now, although useful, this amount would not change their status significantly (this is true for many urban residents, but the money is still welcome—representing over a month's pay—and is even more needed in the countryside). Now, he says, returning relatives don't need to come back hauling large appliances, and even can come back empty-handed if they wish (*liang shou kong kong huilai*). My aunt in Hong Kong says that she hopes the next time she visits her relatives in Guangzhou, they'll take her to dinner. Years ago, they would bring empty plastic bags to the restaurant to carry home leftovers, but they stopped this practice a few years ago. They're all doing well now; most are earning monthly salaries of 1,000 renminbi.

I asked people what their relatives brought when they visited. "Small items," they said, "things made in Hong Kong or abroad that aren't available or are expensive in China." They added that they were often expected to give special local products (*techan*) or take the relatives out to dinner in return. While I was staying with the Lau family in Zhongshan, their relatives from Hong Kong came to visit. They brought with them a tin of Ovaltine, some hard candies, and a couple of polo-type shirts made in Hong Kong. Other common gifts were American ginseng, foreign-made biscuits, Ferrer Rocher or Almond Roca candies, or any kind of brandy or cigarettes. A friend in Guangzhou commented that her relatives now bring toys for their young daughter, but they are at a loss for what they can bring the family that they don't already have.[19]

In some ways the mainland Chinese see the tables as having turned, especially in relation to their neighbors over the border in Hong Kong. I was told a joke about a group of Hong Kong people who went to a restaurant in Shenzhen and were forced to wait downstairs while the local Chinese occupying the exclusive private room finished their meal. Before, the situation had been the reverse. "The feng shui has turned the other way" (*feng shui lun liu zhuan*), commented the joke teller, implying that whereas conditions had previously been good for the Hong Kong people's development, now conditions are favorable on the mainland. They add that some Hong Kong people may not live as well as they do. Many people have returned from Hong Kong to China because they were not able to find work. Further, in anticipation of the 1997 return of Hong Kong to China, many had fled Hong Kong with their capital, resulting in an economic downturn. In addition, Hong Kong manufacturers have increasingly been moving their factories into parts of China and Southeast Asia where labor is cheaper. The following anecdotes illustrate these sentiments:

> Mr. Yeung has the option of buying government-subsidized housing through his unit (*danwei*), a middle school in Shenzhen. He reflected: "Here, some people's level is higher than that of Hong Kong people. In Hong Kong, you can't afford to buy a house; it costs over *bak gei maahn* (H.K.$1 million) for a two-room apartment."

> Liu Xiao, a tenth grade high school student from Shenzhen, says that his uncle has lived in Hong Kong for fifteen years and still lives in a rooftop dwelling. His two sons must share a room.

> A middle school teacher in her thirties is convinced that there must be something wrong with her uncle's ability. He has lived in Hong Kong for more than twenty years and has still not prospered.

> The *South China Morning Post*, an English-language newspaper in Hong Kong, ran a letter in an advice column from a distressed woman whose relatives had just visited from the mainland. They had relentlessly criticized the outdated technology of her refrigerator, television, and other electronics, saying that the equipment they owned in China was much more modern. The columnist replied with the suggestion that the next time their relatives visit she look into renting these items from a local business.

Changes in the Transnational Imaginary

The transformations of the past twenty years have resulted in changes in the way that the majority of Guangdong residents relate to their relatives and friends from abroad. Overseas Chinese, previously the cause of sensation, are no longer seen as so special. The sources of their elevated status—their cultural capital, access to foreign information, living conditions, and currency—have largely been demystified. While the exchange rate between the American dollar and Chinese yuan (basic unit of Chinese currency), and the difference between a Hong Kong and mainland salary, are inarguable, for many Pearl River Delta residents the myth of the world of Chinese overseas being a "heaven" has been debunked.

What previously had served as the basis for the position of privilege of overseas Chinese, their mobility and capital, no longer as clearly defines a relationship of power and dependency between them and their mainland relatives. The transnational imaginary has shifted, reconceptualizing the relationship between the mainland Chinese and their overseas relatives, to form a Cantonese universe centered on the mainland but also reaching abroad to take advantage of opportunities there. If anything, the Guangdong Chinese are beginning to consider themselves on the receiving end of a migration flow that they equate with Chinese having gone abroad. The majority of informants compared the situations of the poor workers from China's inland provinces who come to Guangdong to look for work with that of Chinese emigrating abroad to earn a living, more so in the past than in the present. Emigration is now viewed as a voluntary choice for most people, not for earning money to put food on the table but "for a better life."[20]

Some Guangdong Chinese are beginning to use constructions of the "other," in this case the "other" of non-Chinese societies and their treatment of the Chinese abroad, in negative contrast to their own lifestyles in China. Fear of discrimination, of feeling unsafe, and of having to work doing menial labor abroad all serve to support decisions not to emigrate permanently. One interpretation of this thinking is that it serves as a way for many Chinese to come to terms with the limitations imposed on them by the Chinese government and foreign immigration policies by making these decisions their own. (One informant scoffed at my reports of many people not wanting to emigrate: "They just say that because they have no way of getting out.") But they also see themselves as holding their own form of China-centered non-Western cultural capital, because overseas Chinese are seen as having been assimilated (*tonghua*) to other less civilized cultures and as subjects of discrimination, and therefore not culturally suited for life in China or abroad.

While many young Guangdong residents may still have dreams of becoming wealthy, these visions may not necessarily take place abroad. Their development future, (c. *faat jin chin tou*; md. *fazhan qian tu*), may be brighter in Guangdong. As a young high school teacher told me: "Any young man who is not doing business on the side is foolish." Emigration abroad is viewed by some as a strategy for gaining the foreign citizenship that would allow one the mobility to cultivate business contacts abroad, with the goal of coming back to China to do business. Mr. Cheng, a successful business executive, plans to emigrate to Australia with his wife, a middle school teacher. Their eldest son has been living in Hong Kong for a number of years, where he is married to a Hong Kong Chinese who has Australian citizenship. Their younger son will soon be finishing his undergraduate degree in the United States. The Chengs, neither of whom speak English, don't intend to settle in Australia permanently. After they get Australian citizenship, they hope to return to China to do business.

Emigration is no longer viewed as a one-way prospect. One young Guangzhou student put it this way: "A Chinese can go to America to make money, or an overseas Chinese can go back to China to earn money." In this era of jet travel, emigration no longer has the implications of the long-term, often permanent separation of previous generations. Sallie, a travel agent in San Francisco's Chinatown, observes that this new generation of emigrants usually returns to China for a visit within a year or two. The speed of air travel facilitates this movement.[21]

Mr. Lau's daughter said that her grandmother was deeply saddened when ten years ago her son and his family emigrated to Panama from their village in Zhongshan. For previous generations, this separation was tragic; they did not know when they would see each other again, if at all. In the past in Bai Gong village, travelers would rise before dawn so as to avoid malevolent ghosts, worship the local deities for a safe journey, pay respects to their ancestors, and part in tears. Now, she says, many people going abroad are happy when they leave, excited about the prospect of their opportunities abroad. When her cousins left ten years ago, the family tried to convince her grandmother that they would be back again. It would be easy for them to return by plane. But her grandmother was not fully convinced until she saw how airplanes worked in the movies she saw on Hong Kong television.

The changes detailed in this chapter may seem in their presentation to be quite dramatic and encompassing, and perhaps too clear cut. This perspective is necessary in part to illustrate my central point about the shifts in thinking that have occurred in the more prosperous regions of the Pearl River Delta area. But of course not all Guangdong residents see themselves as better off than their Hong Kong counterparts or feel uneasy about accepting donations of clothing and money from relatives abroad. Many would still jump at the chance of going abroad, despite understandings of the conditions there. And for some, the decision to emigrate may not only be for a better life but also to earn a basic living (c. *wan sic*)—for example, as a restaurant or garment worker. Large differences still exist between various regions of Guangdong, the most pronounced of which is between the poor mountain areas and the cities and prosperous rural areas such as Zhongshan. Even larger differences exist between Guangdong and the other provinces.

While some people are getting rich through private entrepreneurial ventures, others are limited in their opportunities. Sociologist Peter Kwong observes, "The reality is that privatization in China has brought opportunities and unchecked competition, but only those who are young, ambitious and ruthless can prosper" (1994: 3). My fieldwork indicates that in Taishan, a Pearl River Delta emigrant county that claims to have as many Taishan people (including descendants of emigrants) abroad as inside the county, many people still rely on farming for a living. Many with relatives abroad (usually in the United States) place their hopes on eventually going abroad themselves, or on marrying a potential emigrant or U.S. citizen. But many who don't receive remittances from abroad still live as their ancestors have for centuries before them. Those with no close relatives abroad and few skills have little chance of emigrating, and may have trouble making their way even to the county seat to earn a living. The tale of the *Golden Venture*—a ship that ran aground in New York Harbor carrying a cargo of illegal immigrants, mostly from coastal provinces other then Guangdong, who had indentured themselves to "snakeheads" for ($30,000)—illustrates the desperation with which many poor Chinese take high risks to go abroad. Perhaps those on the *Golden Venture* were ill-informed about the opportunities for them in the United States. But it is also likely that they saw no development future for themselves or their families in China. One farmer, when asked if he knew about the hardships faced by illegal immigrants, told the interviewer, "Look, I work on four *mou* land [less than one acre] year in and year out, from dawn to dusk, but after taxes and providing for our own needs, I made $20 a year. You make that much in a day. No matter how much it costs to get there, or how hard the work is, America is still better than this" (quoted in Kwong 1994). The factors of class and economic stability in decisions to emigrate cannot be ignored in this analysis.

Somehow we got there. There were two padlocks on the door—a solid door of wood. Just inside was a dark kitchen, with a door on the left, and an altar to the left of the door. The door was locked, and the two people I as with didn't have the keys, so I couldn't look in. But they told me that one of their relatives used to live there. There was an altar to my right as well, on the same wall as the door we had just walked in. It was kind of by the stove. And just in front of me there was a cupboard, with its two doors falling off. And there was a cupboard to my left. Directly in front of us was a large room. Again, the walls were of stone, the floor was laid with large stone bricks, and there was no dank smell to the air as I might have expected. It was a room half-filled with straw. When I walked in and turned to my left, the left half of the room—my half of the house, was filled with straw. The other half had a bicycle and line-drying clothes. They told me that half the room was ours—my family's, and the other half was theirs. They kept referring to it as "my house," and it seemed very natural that they did so. I was mildly surprised that our house was merely half a room and a kitchen. In front and up above there was a sort of a loft. It filled perhaps a third of the room, and there was a ladder leading up to it.

Perhaps it was the straw which really did it; it was something I had not been expecting at all. I think all of us, to some degree, were treating this trip as an archaeological expedition. I know now that I was, at least. Throughout the program—starting from when we first applied, through the lectures, and up till now, the general atmosphere was that of "finding your roots," "finding your past."

"We will take a two-week trip to China, we'll look for your village, and we'll find your roots. Your family tree."

Perhaps that was why I was surprised by the straw. After all, all of us were making extreme efforts to come back and find our family's houses. And they *were* homes. They weren't just houses. And to come back and see that, after all, my house wasn't isolated, and wasn't regarded as the venerable object I had unconsciously treated it as, was a shock. My home was just an ordinary, everyday object to these people. To my family here. And if storing straw in my house was they best use they could make of it, that was what they were going to do.

—K.Y., 1994

In the preceding chapters I have sketched out the terms that frame the "forged" relationship between Chinese Americans and China. In particular, I examine how the state projects of the PRC and U.S. governments, both of which are invested in shaping Chinese identities, are trying to do so in ways that are challenged by alternative discourses of Chineseness created through transnational processes. This chapter reveals the disjunctures and the alternative popular nationalisms that emerge from interactions between people who identify as Chinese in different ways, as Chinese Americans attempt to reterritorialize their identities amidst socialist ideologies.

The summer Youth Festival (Hai Wai Hua Yi Qing Nian Xia Ling Ning) takes place every July, bringing together participants of various Summer Camp programs (of which the In Search of Roots program is one) for a three-day celebration in Guangzhou. Participants include over four hundred youths of Chinese descent (*huayi*) from Germany, Madagascar, Canada, the United States, France, Tahiti, and Malaysia. The Youth Festival represents a particular ethnographic moment during which mainland Chinese and Chinese Americans construct identities in relation to one another in new ways. As an official state ritual (Kertzer 1988) it highlights the Chinese state's discourses that have been created within the context of mainland China's reopening to the outside world, global economic restructuring, and a renewed world focus on East Asia.[1] The Youth Festival brings together the participants of various Summer Camp programs sponsored by organizations outside of China for a celebration of Chinese culture and origins framed within the context of Chinese nationalism and economic growth. The discourses of Chinese identity that are woven throughout the Youth Festival have their historical roots in turn-of-the-century Chinese nationalism, in which allegiance to the Chinese nation-state was viewed as a natural extension of being "racially" and culturally Chinese (Dikotter 1992; Duara 1997). However, they may not reflect the current conditions under which Chinese identities are negotiated not only in respect to state efforts to shape them but also in relation to alternative discourses of Chinese identity constructed on both "local" and transnational levels. The participation by Roots interns in the Youth Festival illustrates how these multiple meanings of Chineseness as race, culture, and national identity play out.

As previously discussed, ideas about Chineseness as a racial form of identification extending beyond the boundaries of the nation-state (in fact, predating it) have allowed for the designation of a category of people of Chinese descent who no longer live on Chinese soil but are still considered to be racially Chinese.[2] These linkages between national, cultural, and racial identities form the basis for assumptions by Youth Festival organizers about the relationship between Chinese youths from abroad and China.[3] "The discourse of 'Chinese culture' " (Ong and Nonini 1997: 16) has provided the basis for a variety of contemporary narrations of Chinese modernity, both within and outside mainland China. In implementing the Summer Camps and the Youth Festival, the PRC is reaching beyond the boundaries of modern territorial nationalism to employ "extraterritorial narratives of racial and cultural continuity" (Duara 1997: 39) in redefining its relationship with the Chinese abroad who are no longer citizens of the Chinese nation-state. Beginning with the Open Policy in the late 1970s, the PRC has reemerged from its socialist cocoon to engage with the outside world. It has drawn on historically rooted racial ideas of Chineseness (see Ong 1999; Siu 1992) and the assumptions about patriotism and culture that accompany them to call on overseas Chinese patriotic sons to build a new, modern nation of "socialism with Chinese characteristics." Just as the emergence of the Chinese national identity at the turn of the twentieth century required the creation of a broader sense of Chineseness that cut across the variety of existing regional and political allegiances (Duara 1997), it is the challenge of the PRC government today to create a contemporary connection to the Chinese abroad that takes into account the diversity of political, cultural, regional, and generational identities that exist within and outside of the mainland. This goal must be accomplished, however, without the claims of extraterritorial rule that have in the past placed overseas Chinese in precarious positions in the countries in which they resided (see L. Wang 1995; L. Williams 1960).

That these racial discourses and their links to territory and nation provide a subtext for the Youth Festival organizers' plans is evident in an official publication by the Guangdong Provincial Office of Overseas Chinese Affairs (Guangdong Sheng Ren Min Zheng Fu Qiao Ban Gong Shi) published in late 1993, titled *Xin Xi Mu Bang, Gen Zai Hua Xia* (Heart tied to the motherland, roots in the diaspora). Though the publication acknowledges in its title the movement of Chinese roots overseas, it also assumes that affective ties to heritage, traditional culture, and hometown are dormant, waiting to be drawn out through Summer Camp activities.[4] The publication explicitly states the intended effects of the Summer Camp activities in the section subtitled "Retrospective of Guangdong Province's Summer Camps for Youths of Chinese Descent." The five main goals listed are:

1. *Propagate Chinese culture and strengthen the national consciousness.* The younger generation of overseas Chinese living abroad have little understanding of their forefathers' traditional culture, to say nothing of national consciousness. Therefore we've based the camp upon Chinese national culture. We have Chinese [language], Chinese history, geography, Chinese calligraphy, picture-drawing, Chinese folk songs and dances and Chinese *wu shu* . . . so that we can help the participants [get] acquainted with Chinese traditional culture.

2. *Deepen the knowledge of motherland and strengthen the national recognition.* The generation of overseas Chinese youths are gradually assimilated by the countries in which they live. They take both friendly and skeptical attitudes toward China. They come to join the camps with tentative curiosity. On account of this state of mind, we put the stress on the combination of travel and education. Education in travel lays particular emphasis on the influence of images. All camp holding units are asked to organize the participants to visit places of interest, typical representative factories, farms, and schools which can reflect our economic development and scientific results and make them acquainted with the Chinese unity and present situation from different angles. Only in this way can they get a better understanding of our motherland and also their sense of recognition and the sense of ownership.

3. *Foster the participants' attachment to their native place (*xiang tu guannian*) and arouse their nostalgic emotion.* The generation of the overseas [youths] were born and grew up abroad, but they are rooted in China. They come to the place where their forefathers lived, and meet with a warm reception, and they feel their hearts touched when they hear the dialect spoken by their forefathers, and drink the water flowing in the homeland for many years.

4. *Intensify the cooperation and exchange between Chinese and foreign youths and enhance solidarity and friendship.* To develop the mutual understanding and friendship of the Chinese descendants in and out[side] of China, we put more emphasis on all kinds of get-togethers, seminars which attract [those] youths to attend, and enable them to get along with each other and exchange respective points of view on various subjects, and leave the participants a deep and unforgettable impression.

5. *A good summer (winter)⁵ camp can bring about a great advance in our overseas Chinese affairs.* The summer (winter) camps held in our province have attracted a large number of overseas Chinese youths and students as well as their parents and exerted a great active influence in the world of Chinese and brought about a great advance in our overseas Chinese affairs. The camps manifest themselves in the increasing number of students who have taken an active part in joining the camps, [and in] the high quality of holding camps which displays the great vitality of the organizations.⁶

The primary aims of the Youth Festival and Summer Camps were to invoke connections of blood and culture for the *hua yi* in order to reacquaint them with their motherland, which, if they knew better, they would love. These programs took into account the overseas Chinese youths' "friendly and skeptical" attitudes toward China,⁷ in exposing them to their Chinese roots and "traditional" Chinese culture. This was to be accomplished through a combination of travel and education, with a recognition that the Chinese abroad had been assimilated to non-Chinese ways. Such exposure was supposed to build, and in some sense revive, a sense of national consciousness and draw on nostalgic attachments to places to which *hua yi* had never been. The publication, featuring colorful photos of *hua yi* posed in front of various monuments, walking through villages, and even straddling water buffalo,⁸ stands as evidence of the success of the program.

The Youth Festival begins with an opening ceremony that is usually held at one of Guangzhou's larger, upscale hotels, such as the Oriental Hotel (Dongfang Bingguan) or the Garden Hotel (Huayuan Jiudian). The theme of the festival, displayed on large banners hanging from helium balloons outside the hotel, is "Peace, Unity, Friendship, Progress" (*heping, tuanjie, youyi, jinbu*). The welcome includes a procession lined with flag-waving local students, followed by a banquet featuring opening speeches by officials from the city of Guangzhou and from the Office of Overseas Chinese Affairs and, throughout the evening, numerous cultural performances of "tradi-

Welcome by local student musicians outside of the Youth Festival.

Dance performance during at banquet at the 1994 Youth Festival in Guangzhou.

tional" Chinese dance, singing, and martial arts. Each group of *hua yi* is asked to give a performance, which ranges from *wushu* demonstrations to singing Chinese songs (such as "The Cloud over My Hometown") to Tahitian dance. This participatory aspect of the festival marks it as a political ritual that highlights the diversity and similarities among Chinese diaspora cultures while at the same time subsuming these differences within a broader, official statement of Chinese unity. To the government sponsors, the performances are a visual representation of the *huayi*'s love of their homeland. To the *huayi*, they represent an opportunity to contribute to the larger ritual by either marking the distinctiveness of their diasporic identities, as in the Tahitian dance, or displaying their "Chineseness" through a cultural performance.

Festival officials present the *hua yi* participants with souvenirs such as T-shirts, commemorative medals, and a brush, ink, and chop set. The shirts, which give the name of the festival (Hai Wai Hua Yi Qing Nian Huan Jie) in big red letters across the back, and state "Guangdong" in Chinese characters on the front, are to be worn on all public outings. The outings include visits to historic monuments such as the Sun Yat Sen memorial (Sun, considered the father of the nation, was an overseas Chinese himself), where a group picture of all festival participants is taken. (As I stood in my place as part of the mass I commented to the intern next to me, "You can't recognize anybody—all you see is a sea of black heads." "That's the point," he said.) The group is also brought to the Seventy-Two Martyrs memorial, which is constructed from cement blocks inscribed with the names of overseas Chinese groups from around the world. Participants are also taken to other sites of interest, such as a mooncake factory (which proudly displays the "largest mooncake in the world"),[9] and to Shenzhen to see the famous Splendid China and China Folk Culture Village.[10] During my visits, we were also taken to a joint-venture television factory in Shenzhen (in 1995), and to the sports-drink company Jian Li Bao (in 1994), which included a tour of the factory production line where women and men labored who were about the same age as the group participants. Company officials remarked how such successful economic growth would not have been possible without the contributions from overseas Chinese. The message from both factory and government officials consistently linked pride in local economic growth to the contributions of overseas Chinese, under the assumption that these Chinese youths would share in this pride because of their Chinese roots. These sentiments of racial unity based on shared Chinese heritage were captured in a poem, which was printed in Chinese and English on the pamphlet provided for all Youth Festival attendees:

Roots interns visiting a television factory as part of the Youth Festival.

Youth Festival participants at the Jian Li Bao factory visit, wearing the official Youth Festival and Summer Camp T-shirt.

Descendants of the Dragon with Black Eyes
Gathered under the Blue Sky
Their hearts are linked to each other
They cherish the hope of unity, friendship, progress, and peace.[11]

The festival agenda clearly fits within the larger policy that views overseas Chinese as potential investors whose investments represent acts of patriotism—efforts to build the motherland—as well as filial duty to their ancestors buried in China. It is assumed that pride in the motherland could be fostered through the combined exposure to China's recent economic development, and to Chinese traditional arts and heritage sites. These seemingly contradictory references combining tradition and modernity stem from Chinese government discourses in which the Overseas Chinese embody both the Confucian traditions that preserve their Chineseness and also the capitalist know-how to help China catch up with the West (see Ong 1999). However, as I discuss further below, it is uncertain whether the visiting *hua yi* in the Roots program fit this model because most are not particularly patriotic, Confucian, or rich, nor are they necessarily proud to be Chinese. These contradictions were evident in July 1994 at the Youth Festival opening ceremony at the Garden Hotel in Guangzhou, where the audience of Chinese youths from abroad responded enthusiastically to a kung fu performance featuring the music from the popular Wong Fei Hong kung fu series, whereas the earlier playing of the Chinese national anthem had received a distinctly more muted response. However, it is likely that the audience at the Youth Festival was more familiar with the rousing music of the Wong Fei Hong series, and with stylized, kung fu representations of Chinese culture, than it was with the PRC's national anthem and the daily bodily practices associated with these national rituals. The Wong Fei Hong film series has achieved semicult status among kung fu movie aficionados around the world, and the response of the audience at the Youth Festival demonstrated the power of a popular culture production (out of Hong Kong), which references a historical and fantastical China, to evoke a connection to an imagined China for Chinese around the world. This example illustrates that for many, especially those whose connection to China is generations removed, it may no longer be possible to assume a congruence between the acknowledgment of a Chinese heritage and patriotic allegiance to the Chinese nation-state. The old narratives equating Chinese racial heritage with patriotism are being unraveled. Just as youths of Chinese descent outside of China find more familiarity with transnational cultural productions of Chineseness than with state rituals of patriotism, mainland Chinese are beginning to participate in transnational processes that bring the Chinese abroad into the realm of their daily imaginations, providing alternatives to state constructions of an overseas Chinese-derived modernity.

Transnational (Re)connections

Mainland Chinese and Chinese Americans are not linked through social networks and shared cultural or political beliefs, but rather by myths of common origin, rooted in multiply reinforcing discourses that connect race, nation, and territory. However, transnational (re)connections create potential not only for linkages based on shared heritage that are often the subject of transnational scholarship, but also for Chineseness to work within official and nonofficial structures as both a unifying and differentiating factor, exposing the ways that patriotism, cultural identification, and "racial" categorizations are not always neatly correlated. Transnational flows provide the broader context for reshaping Chinese subjectivities that are brought together through rituals of the Chinese state. The experiences of the *hua yi* bring out contradictions that expose deeply rooted tensions within the multiple, and perhaps competing, narratives being produced to describe the transnational linkages between China and the overseas Chinese and the new identities that emerge from these processes.

Through the Youth Festival, Chinese Americans are reconnected to their ancestral places in mainland China amid processes arising out of transnational flows of media, people, ideas, and capital. These flows create new knowledges that reveal differing interpretations of Chineseness within and between the Chinese state, mainland Chinese citizens, and transnational Chinese communities. These tensions arise between the historically rooted assumptions about Chineseness as a racial category and the changing ways of being Chinese (in China and the diaspora) in cultural, "racial," and political terms. My ethnographic analysis of the Youth Festival and related activities reflects in two broad areas the changing dynamics between culture, capital, and the state. First, the increasing contact between mainland China and the Chinese abroad made possible through transnational flows may not only foster a sense of shared Chineseness but also, ironically, within the state-sponsored projects based on these principles, produce new knowledges about different and unfamiliar ways of being Chinese. Transnational flows play an important role in re-creating a sense of Chineseness across national borders, but rather than resulting in a unified, collective transmigrant identity, these Chinese identities are formed in contrast to one another. The irony here is that when those in the diaspora and in the homeland are brought together to take a closer look at one another, differences that were not evident from a distance are revealed (see Bruner 1996). While a unitary sense of being Chinese that equates race with patriotism and cultural knowledge is promoted in official state discourses of Chineseness that form the basis for the Youth Festival,[12] it becomes evident through its execution that these rituals highlight differences among those that they bring together. Chinese American and other *huayi* participants are "racially" Chinese but lack the cultural signifiers and patriotic sentiments that are normally associated with having "black hair and yellow skin." The Youth Festival, which is supposed to produce a sense of transnational Chinese unity by emphasizing connections between "race," culture, and nationalism, is a failed ritual of the state because it results in the production of narratives of identity that complicate official discourses on overseas Chinese.[13] Thus, in contrast to the literature on transnationalism that emphasizes and celebrates the construction of new identities across borders, I argue for a closer examination of how transnational processes allow for the production of contrapuntal identities that further differentiate diaspora populations from the homeland.

The second area concerns how the contradictions that become evident through the ritual of the Youth Festival point to a repositioning of the relative status of mainland Chinese vis-à-vis the Chinese abroad by removing the Chinese overseas from their previously privileged standing. Transnational flows of migration, media, and capital have reconnected mainland China to Chinese populations abroad, without either population necessarily having to move. The wider context for the Youth Festival and Summer Camps is one in which many Guangdong Chinese are now beginning to consider the possibility of Chineseness as race without culture; the possibility of overseas Chinese capital investment without patriotism; and the possibility of a mainland Chinese modernity centered on mainland traditions and self-sufficiency.

It has become evident that the nation-state remains a strong basis for identification; that states in various ways attempt to extend influence over transnational subjects (Smith and Guarnizo 1998; Schein 1998;); and that access to various forms of capital determines the nature and extent of the actors' participation in transnational social fields. An examination of the Youth Festival calls into question the internal homogeneity, degree of nostalgia, and extent of economic practices of *huayi* in relation to China, "the motherland." The Youth Festival illustrates the dynamic and dialectical processes that characterize relations between transmigrant/overseas populations and the state that are neither consistently opposed nor wholly constitutive of their transnational practices.[14] Although the Chinese state apparatus in charge of overseas Chinese affairs is a primary actor in the Youth Festival, the festival represents a collaborative effort between government workers, local Chinese, and the visiting *huayi* and their respective organizations.

Accordingly, it is necessary to recast transnational theories to allow for the complex ways that identities can be situated within transnational fields, in "places" and histories that remain attached to nation-states. More nuanced conceptions of "place" and "tradition" must be reinserted in more nuanced ways into the maelstrom of fluidity, hybridity, movement, and (post)modernity that has come, perhaps inaccurately, to represent discussions of transnationalism. As I discuss in chapter 2, contrary to representing "old" identities, place and tradition can serve as the building blocks for new identities. Thus, identities may be reterritorialized in complex ways that involve "local" ties to multiple places across national borders. The ancestral homeland is a place that is recovered not only through the unfettered work of the imagination but also through the reconstruction of histories and processes of reterritorialization accomplished through a "politics of the local" (Hall 1990). As I discuss in chapter 2 and discuss further in chapter 6, these processes of reterritorialization often ironically depend on the ability to travel and to pull references from multiple places to create a sense of "home" that is not bound in narrow, restrictive ways.

Along these lines, works by Aihwa Ong (1999) and Ong and Donald Nonini (1997) in the field of Chinese transnational studies advocate moving beyond a China-centered view of overseas Chinese studies that privileges the mainland as the center and relegates those in the diaspora to a residual China. Instead, they focus on the formation of alternative modernities built on the discourses of Chinese culture and the historical linkages, kin networks, and trading practices that connect diaspora Chinese to one another. The participants in modern Chinese transnationalism define being Chinese in numerous ways and, according to Ong and Nonini, "through accumulation strategies, mobility, and modern mass media—[they have] engendered complex, shifting, and fragmented subjectivities that are at once specific yet global" (1997: 26).

Ong (1999) notes that tensions and contradictions have arisen from post-Mao reforms that have linked a new Chinese modernity to connections, racial and cultural, with capitalist Chinese abroad. She describes two areas of tension stemming from post—Mao reforms. These reforms link an emerging Chinese modernity to racial and cultural connections with overseas Chinese capitalists. The first area of tension occurs between the interests of the Chinese state and the practices of transnational capital, as overseas Chinese are viewed as the "bearers of capitalist modernity" but also as amoral exploiters of local citizens and therefore threats to national interests. Another contradiction involves inconsistencies between official governmental and folk views of overseas Chinese patriotism and values. The ethnographic case of the Youth Festival allows for an examination of these contradictions from another perspective. Building on Ong's analysis which calls attention to the conflicting interests that sometimes arise from within unifying models of overseas Chinese/Chinese fraternity, my particular focus on *huayi* allows me to address more squarely how contradictions resulting from the dissonance of race, culture, and nation are played out. An examination of the daily practices and interactions between participants, officials, state employees, and local Chinese in the context of the Youth Festival and Summer Camps exposes the gaps within both official and unofficial discourses about the relationship between China and the Chinese abroad. While the Youth Festival may represent a new phase of socialism adapted to market reforms, it is based on historically rooted ideas that no longer necessarily reflect the sentiments of contemporary Chinese citizens or Chinese Americans visiting from abroad. I highlight the ways in which multiple, perhaps competing ideas of modernity (and tradition) and nationalism can emerge through close-up interactions that occur within the festivals.

Another dimension of increased contact between mainland Chinese and overseas Chinese has been traced by scholars who examine the effects of transnational media flows on the renegotiation of Chinese identities. The transnational mass media have created a public sphere that links mainland Chinese to Chinese communities abroad (Yang 1997). Transnational sports television coverage, as a form of transnational media flow, has brought experiences of Chinese outside of China back to mainland audiences, reinforcing a mainland-centered nationalism that is not necessarily consistent with official state discourses (Brownell 1999). In a similar sense, my data point to the ways that transnational contacts between mainland Chinese and the Chinese abroad have strengthened a mainland Chinese identity, but one that is Guangdong-centered and defined in contrast to the Chinese abroad rather than derived from relations with them. Transnational media flows not only create new realms of desire for mainland Chinese, as described by Yang (1997), but provide the basis for oppositional China-based identities that are constructed in contrast to the outside world and that do not necessarily fall along official party lines.

The Youth Festival in Contrast to Village Visits

It is a challenge for the PRC government to (re)establish a relationship with the new generations of Chinese Americans whose cultural and political attitudes differ significantly from those on which mainland Chinese discourse on overseas Chinese is based. *Huayi* view their participation in Youth Festival activities and their visit to their ancestral country in complicated and often conflicting ways. These interactions resonate with larger questions about the tension between transnational forces and the nation-state and the changing relationship between homeland and diaspora under transnationalism.

For the majority of the Roots interns, the village visits, not the Youth Festival, were the highlight of the trip. In the personal narratives and family histories that the interns wrote for the Chinese New Year display of their projects, most focused on the ways in which the visit to China gave them new perspectives on being Chinese American by filling in the missing pieces of their family trees and by helping them understand their grandparents or parents in new ways by learning about what they had been through in China. Thus, they viewed their village visits as their primary purpose for traveling to China, and in many ways they were able to separate their own roots-searching goals and activities from the program's ceremonial structures such as the Youth Festival and the messages of economic development that underlay the Chinese government's sponsorship of their roots-searching activities. As I discuss in chapter 2, Roots participants were able to reference their experiences as Chinese Americans, along with other means of connecting to "Chinese culture" such as popular culture flows from Hong Kong, to create meaning out of their experiences in China. At the same time, the Chinese government's repeated message during the Youth Festival and the Summer Camps about overseas Chinese patriotism and investment was not lost on them.[15] After the Youth Festival's opening ceremony, one intern, Penelope, had remarked, "they must really want us to come back," and another, Christine, said "they're so nice I almost feel an obligation to donate some money."

Indeed the practice of remitting money to China was not unfamiliar to most of the Chinese American participants. Many of their parents were already sending money to relatives, and many interns said that they would like to continue the practice. However, at the same time they began to view some of the official protocol as a distraction from their main work of researching family histories and building genealogies. The daily routine of the village visits often blurred in a whirlwind of activities, as the group was whisked off to banquets and receptions hosted by local officials. These matters of protocol comprised a significant portion of time in the village areas, and although these welcoming receptions helped to formalize and legitimize the experience of "return," some interns wished they could spend more time in the villages. "Relatives, or investment?" asked program intern Tom on numerous occasions after observing that the group had spent a relatively short time in the village because they had to move on to another banquet to be told about the region's growth and development due to overseas Chinese investments. Another intern commented about how she thought that China was "playing it up" to the overseas Chinese in order to encourage the later generations to invest. Still another, in response, said that he doubted how many people really do return to invest.

In contrast to the essentialized and genericized Chinese culture presented at the Youth Festival, most Roots interns identified with the particulars of their ancestral villages introduced to them on their trip that to them represented the Cantonese folk culture from which their families originated.[16] The Youth Festival's emphasis on the grandeur of Chinese "culture" as embodied in more formal traditions represented what many Chinese American Roots participants felt they lacked. In addition, the festival's emphasis on these traditional cultural elements seemed out of place in the rapidly changing society that the interns witnessed on their travels. This mismatch is a reminder of the cultural vacuum on which current policies were crafted. The village visits, in contrast, provided a connection to folk practices and family traditions that meshed more closely with the peasant roots to which most of the interns traced their heritage.

Changing Views toward Overseas Chinese

Just as Chinese Americans in the Roots program begin to poke holes in the narratives constructed to attach them to mainland China, mainland Chinese citizens are also increasingly questioning the Chineseness of the Chinese abroad. As I discuss in chapter 4, the PRC government narratives equating the racial and cultural origins of Chinese Americans with a patriotic devotion to the homeland are also increasingly contradicted by the experiences of everyday mainland Chinese citizens. As mainland Chinese gain access to more information about Chinese from abroad they develop more nuanced understandings of Chineseness as a racial versus cultural or nationalist identification. Lucy, a college student in Guangzhou, observed that while people might have the impression that overseas Chinese are patriotic from television shows featuring those who return to their villages,[17] now people can think more critically about the truth of these statements. Through increased media exposure and personal contact with overseas Chinese, many Guangdong residents are realizing that rather than being patriotic expatriates, overseas Chinese are in many ways different from mainland Chinese.[18] Increasingly, they make distinctions among the Chinese abroad according to class, generation, and country of residence.

John Lim, a Guangdong native in his early thirties who works for a large American corporation in China, has encountered numerous coworkers from Hong Kong and from the United States, including Chinese Americans. He observes: "Chinese think that all Chinese, no matter where they were born, where they live, are Chinese, the descendants of Yan and Huang emperors." But his sentiments are filled with contradictions between ingrained beliefs that he learned in school as a child and in the media and more recent experiences with Chinese from other countries. While he finds that there is less of a "cultural gap" (c. *man fa seung ge cha keuih*) between mainland Chinese and Hong Kong people than between mainlanders and Chinese Americans, he also considers Hong Kong people to be brusque and snobby, viewing themselves as superior to the local Chinese.[19] He further states that American-born Chinese are "high-class Chinese" (c. *gou kup wah yahn*), and that because the place where Chinese Americans live is powerful and rich, so are Chinese Americans. The first time he saw an American-born Chinese, he thought they were "interesting": they don't speak Chinese and they eat Western food. But they still have "Chinese ways." From his interactions with Chinese Americans through his work, he has come to view them as "big children": "They are honest and expose their feelings directly. They tell the truth, without hiding anything. Chinese [in China] keep their attitudes, opinions, and feelings inside, because revealing them can be dangerous. Chinese Americans couldn't get used to living in a Chinese society. They will be fooled by [mainland] Chinese, like a big child."

This "cultural gap" manifested itself in many observations of the *huayi* made by mainland Chinese associated with the Summer Camp programs, and had implications for the perceived effectiveness of these programs. An official from the Qiao Lian (a nongovernmental organization for overseas Chinese affairs) in Taishan County and the driver who worked for the office had encountered a number of Summer Camp groups, mostly from Canada and America, on their visits to their ancestral villages.[20] They remarked that the second and third generations often have different living habits, recalling one *hua yi* who would not eat Chinese food, and another who, unused to squat toilets, had to be taken to another county to use the bathroom. For them, these incidents raised issues about whether *huayi* can be considered culturally Chinese. The official felt that the *huayi* "come back" to have a good time and to take a look at their ancestral house; not necessarily to find their own relatives but to see where their parents and grandparents came from. He has observed that most of the students are curious about the villages, especially the water buffalo and chickens. They like to take items found in the village, such as dried gourds and pipes, back with them to the United States or Canada. For their part the villagers aren't curious about the *huayi* because they have become used to people coming back.[21] They may not comprehend the meaning of searching for roots (md. *xungen*; c. *chahm gan*) but they do understand the intentions of the young people coming back to the village. They talk about it excitedly, saying so and so's granddaughter or son has come back. But they can't communicate with them because they don't speak the same language. They just shake hands and pat each other on the shoulders, and take pictures.

However, the Chinese American youth, clad in T-shirts (some proclaiming Asian American pride) and shorts, loaded down with cameras, water bottles, and coated with insect repellant, looked out of place in the villages. The "cultural gap" between the visiting *huayi* and the local villagers had to be bridged by protocol and formalities, or mediated through the efforts of bilingual guides from the Qiao Ban or China Travel Service, the Chinese American group leader, and some participants. While those interns who spoke Chinese more fluently were able to converse with the villagers, the village visits were orchestrated in a way that constrained much of the dialogue within the boundaries of each group. The Roots interns, who had become familiar with one another, interacted mainly among themselves in the village setting, while the local officials and relatives remained for the most part politely to themselves. And the guides often stood to the side, looking bored.

In general, nonofficial views elicited from informants on why the *huayi* take part in the camps vary in the degree to which they are thought through critically. Many informants in China said that it was because they loved their motherland and wanted to search for their roots (*xungen*). They cited sayings such as *yan huang zixun* ("descendants of the yellow emperor") and *ye luo gui gen* ("the leaf falls back to its roots"), which assumed spiritual, historically rooted connections to China. Others examined the Chinese government's motivations more closely, and said directly that its intentions were to draw investments from the Chinese abroad. Still others said that the *huayi* were merely curious to find out what their village was like.

Mr. Lau, introduced earlier, lives in a small village in Zhongshan County in the San Xiang area. His daughter is a university graduate who I met in Guangzhou and who invited me back to her village to do research and meet her family. When I first told her that I was interested in looking at Chinese from abroad visiting their ancestral villages, she told me that "many 'sisters and brothers' have come back to my village." I had an opportunity to spend time asking her father questions about people from their village who had returned, and his attitudes toward them, which was a rare chance to look at roots searching from the villager perspective.

I asked Mr. Lau whether his family had a c. *juk po* (*zupu*), and why it was important to have one. He brought out a stack of newly photocopied documents, explaining that one was the c. *ga po* (*jiapu*), or family tree, and the other was the *juk po* (*zupu*), or lineage. He explained that a family must have its own c. *chi tong* (ancestral hall) to have its own c. *juk po*. Mr. Lau said that he had copied down his own family's genealogy as a child and had memorized it. Their second great-uncle (c. *yi suk gung*) in Sichuan came back to find the village on his own. He created a *juk po* on his computer and produced an address list of different Lau branches located in Beijing, Taiwan, Japan, Sichuan, and so forth. The Sichuan uncle also asked a historian to do some library research for him on the origins of the Lau family, and this information prefaces his book.

In response to my question, he said that it was important to have a genealogy book so that when people from the outside (abroad) come back you can tell whether they're "real" or not and how they're connected to the family. For example, some relatives from France returned to the village with a piece of paper written by their grandfather that named the village and their relatives there. He checked the paper against the *juk po* and found out how they were related to the family. He said that in doing this they are able to reconnect the different parts of the family. Relatives have returned from Canada, the United States, Panama, France, and other places, and he's happy just to know where his relatives are, even if they don't give him any money or gifts. But there are still many who don't know how to come back (c. *m' sic fan laih*).

Because many people have relations abroad and talk about them with other community members, people are often recognized by village residents when they come back. When Mr. Lau sees them, he nods his head (c. *nap tou*) toward them to show his respect. People in the village emphasize the importance of coming back and bringing back children so they'll have an impression of the native village (*xiang xia;* c. *heung ha*). People return to find their roots in many ways; many people return with official delegations or with tour groups, or with the expressed desire to research more information about their native region. Still others return by themselves (c. *ji gei fan laih*).

Mr. Lau stated that he felt that Chinese living abroad should come back often. If not, their grandchildren will forget where they came from. In fact, often the second or third generation forgets their cultural heritage, and there is a saying that "The first generation is man, the second, as ghost." Some come back and want to eat Western food, and many people, if they left when they were young, have forgotten their hometown language and culture. Although they are of the Chinese race (c. *wong jung yahn*), they don't like to eat rice (c. *m'jungyi sihk faahn*). While not all people who return seem different than the villagers themselves, the ones who seem different have already "accepted Western thinking." Their characters (*xingge*) are different than those of the villagers: they have been affected by foreign ways so they speak more directly.

Over the Chinese New Year the uncle of a friend of the Lau family had returned from Trinidad and Tobago—they called him *cheui leui dah* ("Tobago"). The friend and his uncle had been classmates before he emigrated in his teens, but when he came back last year he couldn't speak a sentence of Chinese. He spoke only (what they thought was) Spanish and couldn't understand what his own mother was saying to him. His *mui fu* took him to see his relatives and he didn't remember them. He looked bored, and after awhile he refused to meet any more people. Mr. Lau thought this was very sad (c. *hou chaam*).

According to Mr. Lau, people who live abroad often have doubts about returning to their village. They have no close relatives in the village and are afraid that others there will ask for things or for them to donate money when they come back. Some return to see if they'll be asked (c. *si tam sik*); if they see it's okay, they'll make more plans to come back but they won't if the people in the village seem greedy. Sometimes when people come back, others will fight for the distribution of money, and sometimes the leaders of the village ask for help for the village. Mr. Lau made the analogy of overseas Chinese being like tortoises—easy to catch—and thus many overseas Chinese are afraid to come back.

I asked Mr. Lau what he does when relatives return. He said that they talk about what they know about the family (such as where other relatives are), and see people (other relatives) so that the visitors can tell people what their hometown is like. They also take photos of houses, especially their ancestral house (c. *jou nguk*), with family members. His daughter said that her father doesn't understand why they only want to celebrate with a banquet in a restaurant (c. *daih sic daih yum*; literally "big eat, big drink") and don't want to go back to the village to see how it's changed.

Rethinking Chinese Identities

Attitudes and assumptions about the Chinese abroad are being reworked in Guangdong, both through renewed interaction with the Chinese from abroad, and through less direct sources of information, such as the mass media, that bring in new perspectives on life outside of China. These new images have done much to complicate the official state model of the wealthy, patriotic overseas Chinese, whose yellow skin and black hair attach him (they are almost always male) and his money to his native country. This model has been inextricably tied to China's birth as a nation-state (with Sun Yat Sen as the model *huaqiao*), and despite the period during Communist rule when connections to overseas Chinese were viewed as subversive, it has enjoyed a dynamic revival in the post-Mao period. However, it is evident that China's new engagement with global capitalism has also brought flows of culture and information that have begun to shape the renewed interaction with overseas Chinese in ways that call into question some of the basic assumptions about the prevailing state discourse on the Chinese abroad. The Youth Festival represents an effort on the part of the PRC government to turn its attention toward the future, as it recognizes that later generations who have never lived in China must be reintroduced to their motherland through cultural rather than political means. But the "cultural gap" that becomes glaringly evident through the experiences of the Roots group and the participants in the Youth Festival is evidence that the model of Chineseness based on race as culture may no longer be applicable to much of the diaspora.

The implications of this realization are many. The Chinese American participants of the Roots program may carry the markers of capitalist modernity in their Western origins and, for most, in their comfortable economic status. However, in the impressions related above of many mainland Chinese the overseas youth in many ways represent a lesser class of Chinese, one that knows little about Chinese "culture" or ways of living, and one that has been negatively affected by racial discrimination in the West. The overseas youth embody a contradiction, because they retain the physical features of Chineseness without the cultural knowledge and attachment to mainland China that is usually assumed to accompany these features. The Youth Festival is perhaps derived from the Chinese government's fear about the future of relations between the PRC and the Chinese abroad, as they see a widening cultural and political gap between the mainland and the Chinese overseas. This gap has encouraged many mainland Chinese to rethink the concept of race as nation and to question the patriotic and nostalgic sentiments of future generations of overseas Chinese for their "motherland."

An additional question that arises from the breakdown of this new nationalist model of an overseas-Chinese-derived modernity is whether capitalist modernity, as represented by the overseas Chinese, can still be seen as a viable future for the mainland. An alternative narrative may be represented by a popular nationalism that emerges as mainland Chinese engage in both direct and indirect interaction with the Chinese abroad. Coexisting with ideas of triumphal capitalism embedded in ethnic Chinese capital networks extending into Southeast Asia are new messages about the status of Chinese abroad, who no longer necessarily occupy positions of privilege in the minds of many Guangdong Chinese. Connections fueled by capital have throughout the history of Chinese emigration stretched the boundaries of and redefined what it has meant to be Chinese (or Chinese American), and in this way have shaped relations between parts of the diaspora.

Chinese emigration itself, and therefore the existence of "Chinese American" as a possible identity, is inextricably linked to the history of migration fueled by the relationship between capital and labor—specifically, the need for cheap labor to feed the growing U.S. economy (Dirlik 1998). Inequalities in access to capital have historically defined relations between mainland Chinese and the Chinese abroad. However, this latest era is marked by a shift in which overseas Chinese no longer are viewed as holding a superior position in terms of access to social and economic capital. New views of the overseas Chinese as victims of discrimination who toil in low-status, low-paying jobs have replaced the old views that privileged them at the same time that the Guangdong Chinese increasingly have access to opportunities to obtain their own social and economic capital. Chinese in Hong Kong, Latin America, the United States, and Canada are viewed as victims of discrimination, living in countries that rob them of their "native" cultures and languages.

As Ong (1999) notes, the model of the overseas Chinese capitalists rests on their ability to retain their Confucian (and therefore Chinese) values while still managing to negotiate within Western capitalist markets. However, the Youth Festival and Summer Camps are an indication that while socialist mainland China may no longer be able to claim Confucianism, it does possess its own Chinese cultural capital in the icons of tradition desired by overseas Chinese—the ancestral villages, genealogy books, and other sites that signify the roots of Chinese heritage. These symbolic resources of heritage coexist with the growing prosperity of the Pearl River Delta Chinese, who are gaining increasing opportunities to earn capital. Perhaps a new stage in the relationship between mainland China and the Chinese abroad is represented by a mainland-centered Chinese modernity that is no longer as dependent on the capitalist knowledge and Confucian values of the Chinese abroad.

. . .

The ethnographic example I offer in this chapter emphasizes the importance of examining more closely the complex ways that Chinese identities are reshaped in the context of global flows, both in ways that are constrained by and challenge preexisting discourses about Chineseness as race and culture. Both mainland Chinese and Chinese Americans participate in the creation of discourses of Chineseness that are attached to flows of capital, both cultural and economic, and that span borders. Increased rates of migration and the transnational cultural flows associated with processes of globalization have created a transnational public sphere that widens the parameters for identity creation beyond the local. Transnational flows of people, capital, goods, and ideas have reworked opportunities for the exercise of the imagination in everyday life (Appadurai 1991). They have allowed Chinese Americans to imagine China and create expectations for their visits even before they set foot there (see Ang 1994). They have created ways for Guangdong Chinese to reevaluate their lives in relation to those of the Chinese abroad, although in ways that demystify life abroad. The result is increased opportunities for both local Chinese and visiting *hua yi* to engage in experimental multiple cultural identities while challenging official forms of China-centered authenticity.

While some transnational scholars view transnational forces as weakening the nation-state, the ethnographic case presented here supports arguments that have been made about the ways that transnational forces can strengthen nationalist projects (Brownell 1999; Glick Schiller and Fouron 1998; Smith and Guarnizo 1998; Ong 1999). My data point to the further possibility that transnational flows may reinforce a type of popular nationalism that departs from official state versions.[22]

An assumption behind the ritual of the Youth Festival and the PRC's vision for the Summer Camps is that it will expose or create a common thread of Chineseness in its participants through their exposure to cultural and historical sites, shared performances, and the stirring of nostalgic emotion for the homeland through contact with its soil. However, Chinese

Americans use their village experiences for the formation of Chinese American identities that are not solely derivative of the "place" of the ancestral village in mainland China (Malkki 1997). In doing so, they complicate an assumption that forms the basis of essentialized characterizations of Chinese identities—that overseas Chinese are loyal to their native places in ways built on nostalgic connections. Indeed, the experiences of most *huayi* may differ significantly from those of a migrant of old returning to his or her native place and once again seeing familiar sites, smelling familiar smells, and reacquainting himself or herself with relatives and friends. The activities of the Roots interns are viewed by some mainland Chinese I interviewed as more of a tourist experience. One intern's aunt commented that the group was not really searching for roots because they were only in the area for half a day. An overseas Chinese from Vietnam said that whereas his own return to the motherland was a return to roots, the In Search of Roots programs were a form of tourism. But as Edward Bruner (1996) notes in his analysis of African Americans "returning" to Elmina castle in Ghana, tourist experiences can be analyzed as part of the larger investigation of travel (Clifford 1997) and the reevaluation of the term "diaspora."

At the same time, the ethnographic example I give here demonstrates the need to rethink the relationships between the nation-state, transnational communities, and cultural flows. The Youth Festival demonstrates the prominence of the Chinese state as an actor in a larger process of reinventing a relationship (almost "from scratch" [Schein 1998]) between the Chinese state and youth of Chinese descent abroad. At the same time, it becomes obvious through the contradictions and ironies that emerge that this complex, multifaceted process of identity building creates a necessity for the PRC government to reassess traditional ideas of what it means to be Chinese. Relationships are being reworked from both ends through access to increased information about Chinese or Chinese Americans made possible through transnational cultural flows.

While there is no doubt that many Youth Festival participants did grow to feel a connection to China, a broader analysis of the festival and a closer examination of the experiences of some of its participants calls into question the underlying existence of a shared Chinese identity and of the festival's ability to create one. Instead, this example points to the existence of multiple narratives of the meaning of Guangdong—as a site of ancestral heritage, as a prospering region increasingly distinguishing itself from both other parts of China and the Chinese abroad, or as a doorway to modernity for the nation as a whole. The festival points to the tensions between the territorial and deterritorialized nation state (see Ong 1999: 11), reminding us that in some cases rather than creating detached, deterritorialized identities, transnational flows sometimes work to reterritorialize identities in new ways. The process of reterritorialization involves interactions between mainland Chinese and overseas Chinese that at the same time raise contrasts between official nationalisms and popular regional identities or nationalisms that emerge from local identities. As previously stated, this form of Guangdong-centered identity increasingly relies upon distinctions that Guangdong Chinese make between themselves and Chinese in other parts of China and abroad. It is interesting, then, that these processes by which Chinese Americans reterritorialize their identities can occur simultaneously with these processes of differentiation on the part of the Guangdong Chinese, even though the two refer to the same geographical location. This may be indicative, however, of the complex ways that identities are formed in relation to places in the context of globalization.

roots narrative)

Home. Hayward became home after the half-hour drive from the hospital in Oakland to the three-bedroom house in the middle of the block. Twenty-three years later, I'm living in Berkeley dorms, houses, and apartments around the Bay Area. But occasionally, I sleep at home.

Home. I left for college to explore life outside the confines of home. But what I saw made me want to run back to the womb, the secure walls of home. Homelessness, racism, sexism, murder—everyday occurrences in the real world. No home here, only plenty of strange, different faces, drained of love. Meanwhile, my dog sits by the window, waiting for me to come home.

Home. "You can't go home again." I left for college as a child and returned home as an adult. Or so I thought. The questions of life I once asked my parents become questions of their politics, policy and practices. I want them to stop being prejudiced. They want me to clean my room. After coming home, occasionally I want to run away. But I still fall asleep in the backseat, as Dad drives from Chinatown back to home.

Home. Certainly China isn't my home, a land thousands of miles away. My history lies in America. Five generations in America, dating back to 1862. Perhaps my great-great-grandfather left his home to sneak to America, but that's where it ends. My history states that home is America. My birth certificate states that home is America, but others say I'm not a real American. Go back home to China, they scream. Like hell.

Home. Again, it's not China. I'm not a Chinese citizen. The country is an abstract, remote place, ancient history. Peasants working in their rice fields, protesting at Tiananmen Square, beggars squatting over holes. Not me. I work in an office. I protest at Sproul. My work is done in a flush toilet at home.

Home. Those American-born-pseudo-Chinese-American (notice the hyphen) authors who go to China for the first time to "find themselves" there—they find the piece of them that is truly Chinese. They feel that they are home. Baloney.

Home. I certainly don't need to travel overseas to find myself. I know who I am, where I stand. Some people like to put it in words. To please you, I'll say this: "I am proud to be a Chinese American" (notice, no hyphen). But words don't define me. Inside, I'm at home with who I am, without having the need to place labels on it.

Home. The façade falls when the Roots brochure materialized in my hand. "The In Search of Roots program involves a year-long course on researching one's Chinese American family history and genealogy. After exploring their Chinese roots in America, participants will explore their roots in China through visiting their ancestral villages." No more excuses. Can't plead ignorant. Put up or shut up. Could China actually be home?

Home. Faced with fears left unresolved which only China could answer. I knew I was Chinese American. I knew I was American. But was I Chinese? Tongue and ears made in the U.S.A., real Chinese would laugh and stare at this American imposter, wouldn't they? *Jook sing.* Hollow bamboo. Banana. Twinkee. Everyone says I'm not real Chinese, and I've been gullible enough to believe them. But could China still be home?

Home. I applied. I endured. I went home. I found home. I came home. I am home. The government of China welcomed me into their home with open arms. I hesitantly entered. My great-granduncle welcomed me into his home with open arms. And I found I was finally at home. Home. Home is not a place, a time, or an object. Home is an emotion. Whatever I touch, whatever I see, whatever I feel becomes a part of me. Whether good or bad, I make a place for these experiences in my home. Home lives in my essence and soul. My essence and soul live in my home. Whether I am in Hayward or in

Berkeley, America or China, I am home. I may be with my family, friends, or alone by myself. I am home.

Home. I now laugh when I once excluded China as my home. How wrong could I have been? It is home. Home of my ancestors. Home of my family line. Home of a month of summer memories. Someday I will return home. But today I am going home.

Home. I park in the driveway. My dog hears the engine cut off and greets me with incessant barking. Dad peers out the window and unlocks the door as I walk up the path. He holds onto the yelping dog as he opens the door for me. Hi Dad, I'm home.

—J. O., 1994

As the narrative that precedes this chapter poignantly communicates, the conception of home held by its author has at various times expanded and contracted in relation to new opportunities to engage with the world outside the family and community in which he was raised. Home initially represented security in contrast to the "real world" environment of Berkeley, but it soon became a place he returned to only occasionally, sometimes to engage his parents in debates based on his newly discovered political ideals. The United States then becomes a metaphor for a safe and secure home when he decides to stay home while the rest of his family visits China. At college, he begins to define himself through Asian American politics as a Chinese American, without having to go to China to validate his identity. But while he resists the idea that China is a central part of his identity, he is still "faced with fears left unresolved which only China could answer" and is still plagued by the fact that "everyone says I'm not real Chinese." He finally decides to attend the Roots program, and while in China he has the opportunity to visit his ancestral village and spend time with his great-uncle. He admits that he feels "finally at home." However, in the end he returns to the comfort of his parents' home, where he is warmly greeted by his father and his dog. Maybe he will return "home" to China someday, and he now realizes that he had been wrong to exclude it as part of his identity. But at the same time he concludes that rather than being something for which he needs to search, home is something that he himself can produce.

The sense of home described by the Roots program intern is not bound by a particular place or time. Rather it is multilocal and multidimensional, contextual and processual. Home extends beyond the physical location he may occupy at any particular time. As I describe in chapters 2 and 3, the process of constructing narratives of home relies simultaneously on Chinese Americans' transnational mobility and their attachments to place(s). This transnational mobility refers not only to their freedom to travel to China (a privilege that was nevertheless a financial strain for many), but also their ability to imagine connections to other places through historical or contemporary cultural linkages. Thus, the Roots program facilitates the transnational travel by the participants that allows them to create attachments to native places in China, yet these attachments are only made meaningful as they relate to their experiences in the United States. The idea that a sense of roots can only be produced through mobility, or that roots themselves can refer to attachments to multiple places, is important in examining identity production in the context of globalization. The notion makes roots searching less a search for authentic, localized, and fixed identities than matter of cultural production. At the same time, the identities are produced in negotiation with both historically and territorially rooted connections and with contemporary plays on these connections by governments trying to shape them. In addition, the ways in which these Chinese Americans create roots differs from those of more mobile transnational actors who are less constrained by state identity-making projects, such as the Hong Kong "astronauts" (Ong 1999, Mitchell 1996). Indeed, this intern's narrative reflects his struggle to negotiate spaces within both U.S. and Chinese efforts to shape Chinese American identities, and the importance of mobility in doing so. His identity-making project and those of other Chinese Americans in the Roots program are facilitated by global circulations of Asian/Chinese culture on multiple levels that allow them to circumvent the more rigid definitions imposed on them.

As discussed throughout this book, constructions of Chineseness play a central role in these negotiations because of the ways in which both the U.S. and Chinese governments define Chinese Americans according to their ancestral origins in China. In the United States, their Chineseness is a means by which they are excluded from U.S. cultural citizenship, while in China it is the means by which they are welcomed "back" to their "motherland." In this way, constructions of shared Chinese heritage can serve both to bring together and to differentiate Chinese people (outside of and within mainland China) from one another.[1] American-born Chinese Americans face the dilemma of both acknowledging a Chinese heritage and creating a modern identity as "Chinese American" that stands on its own in relation to mainland China, which has long been the symbolic center of Chinese identities abroad. At the same time, views of the Guangdong Chinese toward Chinese from both inland China and abroad have changed in the wake of economic reforms and the Open Policy in the region. Conceptions of Chineseness play off one another at these extreme ends of the so-called Chinese diaspora and are brought together through programs jointly sponsored by Chinese American organizations and the PRC government that bring Chinese Americans to visit their ancestral villages in China.

The multisited perspective of this research allows for an examination of how definitions of Chineseness are being reworked as transnational connections bring Chinese from overseas to China. This perspective does not intend to reify the Chinese diaspora but rather to look at those labeled racially Chinese and the connections or disconnections this implies for them. This analysis takes place on several levels. Chineseness can be a national/racial discourse on a scale that is transnational in scope (such as orientalist views of China, or Chinese state discourses of overseas Chinese). It can be part of Western media constructions of capitalist networks or discourses on human rights. In a U.S. context, Chineseness can be framed both as a form of multiculturalism tied to definitions of U.S. cultural citizenship, and as a form of empowered identity within Chinese American activism. Chineseness can become a set of reified, essentialized values and traditions within a Chinese American folk culture concerned with the problem of "passing down" traditions and culture. It can also take on meanings as a sense of family and community in the construction of family histories and Chinese American networks, such as in the experiences of the In Search of Roots group. Finally, particular forms of Chineseness can be used to define Guangdong Chinese in relation to Chinese from other areas of China and abroad.

Meanings of "Chineseness" are diverse, and it is possible to identify at various levels as Chinese or with the Chinese nation-state. Chinese identities are crosscut by a wide range of practices and shifting, multilayered boundaries. At the same time, local and (native) places remain essential as moorings for identities and the accents and dialects with which they are expressed. In one sense, conceptions of Chinese identity are constrained within a historically rooted, Sinocentric worldview that formed the culturalistic conceptions of Chineseness that shaped the form taken by modern Chinese nationalism. These conceptions of Chineseness extended it as a cultural category beyond the borders of the Chinese nation-state and formed the basis for China's relationship with the Chinese abroad. But in another sense, diaspora identities are not only formed in relation to (and perhaps in tension with) the Chinese nation-state but also are responsive to transnational forces as they are manifested locally. Chineseness takes on local forms and is reactive to other conceptions of Chineseness.

Against what are Chinese identities defined? Chineseness can be a differentiating factor that gains its strength from the belief in the racial and cultural sameness of all "Chinese." But visions of a Chinese sameness fall apart at the seams as local forms of identity politics intervene. While Guangdong Province is one of the hometowns of the overseas Chinese—"sons of the yellow emperor" who have gone abroad—there has also been a historical tension with overseas Chinese who are viewed by mainland Chinese as privileged and different. The economic growth and increased information from the "outside" that have accompanied economic reforms in Guangdong have resulted in changes in how Guangdong Chinese see themselves in relation to both Chinese from other parts of China and the Chinese abroad. There is increasing tension between the belief that "we are all Chinese" and the differences they are seeing between themselves and these other Chinese.

Constructing Local Identities: Rootedness and Home

This study has revolved around the central themes of rootedness and home. These concepts are central to all discussions of globalization and migration. Globalization has brought about the destabilization of local places, practices, and identities, even for those who haven't moved. The In Search of Roots program involves a return to roots in the sense that Chinese Americans are brought to visit their ancestral villages in the Pearl River Delta region of China. The meanings of this experience are constructed to some extent in relation to historically based ideas about roots, native place, and Chineseness as they are presented in the educational component of the Roots program and in the official discourses of the Chinese government. But on another level these meanings are crosscut by a variety of other factors that affect how Chinese Americans born and raised in the United States write histories and negotiate identity politics.

As indicated in the intern's narrative at the opening of this chapter, "home" and a sense of place and rootedness may not necessarily refer to ancestral places. For African Americans, a sense of home may be found in the rural South and not Africa. In her book *Call to Home: African Americans Reclaim the Rural South* (1996), Carol Stack tells the story of the return migration, beginning in the 1970s, of generations of African Americans to the impoverished southern counties that they or their parents had left years earlier, showing that migration is not a one-way phenomenon. While African Americans find roots in the rural South, Chinese Americans similarly find roots in their experiences in America. Notions of rootedness are most effective if they refer back to places and spaces that are familiar. Therefore, while Chinese Americans (and perhaps to a greater extent their immigrant parents or grandparents or great-grandparents who were born there) may seek their family roots in the villages of southern China, these desires are also grounded in the immigrant experiences of their ancestors and their own experiences of identity exploration. At various times and in various ways, the Chinese Americans in the Roots program may consider themselves to be Chinese American, Asian American, Cantonese, third generation, Chinese from Peru or Burma, member of a working-class family in Oakland, female/male, lesbian/gay, college graduate, doctor, engineer, community activist, or combinations of these identities as defined through their conceptions of community in the context of their lives in the United States.

Roots interns and Chinese Americans don't passively imagine their Chineseness and their community in a vacuum. They imagine themselves as connected to China not only through family and kinship in a direct sense but also through historical narratives formed within the context of their own roots searching and community building (which may involve peer groups, the formation of a Roots alumni network, relatives met in China, etc.). This is a necessary alternative to a return to a Chinese community in China, which is nearly impossible for these generations.

The In Search of Roots trip to China, and the family history projects presented at the end of the internship, represent a ritual in the creation of identities. The "ritual of return" serves as a rite legitimizing them as Chinese from abroad who have a claim on their ancestral land and heritage. But this "return" is carefully orchestrated by the structure provided by the Qiao Ban and the tour format of the Roots visits. In a similar sense, choosing to learn about aspects of "Chinese culture" and Chinese or Asian American history, language, or arts is a very conscious and structured endeavor that is often undertaken by Chinese Americans through Asian American studies, other academic disciplines, or community programs outside their homes.[2] Rather than being part of a general education as it might be in China, the Chinese culture that Roots interns learn about is infused with specific meanings associated with being Chinese in America.[3]

However, in discussing the Roots program a distinction must be made between family history and genealogy, both of which are a part of the program, and the concept of genealogy writing further examined. As I mention in the introduction, genealogy is the actual tracing of ancestors, usually along patrilineal lines. Family history, however, represents a more general exploration and narration of a family's activities and experiences. This distinction is especially important as it relates to gender, because traditional

Chinese genealogical notions of identity exclude women. The Roots interns, however, chose to write their female relatives and ancestors into both their genealogies and family histories, thus revising the traditional meanings of these practices. In doing so, they create histories that emerge from their identities as contemporary Chinese Americans that although derived from ancestral ties to China are not constrained by them. Thus, while for Chinese Americans tracing one's family back twenty-five generations may foster a sense of family pride, more important is the telling of family experiences and narratives about emigration. Family history focuses on how the family came to the United States (sometimes via Southeast Asia or Latin America), and the lives of grandparents and parents on United States soil. Thus, while genealogies may recover roots in a very literal sense, this knowledge lacks meaning without the flesh-and-bones context of immigrant ancestors and their experiences, and the nature of these roots changes as Chinese Americans "recover" them. The term "ethnic ownership" (B. Williams 1989) describes how taking charge of the knowledge of one's group history or culture can legitimize or create solidarity within oppressed groups. In this context, this knowledge can be viewed as a form of property, and the definition and narration of a group's past can serve as a ritual that creates and legitimates identity.

I want to emphasize, however, that American-born Chinese do not constantly contemplate their Chineseness and are not involved in generational conflict with their elders, as many popular portrayals seem to show. Chinese Americans are not forever in identity crises or waiting for an "epiphany about being Chinese," as one intern termed it. That is not to say that they are not aware of their perceived "difference" and of racial discrimination. But while Chineseness may be a central focus for some people closely tied to personal identity issues within "consciousness-raising" identity politics (Bondi 1993), it is almost never an all-encompassing form of identity.

On one level, Chineseness for the Roots interns is expressed within a structure, such as the Roots program, Asian American studies, or community activism. On another level, it is defined through their relationships with their family and peers, which do not necessarily involve activities that are "traditionally Chinese." The way they imagine other Chinese, even other Chinese Americans, in relation to themselves characterizes their identities as Chinese American and defines their sense of community. Even the way they experience the space of Chinatown, often as an exotic and unfamiliar place, may be different from the way their parents or grandparents did. And while an evening out may involve seeing a Jackie Chan movie and a late-night snack at Sun Hong Kong restaurant, conversation spans a number of topics that can be overheard at any table (many of whom, given the popularity of Hong Kong cinema, are likely to have seen the same movie). At times, attitudes toward Chineseness and roots searching may even be somewhat irreverent, involving a good deal of play, joking, and references to popular culture.

Spontaneous exclamations of "roots!" would be uttered when the group was together. The expression c. *janhaih dak*, roughly translated as "really O.K.!" also became popular within the group to express enthusiasm, even though it didn't make any sense in Chinese. Roots newsletters contain humorous top-ten lists and computer-altered photographs of leaders. The somber saying on which the Roots program is based, c. *yum seui si yuen* ("when drinking water remember the source") is altered to c. *yum seui ogh liu* ("drink water and urinate") and c. *hou yit, yum seui* ("very hot, drink water"—a reference to the hot weather the interns endured when visiting their villages). This play is to some degree experimental. But it also may reflect an ambivalence toward making such a big deal about culture and tradition. In another sense, it might represent a reappropriation of Chinese culture, both "traditional" and popular, for the participants' own means.

The creation of the youth culture that selectively draws on aspects of "traditional" Chinese culture, contemporary Asian popular culture, and Chinese American sensibilities is significant in that it represents the negotiation of a relationship to both China and the United States that reflects the complexity of multigenerational Chinese American identities. Sunaina Maira's work on Indian American youth culture in New York illustrates these processes of identity production that "simultaneously remix elements of 'tradition' and 'modernity,' 'the authentic' and 'the hybrid'" (2002: 194). Indian American youths in New York attend dance parties where bhangra music is mixed with hip hop to produce a "remix" sound that both acknowledges their pride in their Indian heritage and marks them as contemporary youths. Although bhangra music originated in the Punjab region of India as a harvest dance, it was taken up by diaspora youths and transformed into a transnational music trend. As Maira observes, through their creation and participation in this subculture, these youths are exercising a form of "critical nostalgia" through which they "critique this ideology of authenticity and challenge dichotomies of pure/impure ethnicity through the complexity of their everyday practices" (194).

In a similar sense, participants in the Roots program have negotiated a subculture that, while not as clearly connected to other diaspora Chinese youths as bhangra club culture, also critiques and often revises "authentic" traditional cultural practices. What is significant about this subculture is its conscious reclaiming of the United States, and its reworking of Chinese American histories and traditions as legitimate and perhaps even more meaningful alternatives to those they learn about in China. Thus, the subculture of which Roots interns are a part played on ideas of authenticity in ways that consciously made their incomplete knowledge about China and Chinese culture a marker of their Chinese American identities. In contrast to the Indian American youths studied by Maira, the Roots interns identified less with a general pride in Chinese heritage than a pride in their Chinese *American* heritage that they had formed through the Roots experience. This has implications for our understandings of how global flows of popular culture take shape within specific projects of identity formation created by individuals who occupy different generational positions and who have had different experiences with the homeland. Indeed, the organization of the Roots program, focusing on family history and genealogy, and the PRC's hosting of these youths in China, informed the ways that the Chinese American participants drew on popular culture to negotiate new relationships to both Chinese and Chinese American culture. These productions, which incorporate transnational flows of popular youth culture—including the kung fu movies and Japanese *anime* that link Chinese people in China, the United States, and elsewhere—become localized as the interns create their own subculture that is simultaneously transnational by referencing villages in China and localized by referencing the particulars of their own experiences in America.

Honoring Roots

Efforts by In Search of Roots alumni to honor, revise, and ensure the future of the program demonstrate the process of claiming Chinese/Chinese American culture and political space, as well as the contestations and debates that occur as part of this process. The tenth anniversary reunion of the program took place on February 24, 2001, at the Gold Mountain restaurant in Chinatown in San Francisco. The reunion was initiated by former interns who had been planning it for two years. The purpose of the reunion was multifaceted: to honor the sponsors and leaders of the program, to provide an opportunity for former participants to gather, and to organize for the future of the program.[4] An e-mail encouraging people to attend read as follows:

> Hi Roots Gang,
> Time is running out to sign up for the Roots Ten Year Anniversary Dinner!

The dinner is being organized not only to mark a milestone in the In Search of Roots program, but also to thank some key individuals who have made Roots possible: Mark Lai Him (the scholar himself), Hal (the fearless leader), Julia (the behind the scenes organizer), and Tina and Robert Chan (the generous donors and supporters).

Other reasons to go to the Roots X Celebration:

1. YOU THINK "maybe someone will bring a mahjong set."

2. YOU ARE CURIOUS who else will be there.

3. YOU APPRECIATE all the work our honorees have done for us and the community.

4. YOU WONDER if your face will be in the BIG slide show.

5. YOU ARE GUILTY that so many fellow alumni are working so hard JUST for you.

6. YOU ARE CHEAP and know that $35 for a dinner like this is an absolute steal.

7. YOU ARE A DOTCOM-ER and are looking for "networking" opportunities.

8. YOU WANT to renew old friendships and make new ones.

9. YOU CAN'T IMAGINE Hal's hair straight . . . yes, STRAIGHT!

10. YOU BELIEVE in Roots. . . .

See you all on the 24th!

Tom T. (94)

I flew in from Michigan to attend the reunion. I arrived early at the Gold Mountain restaurant with John, a friend and former intern, and his mother. There were already a number of former interns there, members of the organizing committee who were setting up for the evening's events. People were milling around—setting up video equipment, checking-in people, and finalizing speeches. As I chatted with friends and acquaintances and introduced myself to people I had not yet met, I also informed them that I was attending both as a former intern and as a researcher. People began to rib me in a good-natured way about using them as guinea pigs, telling others to be careful about what they said around me.

The room was set up in typical banquet formation, complete with twenty-five tables with lazy susans at the center, each seating ten people. Orchid centerpieces purchased by Gloria Tai, a former Chinese Culture Center director, graced each table. Some interns commented that it seemed like a wedding (people dressed up, banquet food, etc.): they joked that they expected people to come around to greet each table and that they wanted to clink their silverware on their glasses in a signal for the bride and groom to kiss.

The banquet started at around seven o'clock. As the program progressed, various stages of the eight-course meal periodically streamed out of the kitchen: barbeque deluxe combination platter, dry scallop soup, rainbow chicken and prawns, tender beef with greens, Gold Mountain chicken, crispy duck, mushrooms with hearts of mustard greens, and steamed sole. The emcees, two former interns, spoke from the stage at the head of the banquet room. One of the emcees, Ronald, welcomed the guests and thanked the individual and corporate sponsors of the banquet. He reminded the interns that we should leave here tonight knowing how much has been done for us. He then called up Andrew Lee to the stage, who was representing Willie Brown, the mayor of San Francisco. Lee read a proclamation from the mayor commending the Roots program for its accomplishments and declaring February 24, 2001, as In Search of Roots Day in San Francisco. The host and hostess then thanked the various organizations and leaders of the program, and were followed by John, a former intern, who gave the keynote speech. His speech was built on the theme of "teachers, doctors, and engineers," the occupations of the program's leaders and sponsors. He emphasized that we are all teachers, doctors, and engineers in our own way and that Roots has inspired us to become more involved in our communities in various capacities, following the paths of these founders and sponsors. More acknowledgments were then made to former directors of the Chinese Culture Center, other financial supporters, and the organizing committee for the reunion, and a lion dance performed by a local troupe followed.

After the dance came a trivia contest. The prizes were large plastic containers of lychee jellies, the artifically fruit-flavored candies that were very popular among Chinese Americans. The audience laughed when the emcee joked that the prize would go a long way, because after the jellies were consumed the container would most likely have a second life as a storage bin for rice or soup. The first trivia question asked was What were the three principles for the trip to China that the Chinese American leader, Hal, emphasized? Many volunteers raised their hands and one was selected by the emcee, who named the principles: suspend judgment, keep an open mind, and be flexible. At my table, however, people joked how these principles used to include "don't drink the water, don't eat the greens."

The second question, What is the last name of Mark Lai Him (the other leader)? required the knowledge that his Chinese surname was actually the middle part of his English name. What appeared to be his English surname was actually a paper name. The third question, What are the six languages spoken by Julia? (the staff member of the Chinese Culture Center who organized many of the logistics of the program) was answered, correctly, as English, Cantonese, Gwok Yu (Mandarin), French, Portuguese, and Shanghainese). The fourth question involved naming ten exotic foods consumed by Roots interns over the years, and answers included snake, snails, and dog.

The audience members had a great deal of fun with these questions, but what impressed me was that most knew the answers. Although the program had involved ten different cohorts over the years it had been in existence, in many ways a Roots subculture had developed that encompassed all groups. This subculture was neither solely "Chinese" or "Chinese American"— much of it emerged from the daily experiences of program participants and reflected the sense of humor that framed the emotionally and physically grueling process of roots searching in China.

The trivia contest was followed by speeches given by the program leaders, who were the main honorees of the evening. The first leader to speak, Hal, joked that he had prepared a five-minute speech and a one-hour speech, but that he would read the short one. He said that he and Mark Lai Him, the other leader, were a "Chinese odd couple" who worked well together to organize the program, but that he was the fool who took us to China. He thanked the participants' parents, because "without you there would be no interns," and he added "thanks for trusting us with your children." He concluded by saying that the Roots program was about more than finding out about family history. It was about finding out who you are—your identity. He emphasized that the program transmits the Chinese values of family relations, education, hard work, and giving back to the community.

A former intern presented a film on Mark Lai Him that the intern had started as a school project at UCLA. He said that as an Asian-Pacific American filmmaker his work was inspired by Mark Lai Him's work. Indeed, Mark Lai Him has been described as a barefoot historian and the dean of Chinese American history: "You can't write or talk about Asian-Pacific American history without referring to him," said Hal.

Next, Mark Lai Him himself gave a speech. He said that when the program started he still had some black hair (now in his seventies, it is mostly gray) and that he couldn't believe that ten years had passed. "You may think we knew what we were doing, but it has turned into something different than it originally was." He added that the participants might think they learned a lot, but he learned a lot too about the history of China and the geography of Pearl River Delta through locating interns' villages. Just having the books on the shelf was not enough, participating in Roots forced him to use them.

Next, an intern from the 1991 program, Ellen introduced the Pearl River Delta database project, one of the primary initiatives of the alumni group. This database would catalogue information about the region for future roots-searching efforts; however, they needed funds to get it up and running. She noted that there were great things expected of the interns because as we all know we have become "one big Chinese family" (perhaps a reference to overseas Chinese office rhetoric).

To end the program, two interns showed their slideshow called "Roots in Retrospective." It began with an interview with the program's original sponsors, then shifted to a scenic view of the Chinese countryside, accompanied by the booming music from *Once Upon a Time in China*, the same popular music from the Hong Kong kung fu series that was used at a Youth Festival performance in 1995.

The Future of Roots

The Roots tenth anniversary reunion encapsulated a number of issues relating both to what the program has come to represent to the people involved in it and how these various players viewed the future of the program. While a number of former interns have helped out with the program over the years, the reunion was the first intern-initiated effort on a large scale to both honor the program's founders and to redefine the scope of the program's vision. This intense involvement, while obviously a testimony to the program's continued importance in participants' lives, also reflected a particular moment in the program's evolution. The program had been constructed initially to address a generational shift in the Chinese American community, where Chinese Americans, generations removed from China, needed to seize the opportunity to learn from the generations before them before these generations passed on. Through the program, interns were encouraged to interview parents, aunts and uncles, and especially grandparents who had memories of China and of the immigrant experience in America. They learned about Chinese and Chinese American history and culture from the program's coorganizers, who were bicultural and bilingual in both American and Chinese settings. This information was to provide a grounding for them as Chinese Americans.

The program is in no doubt a success, and it has received praise from all involved—the Chinese government sponsors, the Chinese American community sponsors, the Chinese American leaders, the interns, and their parents. It has also received a good deal of media attention. Part of its success can be measured by the extent to which the program produced new generations of scholars, activists, and others who would remain involved in the Chinese American community. Roots interns have built on their experiences in the program in a variety of ways, including individual explorations of China through further study or travel, and involvement in Chinatown organizations, in Roots alumni activities, or as Asian American activists.

One of the issues faced by the program, however, is who will carry it forward in the future. This is a difficult question, given that most participants feel they lack the language skills (knowledge of Cantonese, Mandarin, and village dialects), cultural knowledge, and political connections to support future Roots cohorts in their journeys. At the same time, there is the question of how the focus and direction of the program might evolve to more fully address the changing needs of American-born Chinese Americans. Former interns have been involved in this visioning process, which has raised questions such as: What is the goal of Roots? Is it to research genealogy, locate ancestral homes, and reconnect with Chinese relatives? Is it to produce community leaders, academics and activists? Is it to appreciate what previous generations have sacrificed and to better connect to their experiences? To what extent should the program address contemporary Asian-Pacific American political issues in addition to personal identity questions? What is the relationship between identifying on a broader level as Asian American and on a more specific level with one's ancestral village in China? How do these various goals fit together and to what extent should program leaders shape these processes?

One intern commented that while there is no doubt that the program is life changing, there needs to be more done to help interns address the significance of their experiences in China and relate them back to their lives in America. He observed that narratives are selectively written to focus on existing tropes of roots searching (finding a piece of oneself in China, etc.), and leave out the community building experiences that are also a central part of the Roots experience. In his observation, the narratives focus on how we should honor our grandparents who struggled to come to the United States. They do not interrogate racism but rather talk of fulfilling the American dream of pulling oneself up by one's bootstraps; that if they hadn't come to the United States they'd be poor like the people they saw in China (they ignore the fact that many of their relatives in China are rather prosperous). Interns tend to view their experiences in China as unique and not connected to their lives in the United States or relationships with other Chinese Americans.

Such questions about the future of the Roots program reflect issues raised throughout this book about not only the changing relationship between Chinese Americans and China but also changing relations within the Chinese American community itself. As immigrant generations pass on, what will being Chinese American and being connected to China mean to future generations? Newer generations will in many ways be further removed from China but in other ways through transnational processes, they will be more closely connected than ever before. Will transnational flows facilitate a new type of roots searching that will involve a different understanding of China and one's connections to it? Just as the politics of the 1960s inspired Chinese Americans to create a relationship with China based on Third World revolutionary goals (Louie 2003), so too did the context of the 1990s allow for the crafting of relationships with China that worked both within and against state identity-making projects, multicultural politics, and transnational flows.

Roots as Reterritorialization

The questions raised about the future of the Roots program can push us to theorize transnationalism in a way that addresses the tenuous relationship between American-born generations and the ancestral homeland. Addressing this relationship necessitates an examination of the broader structuring forces that mediate the "return to roots," taking into account not only how broad-scale yet uneven flows of labor and capital produce strategic claims on Chineseness but also how these claims are negotiated by actors as much through disjunctures produced by transnational interactions as through connections. Various actors—from the Chinese government to mainland Chinese citizens to third-generation Chinese Americans—have engaged in the construction of Chinese identities. In the process, they have challenged and reworked notions of family, genealogy, community, gender, and history. As such, examining these constructions of Chineseness has provided an opportunity to study the identity productions that are grounded in the intimate, everyday experiences of family and community but also take place within a context of transnational flows of capital, people, ideas, and goods.

The Roots group traveled to China with very specific purposes, and their visits represented encounters with a China they had imagined and desired from afar. But while each intern sought a specific relationship to China and Chineseness, they would each later use their experiences in China to strategically craft Chinese identities. They create histories that reference China but that ultimately served to define family, community, and identity for the present and the future. Thus, transnational processes of roots searching are accompanied by a complex dynamic involving both deterritorialization and strategic efforts at reterritorialization in relation to both China and the United States.

In a sense, both the Roots program and the Youth Festival provided a necessary structure that guided Roots interns in learning more about their ancestral roots in China and the United States as well as the broader social, economic, and historical contexts that produced them. The program and the festival were each created within specific contexts that shaped the processes through which the Roots interns sought their roots. The politics of racial exclusion in the United States and the discourses of multiculturalism that have arisen in response to this history in many ways shaped the Roots program organizers' desires to help the Chinese American youths find their roots. The Chinese government's search for a path toward modernity with the support of the Chinese abroad resulted in the creation of its Youth Festival and Summer Camps. At the same time, these projects did not solely shape the meanings that the Chinese American participants derived from their experiences. The specific connections and disjunctures that the interns encountered through them (or rather between them or juxtaposed to them) became central to their reworking of their identity narratives. Their physical mobility allowed them to continually move between the past and present, and between the familiar and unfamiliar, to create meanings out of these juxtapositions.

But what about the continuities? Where do family and community, past and present, link up under transnationalism? I end this chapter with the words written in 1994 by a nineteen-year-old Roots intern about her visit to her ancestral village in Taishan, during which she met her aunt and uncle whom she had never before met and whom her father had not seen in twenty-one years. Her words describe a process of reterritorialization that takes shape through the creation of new ties framed in relation to both the past and the present, to China and the United States. In this sense, these continuities only come into view as they are created in the context of transnational linkages. Thus, although her visit might in some ways be considered a romantic "homecoming," it might not have unfolded in the same way without the structure provided by the roots-searching programs. Once enacted, however, these linkages took on a life of their own, invoking familial connections that referred to the past, but also creating possibilities for the present and the future.

• • •

Over and over again, the "continuation" struck me—the sense that I wasn't here to try and find old roots, but that I was here merely to visit and catch up on what I had missed over, say . . . the past few years . . .

The visit left me with a strong sense of the present, not the sense of "going back" for history's sake which I had expected. That sense of "going back" which had seemed to be the whole point of the Roots program, the goal of those who were sponsoring and organizing the trip and lectures. What I found instead was a sense of continuing—not merely moving—forward. [My aunt and uncle in the village] described perhaps once how my grandparents didn't dare come back, but they told me at least ten times which of their daughters were married, where they were living, where their son worked, what he did, and they showed me pictures to try and bring these people to life for me. For all the times I asked to see my house, I received at least one invitation to see my aunt and uncle's house. For each minute I spent in my house, I spent at least two or three in theirs . . .

We did not stare at old artifacts—when I asked about any old artifacts, they said there were none—the Communists cleaned everything out, or else they destroyed things themselves before they could be used as evidence. When I asked more specifically for old pots and bowls, they wondered why I'd want them—this old junk. It wasn't until I explained that my brother and sister hadn't seen these things before that they were able to understand it . . . And still, all along, they did not understand why I would want what they obviously considered old junk, bowls which had remained, all coated with dust, in cupboards with the doors falling off.

As we went back to the bus, my aunt kept telling me to come back and visit. Perhaps in a year, or two, or maybe later. We walked down that long, muddy road again. There were two women . . . They were guiding me so I would walk on the solid dirt, and not on the mud. And sometimes, they pulled me in opposite directions. But I made it without falling, and it was great.

I returned to China most recently in summer 2002. On a hot day in late May, I saw my relatives in Guangzhou for the first time in seven years. My aunt,[1] her husband, and their four-year-old daughter whom I had never met, picked me up from the White Swan Hotel[2] using a van borrowed from the university where they worked. They immediately began telling me about how much Guangzhou had changed—that the environment was much cleaner and traffic much less congested. The city had indeed changed a great deal in the past seven years, so much so that I did not recognize the intersection near Yi Suk Gung's (my great-uncle's) apartment complex. While his apartment remained pretty much the same as I remembered it, although perhaps a bit more run-down, a block away a shopping center, complete with a McDonald's and a Carrefour's department store (JiaLeFu)[3] was being built.

My relatives had changed too. Most everyone was at least a few pounds plumper than before, which they told me was a sign that they were healthy and doing well. Indeed, they did appear to be doing quite well. Each family member, including Yi Suk Gung and his twelve-year-old granddaughter, had their own cell phone. Moreover, instead of eating in their modest apartment, we went across the street to a restaurant set up with banquet-style tables, where we feasted on a multicourse meal. I had brought some gifts with me, which I nervously (recalling my past history of gift-giving faux pas) distributed at the table: American ginseng for Yi Suk Gung, a silver rabbit pin for his wife, and lipstick, earrings, and powder compacts for their three daughters. I also brought envelopes with token amounts of American dollars for each family member, gifts from my father and some of his siblings.[4] They accepted the gifts graciously. At the end of my stay, they gave me some gifts in return—a shirt for my mother, some jade bracelets, and some pearls.[5]

My aunt now lived in a comfortable, new three-bedroom apartment on the grounds of Jinan University where she and her husband worked—she as an office administrator and he as an official in charge of Communist Party affairs on campus. She told me that she thinks her life here in Guangzhou is good—comparable to or better than that of the Chinese in the United States. In turn, she asked how much I made. Afraid that she would view my assistant professor's salary as an indication that I was rich, I told her a slightly more modest figure, noting that houses and other things in America are expensive. However, she did not appear to be too impressed with my salary, commenting that she knew that taxes are also high in the United States. She told me that she and her husband now made fairly decent salaries (she makes 5,000 renminbi per month) and they were even thinking of buying a car within the next year. Her sisters, who work at the luggage inspection section of the Guangzhou railway station make 3,000 renminbi per month. She doesn't believe that anyone in her family wants to emigrate. In fact, she thinks that the life of the Chinese in the United States is probably very tiring (*lei*). Also, she is more familiar with Guangzhou, where her family lives and the surroundings are familiar.

Since I last saw them, they'd increasingly had opportunities to travel abroad. My aunt told me that her plan for her four-year-old daughter after kindergarten was to take her to travel in Guangdong. After primary school she would take her around China, and after college around the world. I asked her specifically where and she said she didn't know yet, but that now it was very common for Chinese people to travel—they can go anywhere. Perhaps they would visit us in America. I asked if other people she knew still wanted to emigrate to the United States or other places, and she said no, only to travel. She repeated what she had told me seven years previously, that she herself would only want to go to America to travel, not to immigrate. She said a friend of hers applied for a visa to travel to Australia, and the visa officials were afraid he would try to stay there. The person had replied that he wouldn't emigrate to Australia even if they allowed him to.

However, my aunt does want her husband's nineteen-year-old niece, Wen Wen, to go to the United States. She was not a good student, having only completed junior middle school (*chuzhong*) and not having passed the test to attend senior middle school. Her parents are poor farmers from the Fujian countryside, and she was living with my aunt and uncle and helping with housework, cooking, and childcare. In return, they sent 500 renminbi back to her parents every month. Because of her lack of education, she could only get a service job as a waitress or store clerk in Guangzhou, but my aunt felt that because she is still young she would have a chance to develop in the United States. They asked me to help find a husband for her in America.

The day before I left, the family met at the restaurant across the street to celebrate Duan Wu Jie (the Dragon Boat Festival). A Lai, one of my aunt's younger sisters, and I talked about life in the United States. She asked me about the price of food in America, pointing to dishes on the table and asking how much they'd cost. I told her that the vegetable dish she was pointing at would cost about u.s. $7. She seemed shocked, announcing the fact to the whole table. My relatives then asked me about other dishes on the table, acting repeatedly surprised over the exorbitant prices in the United States. Later, they queried me about how much my clothing cost in the United States, encouraging me to buy clothes in China because they were cheaper. A Lai also told me that Wen Wen should go abroad, and that I could help her find a husband. But she herself didn't want to leave China. Life is good here. She doesn't speak English. What would she do abroad?

These interactions and others during my time in China reinforced the findings of my research in 1995 about changing attitudes toward emigration in Guangdong. It appears that life has continued to improve for most Guangdong residents, although some still hope to go abroad. While in Shenzhen on the same trip, I visited a Qiao Ban official who I had inter-viewed during my previous stays in Shenzhen. I asked whether he thought that fewer people wanted to emigrate now. He agreed that attitudes toward overseas Chinese and emigration had changed in China, and that the num-ber of people emigrating has been decreasing. He said that it should be so because "we relied on ourselves and made ourselves richer." Thanks to the Open Policy and economic reform, the economy and the living standards are now better, so ordinary people have changed their ideas about the United States. They used to think it was heaven, but not now. But in some backward areas such as in the western and middle parts of China, and in coastal Fujian, people still think the United States is heaven, and they try their best to get there. Many of these people immigrate illegally, although of course the government discourages this. However, usually what they see in the United States is not what they had thought they would see. Some of these people had mistaken the actions of the overseas Chinese who returned from abroad and built three- and four-story houses as a sign of their prosperity, so they think it's easy to make money in the United States.

Indeed, a young businessman from Chaozhou whom I met in Guang-zhou earlier had carefully thought out this issue. He ran a small store outside of the White Swan Hotel selling souvenirs to tourists. When I asked him whether he was interested in emigrating to the United States, he said that he thought that the people in Fujian who paid money to snakeheads to be smuggled into the United States (see chapter 4) were not very wise because it is very difficult to get out of debt in such situations. For the amount of money that one pays for a down payment to a snakehead, he thought, one could instead open a small business in China.

Other people I spoke with also questioned the purpose of trying to emigrate to the United States. A taxi driver in Shenzhen, originally from Hubei Province, asked me and my former student, who is now studying in the United States, whether America was heaven. He observed that America is capitalist and China is socialist, so America is good if you're rich but China will take care of you if you don't have work. In America the poor don't have anything to eat.

People's conceptions of their nearby capitalist neighbor, Hong Kong, have also continued to change. As the Qiao Ban official commented, "Now if you drive someone to Hong Kong [from Shenzhen] they won't stay. Thirty years ago, people swam there." Indeed, while the mainland Chinese economy has continued to grow, Hong Kong has experienced its own economic difficulties. Shenzhen people now boast that they have a Walmart, TGI Friday's, Hard Rock Café, and even a Sam's Club. They live in nicer, newer apartments than most Hong Kong people, and the streets of Shenzhen are newer and wider, with plenty of green space. Many of the teachers at the school where I taught English ten years previously now owned private cars, most of which were made through joint ventures in China for the middle-class Chinese market. People with steady government jobs, such as teachers, were now able to buy on credit. Whereas ten years ago, most teachers lived in fairly modest apartments provided by the school, many now lived in beautifully furnished apartments, complete with wallpaper and interior decorations. Increasingly, people were sending their children abroad for college or for graduate school. Teachers, staff, and former students that I talked with thought that educations in the United States, Europe, or Australia would provide them with opportunities for development in China. Their motivation to go abroad differs in many ways from the people who escaped over the border to Hong Kong thirty years ago, as many planned to return to China to open their own businesses or work for joint-venture companies. Bookstores were full of guidebooks for SAT, GMAT, TOEFL, GRE, and other college entrance examinations for U.S. schools.

Mr. He, an official at the school where I used to teach English, is a loyal party member and patriotic Chinese. When I snapped his picture, he made sure I had included the Chinese and Communist Party flags that were prominently displayed on his desk. While in the past China has worried when sending students abroad about their not returning, he said that they now encourage students to study abroad to "learn advanced things, such as architecture." He is confident that the students will return to China eventually. "Like you," he said, "you came back." He thinks the Open Policy is a good one. Before the policy was too strict but now they have an opportunity to get in touch with the outside world—to study, train, and develop relations with foreigners. Every year the school organizes people to go abroad. They went to Australia in 1995 with twelve students, and in 1996 the Australian students came to China and stayed with families. They have also sent students to France, Germany, Japan, and South Korea. They want their children to see more things. He said that before many people wanted to study and live outside of China. Now China is prosperous and a world market. So students who stay abroad can come back to build their own factories. A former student who graduated from Qinghua University (the most prestigious college in China) with a doctorate wants to build a base in Shenzhen or Shanghai. They will come back because, after all, China is their motherland. Students learn a lot in America and can come back to serve their country. However, he thinks they should finish their basic educations in China and then go to America after university. After they have stayed in China for twenty years they will know more about their own country's history and culture, the roots of their nationality (*minzude gen*). It will be helpful for them their whole life. They should know the motherland first and when they come back they will serve their motherland (*jian shi zuguo*). The students have said that they only go abroad for learning. China is much different from before. The difference between China and other countries is getting smaller. At first the students regarded America as a paradise, but now they know more and they don't think America is a paradise. The living and working conditions in China are better now than in the past. He will encourage students to go abroad and hope that they come back.[6]

These changes in Shenzhen represent a different form of engagement with the outside world, one in which differences between Shenzhen and other large cities appear on some level to be decreasing, and the outside world has become a resource for the development of Shenzhen. On the surface Shenzhen, with its gleaming skyscrapers that appear to pop up overnight,[7] its Western companies and products, and its cosmopolitan population, seems to be overtaking Hong Kong. Indeed, a friend's parents who were visiting her from Chengdu (a large inland Chinese city) in Sichuan Province said that they had not been impressed with Hong Kong at all. Things were expensive, the streets were narrow and crowded, and they saw a lot of poverty. In fact, while they preferred Shenzhen to Hong Kong, they told me that they thought their Chengdu was the best of all.

As the standard of living for many in China continues to improve, Chinese citizens increasingly take control over their own opportunities for development, whether in China or abroad. They are beginning to create their own geographies to describe the relative standards of living both within and outside of China. People I spoke with increasingly took into account not only material comforts but also more intangible markers in assessing their quality of life.[8] Thus, while going to another city or another country may allow one to earn a higher salary, what good is that if one doesn't speak the language and if products are proportionally expensive? My friend's parents told me that the same packet of tea cost H.K.$88 (over U.S.$10) in Hong Kong, 20 renminbi (about $2.50) in Shenzhen, and only a few yuan (less than $1) in Chengdu. One can only speculate as to what the future holds as relations between Chinese people in different parts of China and the world continue to shift. Is it possible, as one scholar of overseas Chinese once told me, that in the future there will no longer be any overseas Chinese; that Chinese people will no longer need to go and stay abroad to develop? What type of relationship, then, will descendants of previous generations of overseas Chinese craft in relation to China, especially because Chinese identities are increasingly constructed through influences not necessarily located in China?

Introduction: On Boundary Crossings

Note: all translations are mine unless otherwise stated.

1 Guangdong, the southernmost province of China (with the exception of Hainan), is located on the South China Sea near Hong Kong. The Pearl River Delta area (Zhujiang San Jiao Zhou) is an alluvial plain system formed by the western, northern, and eastern tributaries of the Pearl River.

2 My great-great-grandfather was the first in our family to emigrate; he moved to the United States during the Gold Rush.

3 All romanizations are in Mandarin pinyin, unless indicated otherwise. Cantonese romanizations are indicated with a "c." In cases where both are used, Mandarin words are indicated with the abbreviation "md."

4 It was common for overseas Chinese to have a second wife as a sign of their new-found prosperity.

5 This sentiment was common among immigrant generations of Chinese. James Watson (1975) has found similar attitudes among Man lineage emigrants from Hong Kong living in England who sent their children back to Hong Kong to be raised by grandparents and educated in Chinese.

6 The family had received a note saying that if they did not pay the requested ransom, the sons would then be kidnapped.

7 All of his siblings ultimately married people they met in the United States.

8 According to my father, the village children, aged eight to twelve, chanted "ABCD" as they rode their water buffalos out to the fields. He recalls that their pronunciation of "ABCD" sounded phonetically like the word "opposite" said slowly in English, followed by a "dee" sound.

9 Indeed, my grandfather's first wife had remained in China. My grandmother, the second wife, was chosen to come to the United States because life in the United States was considered a hardship.

10 In between my father's return in 1948 and my own visit in 1993, there were numerous twists and turns in PRC policy toward overseas Chinese. At times, overseas Chinese (and their capital) were welcomed, while at other times overseas connections were cause for persecution.

11 These varied ways of relating to the ancestral village show in one sense that the moment of emigration is neither a permanent nor an irrevocable one. But although emigration has been studied as a flexible phenomenon in earlier research on return migration, as well as through works informed by the transnational literature, less attention has been paid to the ways in which these patterns unfold beyond the first, more mobile generations. The late-nineteenth and early-twentieth-century history of Chinese emigration from coastal Guangdong to the United States demonstrates a pattern that represents neither a unidirectional movement toward assimilation nor a straightforward back-and-forth movement between the homeland and places abroad. U.S. immigration laws, political upheaval in China resulting in varied and often contradictory policies toward the Chinese abroad, and Sino-U.S. relations shaped the possibilities for the maintenance of ties with people in China and for identification with China in a broader sense. Although the century-old pattern of return migration to China was (not wholly voluntarily) maintained to an extent by later generations such as my father's, who retained ties of language and kinship to the village, it was certainly not characterized by the definite sense of purpose (getting married, fathering children, building a house, returning to retire) of previous generations, nor was it marked by the smooth transitions back and forth that often are assumed on behalf of transmigrant generations. It is this historical and processual dimension that is often lacking in many discussions of transnational relationships, which in their emphasis on the maintenance of linkages between transmigrants and their places of origin, often render static the social practices associated with transnational movements over time and across generations.

12 Research on new types of transnational relationships across nonbounded field sites has necessitated the practice of multisited fieldwork and an "itinerant" (Schein 1998) type of anthropology. In her study of Hmong/Miao forged transnationality, Louisa Schein discusses the ways in which she served as a nexus and translator, often facilitating "identity exchanges," between Miao from mainland China and Hmong living in the United States. Her project itself was multilocal, consisting largely of arranged and rather infrequent encounters between Hmong and Miao in a variety of forums, from international conferences to smaller-scale visits.

13 One of the leaders of the Roots program referred to other programs sponsored by various organizations in the United States and other countries outside of China as having a "buffet"-style approach to Chinese culture. By this, he meant that participants received only a superficial sampling of Chinese culture during their relatively short visits to China. In contrast, the Roots program was a year-

long venture, beginning with family history and genealogical research and ending with presentations built on this research as well as visits to ancestral villages.

14 The China-sponsored portion of the program will be discussed further in chapter 1. The Office of Overseas Chinese Affairs is represented at all administrative levels of government in most parts of Guangdong Province, from district (*zhen*) to province (*sheng*). It is also an official branch of the national government's central committee.

15 More recently, research by historians such as Madeline Hsu (2000) and Yong Chen (2000) has redefined early Chinese immigration as a form of transnational practice.

16 Not all participants were able to find family records in the archives. Some families had emigrated to Hong Kong, or to places in Southeast Asia or in Latin America before entering the United States. Therefore, many families entered after the repeal of the Exclusion Acts in 1943.

17 To use such "paper names," immigrants would have to memorize the information pertinent to paper-name identities to pass the interrogation of immigrant officials under a system that was designed to make entry very difficult.

18 Coaching books were handwritten "crib sheets" that potential immigrants studied and then threw overboard before going through interrogation by U.S. immigration officals during the exclusion era (1882–1943). Because many immigrants assumed paper names and the family histories that went along with them, it was important that they record this information for later arrivals so that their stories would match, thus convincing immigration officials that they were legitimate relatives and not "paper sons."

19 *Zhongguoren* implies citizenship in the Chinese nation-state (although it is also used colloquially to apply to Chinese abroad), while *hua ren* implies Han ethnicity on the mainland or abroad. *Huaqiao* has connotations of extraterritorial rule, and according to current PRC definitions it applies only to Chinese nationals living outside of China who retain their citizenship. *Meiji huaren* refers to a Chinese person with American citizenship, while *huayi* refers to descendants of Chinese abroad who are not citizens of the PRC.

20 Like concepts of native place (*jiguan, jiaxiang*), *tongxiang* (hometown mate) boundaries were flexibly drawn depending on the situation, similar to the ways that Evans Pritchard (1968) described segmentary opposition among the Nuer. Sometimes one's *tongxiang* may come from the same village (*cun*), other times the same country (*xian*), and at others times the same province (*sheng*).

21 Descent is usually traced on the father's side. It was actually my mother's side that was from Taishan County, but my father's village was located in neighboring Heshan County and both regions were part of the cultural area known as the five counties (formerly four) that included a cluster of emigrant counties on the western edge of the Pearl River Delta. The Taishan region is well known in China for its emigrant way of life (local officials bragged that there are more

Taishan people outside of China than in China), so it was easier for people to place me there.

22 This was also the name of a publication based in Guangzhou, focusing on Guangdong and Hong Kong culture, that was circulated nationwide.

23 These statistics are taken from Yeung and Chu 1994.

24 The question of Taiwan, especially in light of the independence movement, greatly complicates the claims that I make here. Taiwan holds youth programs, similar to the Roots program, in which Taiwan is described as a location for the preservation of Chinese culture and language. Still, as one leader of the program observed, mainland China has the advantage of appealing to a wider group of overseas Chinese because of the connections that can be drawn to ancestral villages.

25 By "bifocality" I mean a dual perspective that allows for a more complex view of where one is located in relation to people in other places and that is facilitated by travel and transnational flows of ideas and information.

26 As I discuss later in this volume, the definition of Chineseness as a racial identity closely tied to nationalism stems from turn-of-the-century nationalist efforts in China that continued to be reflected in policies toward overseas Chinese and in folk Chinese attitudes until the present. Overseas Chinese, who played a significant role in the 1911 revolution, also subscribed to these ideas (Sun Yat Sen was an overseas Chinese, and other reformers and revolutionaries at the turn of the century campaigned abroad to win the support of the overseas Chinese for their efforts).

27 In a sense, the idea of Chineseness has always been a fiction uniting the very diverse and often antagonistic subgroups within the (sometimes flexible borders of the) territory of China. Scholars of nationalism and Chinese ethnicities have pointed out the various ways that Chineseness breaks down into alternative allegiances (Honig 1992; Crossley 1990). Although the boundaries of these groups are porous, some of these divisions within Chineseness include the distinction between minority and Han Chinese, between rural versus urban, and among regions. For example, some scholars have pointed out a potential, past and present, for a regional Guangdong-centered nationalism stemming from its connections to the outside world via the overseas Chinese. These connections have brought relative prosperity to the region, setting it apart from other areas of China. This separatism has historical roots in a variety of cultural and political expressions of Cantonese independence, expressed in the 1989 discovery and preservation of the king of Nan Yue tomb in downtown Guangzhou, which signified the past (and potential future) glory of an independent southern region (Lary 1996). Separatism has been more recently expressed as a form of alternative Chinese modernity in post-Mao China, derived from transnational connections with overseas Chinese capitalists (Ong 1999).

28 Chineseness as a form of identity coexists with other dimensions of identifica-

tion: gender, class, region, politics. I also do not intend to imply that Chinese-ness is something that should be reclaimed through a communion with any form of essentialized Chinese culture rooted on the mainland Chinese territory.

29 Or when Chineseness becomes something that one is trying to define oneself against.

30 Such readings of Chinese American cultural citizenship, many have argued, are rooted in the contradiction between capital and labor on which Asian immigration into the United States was built (Dirlik 1998; Lowe 1996).

31 See Louie (2003) for a discussion of how relations with the Chinese homeland are shaped for specific historical and political contexts in the United States.

32 Ye Yang, ed. 2002. "Shenzhen Museum." Shenzhen City: A Shenzhen Museum Publication.

33 Territorial roots are a universal metaphor for the grounding of identities in particular places and historical times. At the same time, the relationships of people with their place of origin have never been simple. As Liisa Malkki notes: "To plot only 'places of birth' and degrees of nativeness is to blind oneself to the multiplicity of attachments that form to places through living in, remembering, and imagining them" (1997: 72). In other words, in describing ties to place and the claims to authenticity that usually accompany them, both folk and academic discourses often inappropriately privilege immediate physical or temporal connections over the complex and varied forms of attachment to places that are central to processes of place making. Hierarchical notions of authenticity based on the closeness and immediacy of association with places portray places, and notions of culture derived from them, as falsely bounded and static entities rather than as dynamic, contested spaces. In fact, those groups that construct identities in relation to places from a temporal or spatial distance, perhaps more than those that physically occupy them, bring contested meanings to places. Malkki notes that homelands are increasingly invented from afar, in relation to places that those imagining them no longer physically occupy (52).

Ideas of "origins" and "nativeness" as associated with place are further problematized within academic discourses on place, space, and identity. Akhil Gupta and James Ferguson (1997) argue that the simple equation of identities with neatly bounded places is an increasingly inaccurate reflection of the complex relationships between places and identities amidst global flux.

Given the ways that Chinese American identities are fixed to places in China through various forms of cultural politics, the question remains how these identities (which have been relegated to the rural villages of the past) can be reconceived as processual, dynamic, and multiply rooted through a progressive politics of place in which places are conceived of as comprised of competing, negotiated meanings (Massey 1994; Dirlik 1999b). These tensions between territorially rooted and dynamic aspects of identities raise questions that are at the heart of discussions of transnational and diasporic politics. Why do associations with places and territories continue to remain central to identities, even as people increasingly move away from their places of origin and these places themselves change under globalization?

1 *Identities Fixed in Place: Ancestral Villages and Chinese/Chinese American Roots*

1 Ironically, this leader, who had grown up in the Philippines, did not know how to *bai san* until he came to the United States. His mother's funeral in the Philippines had been Western in style.

2 Genealogy books, or *zupu*, trace patrilineal descent over multiple generations, indicating lineage membership. The village visits will be discussed in further depth in chapter 2.

3 Politics, specifically the forced separation entailed by Communist China's isolation from the outside world from the 1950s until the 1980s, has played a central role. And in many ways these changes may appear to be an inevitable consequence of the passage of time. The transformation of this transnational community will be discussed in further depth later.

4 Yu's political history incorporates Chinese-language newspapers, interviews, and archival materials from the CHLA and other sources.

5 The KMT, or Guomindang, is the name of the Chinese nationalist party, which held power in China from 1928 to 1949.

6 Yu observes: "In their struggle to maintain their independence and resist the KMT's authoritarian control, many Chinese Americans demonstrated a new kind of overseas Chinese nationalism through their own organizations, such as the CHLA. The essence of this new nationalism included an awareness of the basic political rights of citizens and the willingness to claim these rights, the development of political consciousness and the courage to voice political criticism, and most significantly, the use of political concepts learned in American society to criticize China's politics. . . . Moreover, because these Chinese Americans consciously linked their struggle for survival in America to China's national salvation movement, they even began to develop a new consciousness of themselves as Chinese Americans" (1992: 94).

7 This term signifies ancestral villages in various contexts within mainland Chinese official and folk discussions. *Jiguan* and *zuji* have associations with official residence, while *guxiang, jiaxiang,* and *xiangxia* are folk usages invoking rural origins and family connections. According to the ethnographic interviews I conducted with mainland Chinese in Shenzhen, Guangzhou, and other parts of the Pearl River Delta, consensus did not always exist on the meanings of these terms. Was one's *jia xiang* where one's father was born? One's grandfather? Would Shenzhen one day become their *jiaxiang*?

8 Gupta and Ferguson explain the relation between place and space: "Keeping in mind that notions of locality or community refer both to a demarcated physical space and to clusters of interaction, we can see that the identity of a place

emerges by the intersection of its specific involvement in a system of hierarchically organized space within its cultural construction as a community or locality" (1997: 8).

9 In late-nineteenth and early-twentieth-century Shanghai, native-place loyalties translated into larger urban and national levels of identification (Goodman 1995a, 1995b). Native-place identities were formed according to the belief that a "traveler's identity would not change along with place of residence" (1995b: 5). Children of immigrants who had been outside their native place for several generations inherited the *jiguan* of their ancestors (5). Absence from one's hometown was supposed to bring about a nostalgia for its familiarities and a suffering due to the deprivation of these things, and one returned to one's hometown for important festivals and for burial. The native-place communities formed by sojourners in the city bonded through attachments of "territory, culture, and language" shared by an "imagined community" of fellow provincials living and working outside their native place (389). Native place, urban, and national levels of identity (26) did not contradict one another. Rather, "quasi-Confucian" concepts that constructed identities as a series of concentric circles viewed loving and strengthening one's native place as "morally excellent" (12). Thus, although native-place identities marked cultural differences, they also allowed for the formation of a common Chinese identity by "locating the abstract entity of the nation in familiar local situations and practices" (414).

10 Listings of these local products have increasingly begun to include famous locally produced industrial products.

11 From 1882 to 1943, Chinese immigration was severely restricted by the U.S. government in an effort to reduce labor competition. Only select classes, such as merchants and students, and the children of citizens were allowed to enter the United States during this time period. Because of this exclusion policy families could not be brought to the United States.

12 As Appadurai (1990, 1991) and others have observed, these processes can also occur from afar without travel being necessary.

13 Reforms have also been made in rural and urban sectors outside the SEZs, and many industries have moved to smaller urban centers in the Pearl River Delta area such as Dongguan, Zhongshan, and Jiangmen where labor is cheaper and immigration controls for workers from inner provinces are less strict.

14 The television documentary *He Shang* (River elegy) is an oft-cited example of this critique of China's insularity.

15 In many ways, this harks back to a historical basis for Chinese unity that emphasized (the belief in) common ritual practices over shared ideologies and beliefs. James Watson (1993) discusses the emphasis in late imperial China on orthopraxy (common ritual practices) over orthodoxy (common beliefs) as essential to uniting the diverse cultures within the Chinese empire.

16 For a more detailed discussion of the Chinese government discourses of blood and race, see Dikotter (1992, 1994).

17 Connie Clark was very helpful in sharing this information with me.

18 Mr. Lau, interview by the author, Zhongshan County, 1995.

19 Mr. Xin, interview by the author, Shenzhen, 1995.

20 It is unclear exactly how much the PRC government spends on the camps and on the Youth Festival. Many activities are organized on a city or county level. The Guangzhou-based Youth Festival itself must require a substantial budget, however, given the quality of the accommodations and food given to the participants.

21 Personal conversation with Him Mark Lai, 1996.

22 Zhongshan City Chinese American Youth Language and Cultural program pamphlet, 1994.

2 Welcome Home!(?): Crafting a Sense of Place in the United States through the In Search of Roots Homeland Tour

Unless otherwise indicated, all quotes come from field notes and interviews conducted from 1994 to 1995.

1 It should be noted that although this group of Chinese Americans was able to exercise the privilege of mobility through participation in a heritage trip to China, this type of mobility must be differentiated from the speed, ease, and frequency of mobility that characterized elite transnationals such as the "astronauts" studied by Ong (1999) and others, and from the regularized movements of migrants across borders studied by Rouse (1992) and others. The families (usually the parents' generation) of most of the Chinese Americans in my study communicated infrequently with relatives in China, and many Roots interns were visiting China for the first time.

2 These interactions operate within broader contemporary discourses and processes: within multicultural politics and cultural citizenship in the United States; within Chinese government conceptualizations of patriotic overseas Chinese who will help China develop; and within changing conceptions of opportunities for mobility and prosperity within China.

3 The idea of racialization refers to the ways that meanings of racial difference are assigned to particular groups within particular political and historical contexts (see Omi and Winant 1994).

4 The concept of perpetual foreigner refers to the idea that people of Asian descent in the United States are viewed by other Americans as being unassimilated or somehow less American because of both their cultural and racial backgrounds. Thus, Asian Americans who have lived in the United States for generations are sometimes complimented on the quality of their English (when it may be the only language they speak), or are asked where they are "really" from, as though they do not belong in the United States. The idea of Asians as perpetual foreigners stemmed from public discourses that surrounded efforts to legally exclude Chinese and other Asians from entry into the United States.

Though the nativists who opposed Asian immigration probably felt threatened primarily by the labor competition that these immigrants represented, their hostility was couched in racist terms. Chinese were portrayed in political cartoons and in writing as less evolved, disease ridden, and sneaky. The extent of their essential difference was supported by orientalist constructions of the East by the West, which portrayed the region as dark, mysterious, and untameable.

5 Works on cultural tourism have revealed the complexities of experiences of "return" to places where tourists have ancestral roots (see Bruner 1996; Ebron 1999).

6 See Louie 2003 for a more in-depth discussion of cultural heritage tours in relation to tourism.

7 The Qiao Ban has branches at all regional levels. The Guangdong Province Office of Overseas Chinese Affairs sponsored the China portion of the In Search of Roots program's visit to China.

8 In recent years, participants have had the opportunity to visit both maternal and paternal villages through the program.

9 The primary emigrant regions are represented by the cultural/geographical areas of San Yi, Si Yi, Zhongshan, and Bao An.

10 Perhaps Kevin was struck by the number of workers from inner areas living on the streets of the city. Guangdong's economic prosperity has attracted throngs of workers from rural inland China, who arrive without residence rights and receive little support from the city. They are viewed as the major source of social problems and are treated poorly.

11 The group leader in this case was a community educator involved in the Chinese Culture Center. He spoke a number of local Chinese dialects and played many roles during the trip, from dealing with local officials to resolving logistical issues to playing the role of translator and cultural mediator during the village visits.

12 This was done in a playful but respectful manner. The humor in this incident was not in the use of an Indian accent but rather in the lack of fit of the accent to the situation.

13 Emigrant villages can often be identified by the distinctive Western-influenced architecture of some of the homes built with overseas Chinese money, and by the predominance of schools, roads, or other things donated by the overseas Chinese.

14 In their attempt to revive the pre-Communist glory of the complex lineage system that had organized the Guan lineage of (Kaiping) since the seventeenth century, overseas Chinese contributed to the building of schools and the Guan lineage library, as well as to renovations projects (Woon 1989).

15 Much time was spent at night markets and shopping arcades, buying bootleg CDs, posters of Hong Kong movie and film stars, Japanese comics, and souvenirs.

16 This Hong Kong kung fu series was also very popular in the United States and in Southeast Asia.

17 The glossy red envelopes, designed to contain money for the Chinese New Year celebration, a birthday, or a gift, are called *hongbao*.

18 Arif Dirlik (1999b) suggests a "place consciousness" that takes into account social categories such as class, race, and gender, to reinsert the idea of place into discussions of the local and the global.

19 In a sense, understandings of family/clan by Chinese Americans may have more in common with a broader U.S. interest in genealogy than traditional Chinese clan ties.

20 Thus, although PRC programs emphasize dance, food, and costume as part of their official welcomes, Chinese American connections go beyond these generic characteristics. However, as Kong (1999) observes, these are the aspects of Chineseness that become the focus of efforts to define ethnic markers. Perhaps this is because beyond the idea of Chineseness as a racial categorization (black hair, yellow skin), these symbolic aspects of "culture" are generic enough to encompass people who may hold different nationalities, speak different languages, and believe in different politics.

3 Crafting Chinese American Identities:
Roots Narratives in the Context of U.S. Multiculturalism

1 Community in this sense was envisioned as a discrete geographical location rather than the population dispersed throughout the city and suburbs.

2 A cartoon strip, *Angry Little Asian Girl*, makes fun of these assumptions. In this strip the girl walks into a classroom and the teacher says, "Oh my, you speak English so well, where did you learn to speak so well[?]" The girl says, "I was born here, you stupid dipshit, don't you know anything about immigration? Read some history, you stupid ignoramus."

3 This process of cultural innovation is driven largely through ritual exercises of solidarity that incorporate powerful symbols (Kertzer 1988). These symbols, whether of unity, protest, authority, or equality, are the language in which cultural battles are fought. The power of symbols and their ritual exercise lies in their ability to remain stable in form yet flexible in the content of the message they present. Symbols can be co-opted and reinterpreted, empowered and disempowered, through manipulation by social actors. Kertzer argues that because of the existence of this symbolic diversity, symbols can play a role in fueling and legitimizing alternative viewpoints.

4 One intern commented: "I think that Roots was [my] first feeling of the cultural and political feeling of being a part of the Asian American community. That was the first experience I had that gave me a sense of that community outside my family."

5 Here she refers to the National Archives, which houses INS records and interrogations from Angel Island Immigration Station.

6 After a Roots meeting, a small group went out to dinner at a family-style Chi-

nese restaurant. One of the dishes ordered was c. *yuk beng* (*zhu rou bing*), which consists of minced steamed pork mixed with eggs. Susan looked at the dish with surprise, recognizing it as something her mother cooks at home—something she always had thought was a type of American meatloaf.

7   Nee and Nee's *Longtime Californ'* (1986) is about San Francisco's Chinatown, and Lai, Lim, and Yung's *Island* (1991) is on the history and poetry left by detainees at Angel Island Immigration station.

8   When this research was conducted, there were fifty-six people who had participated in the Roots program, organized as cohorts of nine to ten interns each year since 1991. The number of women was over 50 percent. Seventeen interns were in high school at the time of participation, thirty-eight were college students, and fourteen worked full time. Of the total, 56 percent were second generation, 27 percent third generation, 8 percent first generation, 6 percent fourth generation, and 3 percent fifth generation (thanks to Him Mark Lai for providing these statistics). The discussion section that I organized was attended by twelve interns from three different cohorts, and many knew each other already. The group went out for dim sum and the discussion was held afterward in a private room upstairs in the Chinese Culture Center.

9   Another intern, raised in Chinatown, elaborated on why Chineseness may be held onto as a commodity by some of the more recent immigrants in the Chinatown community. In her view, it was a way for them to assert themselves, as well as to distinguish themselves from American-born Chinese: "I think that a lot of my peers criticize people for not 'being Chinese enough' because that's all they have; I mean, they don't have class privileges, they don't grow up in the suburbs, and language proficiency is the only thing they have that middle-class Asian Americans don't have, and that's the only thing they have to hold onto."

10 Similarly, a stereotype prevalant among Asian Americans in the 1990s is the image of driving an Acura Integra and carrying a cell phone. The interns joked about whether this could be considered part of Chinese American culture.

11 Of course, as Brownell and Wasserstrom (2002) observe, genealogical forms are also changing in mainland China. Thanks to Susan Brownell for pointing out this parallel to me.

12 *Fa* (c. *faat*), meaning hair, sounds similar to the word *fa*, which means to prosper.

13 *Jung* are somewhat like tamales—sticky rice wrapped in leaves, formed into particular shapes, and filled with particular ingredients according to the region.

4 The Feng Shui Has Taken a Turn (feng shui lun liu zhuan): Changing Views of the Guangdong Chinese toward Life Abroad Following the Open Policy

1   This region encompasses the major metropolitan areas of Guangzhou, Dongguan, Foshan, Zhongshan, and the special economic zones of Shenzhen and Zhuhai, as well as many rural counties that have in past years sent many emigrants abroad.

2 It is debatable, however, whether this southern culture represents a leading edge or a desert culture (Friedman 1994).

3 Indeed, Asian popular culture is often featured in magazines and zines read by Asian Americans, such as *Giant Robot*, which has run articles on Ultraman and Michelle Yeoh in addition to pieces on Japanese internment and Asian American history.

4 Appadurai states: "One important source of this change is the mass media, which present a rich, ever-changing store of possible lives, some of which enter the lived imaginations of ordinary people more successfully than others. Important also are contacts with, news of, and rumors about others in one's social neighborhood who have become inhabitants of these faraway worlds. The importance of media is not so much as direct sources of new images and scenarios for life possibilities, but as semiotic diacritics of great power, which also inflect social contact with the metropolitan world facilitated by other channels" (1991: 198). Note, however, that Ong (1999) criticizes Appadurai for not distinguishing between the differential access to mobility available to different people, and the role of nation-states in controlling this mobility.

5 While Appadurai has been criticized by Ong (1999) and others for not adequately taking into account the controlling structures of the state, this case study shows how these fantasies are filtered through state controls and even when they provide alternatives they remain constrained within them.

6 This viewpoint is not solely the result of government constructions of the Chinese abroad, although through its attempts to communicate this image of overseas Chinese the state has presented a skewed image of them as rich capitalists, and has made specific efforts to give those who contribute to China official praise and recognition.

7 The difference here is one of comparison between individuals and communities, and among nations (Connie Clark, personal communication). While there have been long-recognized status differences within China, the discourse of underdevelopment, which involves a hegemonic process of convincing the "poor" that they are poor, brings in power differentials between nations that produces this consciousness on a national level.

8 This is not to say that no gains were made during the Maoist period. Potter and Potter (1990) clearly illustrate progress made in a rural village near Dongguan as a result of Maoist reforms.

9 The number of color televisions owned by Guangzhou households increased from 40 percent in 1986 to 90 percent in 1990 (Cheng and Taylor 1991).

10 People also listened to Hong Kong radio. According to White and Cheng (1993: 170) by 1985 85 percent of radios in Guangzhou were tuned to Hong Kong stations.

11 Some of these changes in the effect of these images may be due to the reporting of real economic shifts that have occured in the American economy. Also, more news/information shows from the United States have become available on

Hong Kong television. Hearing about these conditions from "Americans" themselves (through these television reports) versus the Chinese state media may make these images seem more authoritative.

12 According to Yeung and Chu (1994), in 1990, visitors to Guangdong numbered 25,275,400. Of this total 3.4 percent were foreigners, 94.5 percent were from Hong Kong and Macau, 1.9 percent from Taiwan, and 0.3 percent were overseas Chinese. Before 1979, there was little tourism in Guangdong: the number of international visitors received by Chinese travel agencies increased from 698,000 in 1979 to 5,414,800 in 1990.

13 The Cantonese words *heung ha* (literally, "countryside") were added on to the words for "boy" or "girl" to describe the young men and women from the countryside (often from outside of Guangdong) who came to Guangdong to search for work. They were viewed as simple, ill mannered, unfashionable, unskilled, and unsophisticated. These words were also combined with specific nouns and used as adjectives to describe these objects as crude, unfashionable, or unsophisticated. The phrase c. *Heung ha tau* (*tau* means "head") refers to a bad or crude haircut and *heung ha saam* to clothing that is out of fashion, as one informant contemptuously described the school uniform that teachers were required to wear.

14 Mayfair Yang, in her book *Gifts, Favors, and Banquets* (1994), describes how the ethics and emotion, and giving and sharing, involved in kinship are applied in urban settings to *guanxi* relationships, which are the basis for social relationships in China. Yang describes some of the principles of kinship relations rooted in Confucian ritual, which relate them to *guanxi* practices. "Kinship bonds are maintained by acts of giving and sharing," acts that define "the proper form of ethical kinship conduct" (112). However, kinship bonds differ from *guanxixue*, she says, because the obligations they imply do not necessarily result in mutual benefits for both parties. She observes that "a close kinship can entail deep 'emotional feelings' (*ganqing*) of attachment," but that "at the same time, there can also be considerable indifference, even hostility in kinship" (112). Some of her informants described kinship relations as being too complicated (*fuza*), and therefore preferred some of the other potential bases of *guanxi* over them.

According to Yang, the use of personal connections and the practice of gift giving in *guanxixue* are distinguished from bribery not only in terms of the networks of kin, *lao xiang*, friends, and neighbors that they are based on, but also in their use of *renqing, yiqi, and ganqing*. The concepts of *renqing* and *ganqing* are particularly useful as they relate to questions of gift giving as a demonstration of sentiment in Chinese culture. She cites Befu's (1967) analysis of "expressive gifts" versus "instrumental gifts" in Japan. While "instrumental gifts" are given with the expectation of certain returns, " 'expressive gifts' reinforce *ganqing*, the affective sentiments and feeling of obligation that accompany kinship, friendship, and superior-subordinate ties" (112). The concept of *ren-*

qing, literally "human feelings," is based in Confucian discourse and is viewed as encompassing both the ethical and emotional. It is part of the "intrinsic character of human nature" and entails proper conduct and obligations of reciprocity. The concept of *ganqing* is found between relatives and friends and results from an "intimate social bond." It entails an element of "sacrifice in giving" (121).

15 On a more recent visit with my relatives in 2002, I stayed with my aunt and realized that she really was a very busy person, and also a little forgetful. Thus, I may not have committed the faux pas I originally thought was the cause of our lack of communication. What is significant, however, is that my Chinese friends thought I had. On my visit in 2002 I attempted to rectify any of my past misdoings by buying my aunt and her two sisters some nice gifts, including earrings. Although I mistakenly gave them earrings for pierced ears, they told me it was okay because it's the thought that counts.

16 Mainland Chinese are now expected to give gifts, such as special local products (*te chan*), back to their relatives.

17 In an official sense, however, China did not see itself as relying on the Chinese abroad, as I was reminded when an overseas Chinese official corrected me when I used that term.

18 Potter and Potter (1990) refer to the concept of "negative egalitarianism" (338) as the unwillingness for one's neighbors to do better than oneself. In some ways, this principle is useful in understanding attitudes of resentment that could occur toward more wealthy overseas relatives, as well as the desire to see that they are not as well off as previously thought.

19 When I visited Guangzhou in summer 1993, I came with over US$300 in cash for the purchase of a color television for my great-uncle. He had called my oldest uncle in America, asking him to ask his ten brothers and sisters (nieces and nephews to my uncle) to help him buy a new TV because his old one was wearing out. To my great-uncle this was a reasonable favor to ask, given that our kinship relationship was so close and that he had ten close relatives in the United States whose incomes were much greater than his. For him, this transaction not only yielded a new nineteen-inch color remote-control Panasonic set but also a demonstration of his U.S. relatives' *qinqing* for him.

20 Most informants used the Cantonese equivalent of *wei shenghuo hao yidian*.

21 See Ong 1993 and Wakeman 1989 on the role of air travel in creating and maintaining transnational linkages.

5 *The Descendants of the Dragon Gather: The Youth Festival as Encounter between the Chinese and Chinese American Other*

1 According to Kertzer (1988), rituals are important vehicles for both legitimating and changing political systems. Rituals are used to create and display a sense of political unity or collective identity, because they can be called on to symbolically

unite the constituent parts of a political party, an organization, a tribe, or a nation. Rituals are powerful in that they are able to combine a variety of diverse sentiments under a common set of symbols (a national flag, a sacred relic) and create a sense of unity through collective participation. The Youth Festival invokes the power of ritual to be stable in form yet flexible in content, and in this way subsumes a diversity of Chinese identities within a display of unity.

2   The treaty of Nanjing in 1842 proclaimed the Qing empire's responsibility for its overseas subjects (Wang 1988: 121). In the early 1900s the Qing took a more aggressive stance on overseas Chinese affairs: "To protect huaqiao became directly linked to the policy of protecting Chinese merchants generally against foreign competition. This, in turn, led to the crucial matter of who was and who was not a Chinese subject and how to induce the Chinese to remain Chinese" (124). Qing policy set the precedent for later *jus sanguinis* policies of the Republic, Nationalist, and Communist governments (Fitzgerald 1972: 6), which "claims in theory jurisdiction over all persons of Chinese blood, no matter for how many generations their ancestors have lived abroad" (T. Chen 1940: 2). In 1954, the PRC chose to abandon the policy of *jus sanguinis* and entered a period of "decolonization" of the overseas Chinese in Southeast Asia. In his speech in Rangoon in 1957, Chou En Lai encouraged the Chinese there to assimilate to the local environment, acknowledging that overseas Chinese were *hua yi*, people of Chinese descent, and citizens of their countries of residence in Southeast Asia.

3   As one reader of a draft of this chapter observed, the use of the term "abroad" implies a mainland-centered position. Throughout this chapter I use this term when referring to mainland Chinese perspectives that view those of Chinese descent living outside of China as *haiwai huaren* (literally, overseas Chinese). This terms implies not so much a political affiliation with the Chinese nation-state (as does the term *huaqiao*) as a culturalistic and racial idea that although they may no longer be citizens of China they are still "Chinese" by virtue of their ancestry. I discovered, in searching for an alternative vocabulary positioned from the point of view of Chinese outside of China, that it is very difficult to describe ethnic Chinese identities without referring to China as the center (as in the terms Chinese diaspora, Chinese abroad, and overseas Chinese).

4   These programs were jointly organized by the Office of Overseas Chinese Affairs (Hua Qiao Shi Wu Ban Gong Shi) and the China Travel Service (Zhong Lu). The China Travel Service, which is government owned, handled many of the logistical aspects of the daily trips and supplied guides.

5   The Summer Camp program has both summer and winter sessions in order to accomodate the school vacations of various countries.

6   The text from *Xin Xi Mu Bang* quoted here was translated by Xing Qingshen.

7   The reference to "skeptical" attitudes perhaps refers to the fact that on China's initial reopening to the outside world, both government officials and folk realized that during its long isolation the country had fallen behind. Overseas

Chinese were called on to help bring China into the modern world and, as Ong (1999) explains, to allow for development without deracination. The participation of overseas Chinese was explained in official discourses in terms of their love for the motherland, and it was expressed in patriotic language. This reference may also refer to the danger for many Chinese abroad of being associated politically with mainland China during much of the cold war era.

8   This produced a disgusted response from one local official who was viewing the book with me. Water buffalo are seen as dirty work animals, and a number of mainland Chinese I interviewed commented on the strange fascination that the overseas Chinese youth seemed to have with them.

9   Mooncakes (*yuebing*) are traditionally served during the Mid-Autumn Festival. They are typically filled with lotus-seed paste or black-bean paste, and are deep fried. The mooncake on display was made by the Qu Xiang Bakery in Guangzhou and weighed 208 kilograms and measured 1.5 meters in diameter (mooncakes are normally a few inches in diameter). A souvenir postcard called it "the crystallization of wisdom and art of cakes-making. It also displays the productive capacity of the enterprise."

10 Perhaps fitting the theme of combining overseas capital for development while retaining cultural pride as Chinese, the group traveled from Guangzhou to Shenzhen on a new modern superhighway that had been build with overseas capital. At the Splendid China and China Folk Culture Village, participants were to soak in Chinese "tradition" in the form of miniaturized Chinese monuments and singing Chinese minorities.

11 Guangdong Provincial Office of Overseas Chinese Affairs. Program for Overseas Chinese Youth Festival, 1995.

12 As Susan Brownell (1999: 209) notes, official state discourses often define the terms of public culture debates "either because it seeks to control them, or because counterdiscourses emerge in almost direct opposition to it" (1999: 209). In a similar sense, official policies toward the Chinese abroad that shape the Youth Festival set the stage for debates about meanings of Chineseness surrounding the festivals.

13 Thanks to Diane Mines for helping me to clarify this point.

14 Here, I draw on Schein's (1998) argument about the dialectical processes between transnational populations and the state, made in relation to her research on Miao/Hmong transnationalism.

15 It is likely that encouraging immediate investment may not have been the primary goal of the Youth Festival and Summer Camp programs because most participants were not in a position to do so. The official literature describes a more basic goal for the activities as being the fostering of a "hometown concept" (*xiangtu guannian*) and nostalgic emotion for the village through the visits to China.

16 This identification with the Cantonese working-class origins of most Roots interns is discussed in chapter 3.

17 These overseas Chinese are usually prominent and quite wealthy businessmen, who donate to or invest in their hometowns.

18 See Yang (1997) for a detailed description of how overseas Chinese have become part of the mainland Chinese imaginary through various forms of media.

19 As Smart and Smart (1998) note, despite linkages between Hong Kong and Guangdong Chinese based on shared origins, there also exist more negative perceptions of the "ugly Hong Konger."

20 The majority of emigrants who settled in major U.S. Chinatowns in the late nineteenth and twentieth centuries were from the Taishan County region, which boasts that there are more Taishanese living abroad than living on the mainland.

21 The word "return" (*hui lai*; c. *fan laih*) is used, even though it is known that most of the Chinese youth had never been to their villages before.

22 Thanks to Susan Brownell for helping me clarify this point.

6 Remaking Places and Renegotiating Chineseness

1 Helen Siu (1993) uses the terms "unifying and differentiating" to describe the formation of Chinese identities during the settlement of the Pearl River Delta area.

2 Chinese Americans who become reethnicized to an extreme are sometimes called "born-again Chinese."

3 David Scott (1991) observes that tradition is sometimes used to support a revitalization of cultural practices and meanings in a new context, as in the conscious adoption of elements of African culture by the African American community. Errington and Gewertz (1996) talk about the conscious invocation of "culture" and efforts to negotiate its meanings as a means of empowerment or economic gain in negotiating with a developing Papua New Guinean modernity.

4 While preparing for the ten-year anniversary dinner, we came up with the tentative goal "to sustain, promote, and enhance the In Search of Roots program." We came up with the following areas: 1. Marketing / Outreach (e.g., recruitment); 2. Networking / Alumni Relations; 3. Fundraising; and 4. Program Development (including mentoring, classes, special projects, etc.).

Epilogue

1 My great-uncle told me to address her as "aunt" (*guma*) instead of by her first name, even though she is only a few years older than I am. This is because she is the same generation as my father. Because of this, her four-year-old-daughter referred to me as "big sister."

2 I had been staying there as part of my new research project while accompanying a group of adoptive parents to China to receive their children.

3   This French chain had stores in other big cities such as Wuhan and Beijing. It carried both Chinese-made and imported products, and it seemed quite popular among local middle-class Chinese people. Its French name had been translated into the Chinese characters for family (jia), happiness (le), and good fortune (fu).

4   The issue of whether or not people were obligated to donate to the gift had indeed been a contentious one, as my oldest uncle in the United States felt that the U.S. relatives were obligated by our relative privilege to give a gift to our relatives in China. Others felt that this was not necessary, particularly because they did not know Yi Suk Gung that well or had not gotten along with him when they were in China.

5   In perhaps another cross-cultural gift-related misunderstanding, I had been a bit surprised to find out later that the jewelry gifts I received had previously been given by my aunt to her parents, who had in turn given them to me as gifts. When I returned to my aunt's house she asked to see the gifts, and she gave me the details of where she had gotten them, and so forth. I am still not sure how to interpret the fact that they passed them on to me, and why my aunt didn't seem to mind that they had done so.

6   The high school headmaster's son went to Sweden to study. The son said that the Chinese abroad may become rich but they can't get along well with white people. He said that it was because they are yellow-skinned people. He wants to work in an Asian country. When he sees yellow-skinned people he regards them as his own relatives. Mr. He said that he regards me as Chinese, so our relations are good and he wanted to make the time to talk to me for this interview.

7   A former student told me that Shenzhen was developing so rapidly that he would have trouble finding his way around it after having been away at college in Guangzhou for a few months.

8   At the same time it is important to remember that conditions for the floating population from poorer regions of China have not improved.

BIBLIOGRAPHY

Anderson, Benedict. 1983. *Imagined Communities: Reflections on the Origin and Spread of Nationalism*. London: Verso.

Ang, Ien. 1985. *Watching Dallas: Soap Opera and the Melodramatic Imagination*. New York: Methuen.

———. 1994. "On Not Speaking Chinese." *New Formations* 24 (winter): 1–18.

Appadurai, Arjun. 1990. "Disjuncture and Difference in the Global Cultural Economy." *Public Culture* 2(2): 1–24.

———. 1991. "Global Ethnoscapes: Notes and Queries for a Transnational Anthropology." In *Recapturing Anthropology*, ed. R. Fox. Santa Fe, N.M.: School of American Research Press.

Basch, Linda, Nina Glick Schiller, and Christina Szanton-Blanc, eds. 1994. *Nations Unbound: Transnational Projects, Postcolonial Predicaments, and Deterritorialized Nation-States*. Langhorne, Pa.: Gordon and Breach.

Befu, Harumi. 1966–67. "Gift-Giving and Social Reciprocity in Japan: An Exploratory Statement." *France-Asie/Asia* 21 (188).

Bisharat, George. 1997. "Exile to Compatriot: Transformations in the Social Identity of Palestinian Refugees in the West Bank." In *Culture, Power, Place: Explorations in Critical Anthropology*, ed. Akhil Gupta and James Ferguson. Durham, N.C.: Duke University Press.

Bondi, Liz. 1993. "Locating Identity Politics." In *Place and the Politics of Identity*, ed. Michael Keith and Steve Pile. London: Routledge.

Borofsky, Robert. 1987. *Making History: Pukapukan and Anthropological Constructions of Knowledge*. New York: Cambridge University Press.

Bourdieu, Pierre. 1977. *Outline of a Theory of Practice*. Trans. Richard Nice. Cambridge: Cambridge University Press.

———. 1984. *Distinction: A Social Critique of the Judgement of Taste*. Trans. Richard Nice. Cambridge: Harvard University Press.

———. 1994. "Structure, Habitus, Power: Basis for a Theory of Symbolic Power." In

Culture, Power, History: A Reader in Contemporary Social Theory, ed. Nicholas B. Dirks, Geoff Eley, and Sherry B. Ortner. Princeton: Princeton University Press.

Brownell, Susan. 1999. "Strong Women and Impotent Men: Sports, Gender, and Nationalism in Chinese Public Culture." In *Spaces of Their Own: Women's Public Sphere in Transnational China*, ed. Mayfair Mei-Hui Yang. Minneapolis: University of Minnesota Press.

Brownell, Susan, and Jeffrey Wasserstrom, eds. 2002. *Chinese Femininities / Chinese Masculinities: A Reader*. Berkeley: University of California Press.

Bruner, Edward. 1996. "Tourism in Ghana: The Representation of Slavery and the Return of the Black Diaspora." *American Anthropologist* 98 (2) (June): 290–304.

Bruner, Edward M., and Barbara Kirshenblatt-Gimblett. 1994. "Maasai on the Lawn: Tourist Realism in East Africa." *Cultural Anthropology* 9(4): 435–70.

Chan, Su Cheng. 1991. *Asian-Americans: An Interpretive History*. Boston: Twayne.

Chen, Nancy N., Constance D. Clark, Suzanne Z. Gottschang, and Lyn Jeffery, eds. 2001. *China Urban: Ethnographies of Contemporary Culture*. Durham, N.C.: Duke University Press.

Chen, Ta. 1940. *Emigrant Communities in South China*. New York: Institute of Pacific Relations.

Chen, Yong. 2000. *Chinese San Francisco: A Study of a Transpacific Community, 1890–1943*. Stanford: Stanford University Press.

Cheng, Elizabeth, and Michael Taylor. 1991. "Delta Force: Pearl River Cities in Partnership with Hong Kong." *Far Eastern Economic Review* (May 16): 64–66.

Chin, Frank, Jeffery Paul Chan, Lawson Inada, and Shawn Wong, eds. 1974. *Aieee! An Anthology of Asian American Writers*. Seattle: University of Washington Press.

Choy, Philip, Lorraine Dong, and Marlon Hom, eds. 1995. *The Coming Man: Nineteenth-Century American Perceptions of the Chinese*. Seattle: University of Washington Press.

Clifford, James. 1997. *Routes: Travel and Translation in the Late Twentieth Century*. Cambridge: Harvard University Press.

Cohen, Myron. 1991. "Being Chinese: The Peripheralization of Traditional Identity." *Daedalus: The Living Tree—The Changing Meaning of Being Chinese Today* 120(2): 113–35.

Cohn, Bernard C. 1981. "Anthropology and History in the 1980s: Toward a Rapproachment." *Journal of Interdisciplinary History* 12(2): 227–52.

——. 1987. *An Anthropologist among the Historians and Other Essays*. New York: Oxford University Press.

Crossley, Pamela Kyle. 1990. "Thinking about Ethnicity in Early Modern China." *Late Imperial China* II (June): 1–34.

Cushman, Jennifer, and Wang Gungwu, eds. 1989. *Changing Identities of the Southeast Asian Chinese since WWII*. Hong Kong: University of Hong Kong Press.

de Certeau, Michel. 1984. *The Practice of Everyday Life*. Trans. Steve Randall. Berkeley: University of California Press.

Dikotter, Frank. 1992. *The Discourse of Race in Modern China*. Stanford: Stanford University Press.

——. 1994. "Racial Identities in China." *China Quarterly* 138 (June): 404–12.

Ding, Loni. 1996. *Ancestors in America: Coolies, Sailors, Settlers*. San Francisco: Center for Educational Telecommunications. Video.

Dirlik, Arif. 1993. "Introduction." In *What Is in a Rim? Critical Perspectives on the Pacific Rim Idea*, ed. Arif Dirlik. Boulder, Colo.: Westview Press.

——. 1999a. "Asians on the Rim: Transnational Capital and Local Community in the Making of Contemporary Asian America." In *Across the Pacific*, ed. Evelyn Hu Dehart. Philadelphia: Temple University Press.

——. 1999b. "Place-Based Imagination: Globalism and the Politics of Place." *Review* 22(2): 151–88.

Duara, Prasenjit. 1993a. "De-Constructing the Chinese Nation." *Australian Journal of Chinese Affairs* 30 (July): 1–26.

——. 1993b. "Provincial Narratives and the Nation: Centralism and Federalism in Republican China." In *Cultural Nationalism in East Asia*, ed. Harumi Befu. Berkeley: Institute of East Asian Studies, University of California.

——. 1997. "Nationalists among Transnationals: Overseas Chinese and the Idea of China, 1900–1911." In *Ungrounded Empires: The Cultural Politics of Modern Chinese Transnationalism*, ed. Aihwa Ong and Donald Nonini. New York: Routledge.

Ebron, Paulla. 1999. "Tourists as Pilgrims: Commercial Fashioning of Transatlantic Politics." *American Ethnologist* 26(4): 910–32.

Ebron, Paulla, and Anna Tsing. 1995. "From Allegories of Identity to Sites of Dialogue." *Diaspora* 4(2).

Errington, Frederick, and Deborah Gewertz. 1996. "The Individuation of Tradition in Papua New Guinean Modernity." *American Anthropologist* 98(1): 114–26.

Escobar, Arturo. 1995. *Encountering Development: The Making and Unmaking of the Third World*. Princeton: Princeton University Press.

Espiritu, Yen Le. 1992. *Asian American Panethnicity: Bridging Institutions and Identities*. Philadelphia: Temple University Press.

Evans-Pritchard, E. E. 1940. *The Nuer: A Description of the Modes of Livelihood and Political Institutions of a Nilotic People*. Oxford: Clarendon Press.

Faure, David. 1989. "The Lineage as Cultural Invention: The Case of the Pearl River Delta." *Modern China* (January): 4–36.

Faure, David, and Helen F. Siu. 1995. *Down to Earth: The Territorial Bond in South China*. Stanford: Stanford University Press.

Featherstone, Mike. 1990. *Global Culture: Nationalism, Globalization, and Modernity*. London: Sage.

——. 1996. "Localism, Globalism, and Cultural Identity." In *Global/Local: Cultural Production and the Transnational Imaginary*, ed. Rob Wilson and Wimal Dissanayake. Durham, N.C.: Duke University Press.

Fiske, John. 1987. *Television Culture*. London: Methuen.

Fitzgerald, Stephen. 1972. *China and the Overseas Chinese: A Study of Peking's Changing Policy, 1949–1970*. Cambridge: Cambridge University Press.

Foucault, Michel. 1979. "Two Lectures." In *Power/Knowledge*. New York: Vintage.

Fox, Richard. 1990. "Introduction." In *Nationalist Ideologies and the Production of National Cultures*. American Ethnological Society monograph series, no. 2. New York: American Anthropological Association.

Friedman, Edward. 1994. "Reconstructing China's National Identity: A Southern Alternative to a Mao-Era Anti-Imperialist Nationalism." *Journal of Asian Studies* 53(1) (February): 67–91.

Gable, Eric, Richard Handler, and Anna Lawson. 1992. "On the Uses of Relativism: Fact, Conjecture, and Black and White History at Colonial Williamsburg." *American Ethnologist* 19(4) (November): 791–805.

Gilroy, Paul. 1993. *The Black Atlantic: Modernity and Double Consciousness*. Cambridge: Harvard University Press.

Glick Schiller, Nina. 1997. "The Situation of Transnational Studies." *Identities: Global Studies in Culture and Power* 4(2): 155–66.

——. 1999a. "Transmigrants and Nation-States: Something Old and Something New in U.S. Immigrant Experience." In *Handbook of International Migration: The American Experience*. ed. C. Hirschman, Josh DeWind, and P. Kasinitz. New York: Russell Sage Foundation.

——. 1999b. "Who Are These Guys? A Transnational Perspective on National Identities." In *Identities on the Move: Transnational Processes in North America and the Caribbean Basin*, ed. Liliana Goldin. Austin: University of Texas Press.

——. 1999c. "Citizens in Transnational Nation-States: The Asian Experience." In *Globalisation and the Asia Pacific: Contested Territories*, ed. P. Dicken, P. Kelley, L. Kong, K. Olds, and H. Wai-chung Yeung. London: Routledge.

Glick Schiller, Nina, Linda Basch, and Christina Blanc-Szanton. 1992. *Towards a Transnational Perspective on Migration: Race, Class, Ethnicity, and Nationalism Reconsidered*. New York: New York Academy of Sciences.

Glick Schiller, Nina and Georges Fouron. 1998. "Transnational Lives and National Identities: The Identity Politics of Haitian Immigrants." In *Transnationalism From Below*, ed. Michael Peter Smith and Luis Eduardo Guarnizo. New Brunswick, N.J.: Transaction Publishers.

Gladney, Dru. 1991. *Muslim Chinese*. Cambridge: Harvard Council on East Asian Studies.

Goodman, Bryna. 1995a. "The Locality as Microcosm of the Nation?: Native Place Networks and Early Urban Nationalism in China." *Modern China* 31(4) (October): 387–419.

——. 1995b. *Native Place, City, and Nation: Regional Networks and Identities in Shanghai, 1883–1937*. Berkeley: University of California Press.

Grewal, Inderpal, Akhil Gupta, and Aihwa Ong, 1999. "Introduction: Asian Transnationalities." *positions: east asia cultures critique* 7(3): 654–66.

Gupta, Akhil and James Ferguson, eds. 1997. *Culture, Power, Place: Explorations in Critical Anthropology*. Durham, N.C.: Duke University Press.

Hall, Stuart. 1990. "Cultural Identity and Diaspora." In *Identity: Community, Culture, Difference*. London: Lawrence and Wishart.

———. 1991. "The Local and the Global: Globalization and Ethnicity," and "Old and New Identities: Old and New Ethnicities." In *Culture, Globalization, and the World-System: Contemporary Conditions for the Representation of Identity*, ed. Anthony D. King. Binghamton: Department of Art and Art History, SUNY—Binghampton.

Handler, Richard. 1988. *Nationalism and the Politics of Culture in Quebec*. Madison: University of Wisconsin Press.

Handler, Richard, and Jocelyn Linnekin. 1984. "Tradition, Genuine or Spurious?" *Journal of American Folklore* 97(384): 273–90.

Hing, Bill Ong. 1993. *Making and Remaking Asian America through Immigration Policy, 1850–1900*. Stanford: Stanford University Press.

Hobsbawm, Eric. 1983. "Introduction: Inventing Traditions." In *The Invention of Tradition*, ed. Eric Hobsbawm and Terence Ranger. New York: Cambridge University Press.

Honig, Emily. 1992. *Creating Chinese Ethnicity: Subei People in Shanghai, 1850–1980*. New Haven: Yale University Press.

Hsu, Madeline. 2000. *Dreaming of Gold, Dreaming of Home*. Stanford. Stanford University Press.

Hu Dehart, Evelyn. 1999. "Introduction." In *Across the Pacific*, ed. Evelyn Hu Dehart. Philadelphia: Temple University Press.

Jackson, Jean. 1995. "Culture, Genuine and Spurious: The Politics of Indianness in the Vaupes, Colombia." *American Ethnologist* 22(1) (February): 3–27.

Kearney, Michael. 1986. "From the Invisible Hand to Visible Feet: Anthropological Studies of Migration and Development." *Annual Review of Anthropology* 15: 331–61.

———. 1995. "The Local and the Global: The Anthropology of Globalization and Transnationalism." In *Annual Review of Anthropology*. Palo Alto, Calif.: Annual Reviews, Inc.

Keith, Michael, and Steve Pile. 1993. "Introduction: The Politics of Place," and "Introduction: The Place of Politics." In *Place and the Politics of Identity*. London Routledge.

Kertzer, David. 1988. *Ritual, Politics, and Power*. New Haven: Yale University Press.

Kondo, Dorinne. 1990. *Crafting Selves: Power, Gender, and Discourses of Identity in a Japanese Workplace*. Chicago: University of Chicago Press.

Kong, Lily. 1999. "Globalisation, Transmigration, and the Renegotiation of Ethnic Identity." In *Globalisation and the Asia Pacific: Contested Territories*, ed. P. Dicken, P. Kelley, L. Kong, K. Olds, and H. Wai-chung Yeung. London: Routledge.

Kuah, Khun Eng. 2000. *Rebuilding the Ancestral Village: Singaporeans in China*. Burlington, Vt.: Ashgate Press.

Kwong, Peter. 1994. "China's Human traffickers: Wake of the Golden Venture." *Nation* 259(12) (October 17): 422–25.

Lai, Him Mark. 1992. "Development of Organizations among Chinese in America since World War II." Paper presented at the Luo Di Sheng Gen conference, Berkeley.

Lai, Him Mark, Genny Lim, and Judy Yung, eds. 1991. *Island: Poetry and History of Chinese Immigrants on Angel Island, 1910–1940*. Seattle: University of Washington Press.

Lam, Andrew. 1997. "An Asian American Argues It's Better to Be Feared than to Be Invisible." Pacific News Service, http://www.pacificnewsservice.com.

Lary, Diana. 1996. "The Tomb of the King of Nanyue—The Contemporary Agenda of History: Scholarship and Identity." *Modern China* 22(1) (January): 3–27.

Leonard, Karen. 1997. "Finding One's Own Place: Asian Landscapes Re-Visioned in Rural California." In *Culture, Power, Place: Explorations in Critical Anthropology*, ed. Akhil Gupta and James Ferguson. Durham, N.C.: Duke University Press.

Liu, John, and Lucie Cheng. 1994. "Pacific Rim Development and the Duality of Post-1965 Immigration to the U.S." In *The New Immigration in Los Angeles and Global Restructuring*, ed. Paul Ong, Edna Bonacich, and Lucie Cheng. Philadelphia: Temple University Press.

Louie, Andrea. 2000. "Reterritorializing Transnationalism: Chinese Americans and the Chinese Motherland." *American Ethnologist* 27(3): 645–69.

——. 2001. "Crafting Places through Mobility: Chinese American 'Roots Searching' in China." *Identities: Global Studies in Culture and Power* 8(3): 343–79.

——. 2003. When You Are Related to the "Other": (Re)locating the Chinese Homeland in Asian American Politics through Cultural Tourism." *positions: east asia cultures critique* 11(3) (winter): 735–63.

Lowe, Lisa. 1991. "Heterogeneity, Hybridity, Multiplicity: Marking Asian American Difference." *Diaspora* 1 (spring): 24–44.

——. 1996. *Immigrant Acts: On Asian America Cultural Politics*. Durham, N.C.: Duke University Press.

Lowenthal, David. 1985. *The Past Is a Foreign Country*. New York: Cambridge University Press.

Lull, James. 1989. *China Turned On: Television, Reform, and Resistance*. New York: Routledge.

Madsen, Richard. 1995. *China and the American Dream: A Moral Inquiry*. Berkeley: University of California Press.

Mahler, Sarah. 1998. "Theoretical and Empirical Contributions toward a Research Agenda for Transnationalism." In *Transnationalism from Below, vol. 6: Comparative Urban and Community Research*, ed. M. P. Smith and Luis Guarnizo. New Brunswick, N.J.: Transaction Publishers.

Maira, Sunaina. 2002. *Desis in the House: Indian American Youth Culture in New York City*. Philadelphia: Temple University Press.

Malkki, Liisa. 1997. "National Geographic: The Rooting of Peoples and the Territorialization of National Identity among Scholars and Refugees." In *Culture,*

Power, Place: Explorations in Critical Anthropology, ed. Akhil Gupta and James Ferguson. Durham, N.C.: Duke University Press.

Marcus, George, and Michael Fischer. 1986. *Anthropology as Cultural Critique: An Experimental Moment in the Human Sciences*. Chicago: University of Chicago Press.

Massey, Doreen. 1993. *Space, Place, and Gender*. Minneapolis: University of Minnesota Press.

Mauss, Marcel. 1950. *The Gift: The Form and Reason for Exchange in Archaic Societies*. New York: Norton.

McKeown, Adam. 1999. "Conceptualizing Chinese Diasporas, 1842–1949." *Journal of Asian Studies* 58(2): 306–37.

Mitchell, Katherine. 1996. "In Whose Interest? Transnational Capital and the Production of Multiculturalism in Canada." In *Global/Local: Cultural Production and the Transnational Imaginary*, ed. Rob Wilson and Wimal Dissanayake. Durham, N.C.: Duke University Press.

Nader, Laura. 1972. "Up the Anthropologist: Perspectives Gained from Studying Up." In *Reinventing Anthropology*, ed. Dell Hymes. New York: Vintage.

——. 1997. "Controlling Processes: Tracing the Dynamic Components of Power." *Current Anthropology* 38(5) (December): 711–37.

Omi, Michael, and Howard Winant. 1984. *Racial Formation in the United States: From the 1960s to the 1980s*. New York: Routledge.

Ong, Aihwa. 1993. "On the Edge of Empires: Flexible Citizenship among Chinese in Diaspora." *positions: east asia cultures critique* 1(3) (winter): 745–78.

——. 1996. "Cultural Citizenship." *Current Anthropology* 37(5): 737–61.

——. 1999. *Flexible Citizenship: The Cultural Logics of Transnationality*. Durham, N.C.: Duke University Press.

Ong, Aihwa, and Donald Nonini. 1997. *Ungrounded Empires: The Cultural Politics of Modern Chinese Transnationalism*. New York: Routledge.

Ong, Paul M., Edna Bonacich, and Lucie Cheng, eds. 1994. *The New Asian Immigration in Los Angeles and Global Restructuring*. Philadelphia: Temple University Press.

Peterson, Glen D. 1988. "Socialist China and the Huaqiao: The Transition to Socialism in the Overseas Chinese Areas of Rural Guangdong, 1949–1956." *Modern China* 14 (July): 309–35.

Portes, Alejandro, Luis E. Guarnizo, and Patricia Landolt. 1999. "The Study of Transnationalism: Pitfalls and Promise of an Emergent Research Field." *Ethnic and Racial Studies* 22(2): 218–22.

Potter, Sulamith H., and Jack M. Potter. 1990. *China's Peasants: The Anthropology of a Revolution*. New York: Cambridge University Press.

Pritchard, E. 1968. *The Nuer: A Description of the Modes of Livelihood and Political Institutions of a Nilotic People*. Oxford: Clarendon Press.

Rouse, Roger. 1992. "Making Sense of Settlement: Class Transformation, Cultural

Struggle, and Transnationalism among Mexican Migrants in the United States."
In *Toward a Transnational Perspective on Migration: Race, Class, Ethnicity, and Nationalism Reconsidered*, ed. Nina Glick Schiller, Linda Basch, and Cristina Szanton-Blanc. New York: New York Academy of Sciences.

——. 1995. "Thinking through Transnationalism: Notes on the Cultural Politics of Class Relations in the Contemporary United States." *Public Culture* 7 (2) 353–402.

Said, Edward. 1978. *Orientalism*. New York: Pantheon Books.

Sassen, Saskia. 1988. *The Mobility of Labor and Capital: A Study of International Investment and Labor Flow*. New York: Cambridge University Press.

——. 1992. "Why Migration?" *NACLA Report on the Americas* 26(1) (July): 14–19.

Schein, Louisa. 1998. "Forged Transnationality and Oppositional Cosmopolitanism." In *Transnationalism from Below*, ed. Luis Eduardo Guarnizo and Michael Peter Smith. New Brunswick, N.J.: Transaction Publishers.

Schiefellin, Edward, and Robert Crittenden. 1991. *Like People You See in a Dream: First Contact in Six Papuan Societies*. Stanford: Stanford University Press.

Scott, David. 1991. "That Event, This Memory: Notes on the Anthropology of African Diasporas in the New World." *Diaspora* 1(3): 261–84.

Segal, David A., and Richard Handler. 1995. "U.S. Multiculturalism and the Concept of Culture." *Identities* 1 (4): 391–407.

Sinn, Elizabeth. 1992. "Xin Xi Gu Xiang: A Study of Regional Associations as a Bonding Mechanism in the Chinese Diaspora: The Hong Kong Experience." Paper presented at the Luo Di Sheng Gen Conference, Berkeley.

Siu, Helen F. 1990. "Recycling Tradition: Culture, History, and Political Economy in the Chrysanthemum Festivals of South China." *Comparative Studies in Society and History* 32 (October): 765–94.

——. 1993. "Cultural Identity and the Politics of Difference in South China." *Daedalus: The Exit from Communism* 122(3) (spring): 19–43.

Smart, Josephine, and Alan Smart. 1998. "Transnational Social Networks and Negotiated Identities in Interactions between Hong Kong and China." In *Transnationalism from Below*, vol. 6, Comparative Urban and Community Research, ed. Michael P. Smith and Luis Eduardo Guarnizo. New Brunswick, N.J.: Transaction Publishers.

Smith, Michael P., and Luis Eduardo Guarnizo, eds. 1998. *Transnationalism from Below*, vol. 6, Comparative Urban and Community Research. New Brunswick, N.J.: Transaction Publishers.

Solinger, Dorothy. 1999. *Contesting Citizenship in Urban China: Peasant Migrants, the State, and the Logic of the Market*. Berkeley: University of California Press.

Stack, Carol. 1996. *Call to Home: African Americans Reclaim the Rural South*. New York: Basic Books.

Tien, Ju-Kang. 1953. *The Chinese of Sarawak: A Study of Social Structure*. London: London School of Economics Monograph in Social Anthropology # 12.

Tsai, Shin-Shan Henry. 1983. *China and the Overseas Chinese in the United States, 1868–1911*. Fayetteville: University of Arkansas Press.

Tu, Wei Ming. 1991. "Cultural China: The Periphery as Center." *Daedalus: The Living Tree—the Changing Meaning of Being Chinese Today* 120(2): 1–32.

———, ed. 1994. *China in Transformation.* Cambridge: Harvard University Press.

Visweswaran, Kamala. 1998. "Race and the Culture of Anthropology." *American Anthropologist* 100(1): 70–83.

Vogel, Ezra. 1989. *One Step Ahead in China: Guangdong under Reform.* Cambridge: Harvard University Press.

Wakeman, Frederic, Jr. 1977. *Strangers at the Gate: Social Disorder in South China, 1839–1861.* Berkeley: University of California Press.

———. 1989. "All the Rage in China." *New York Review of Books,* March 2.

Wang, Gung Wu. 1991a. "Among Non-Chinese." *Daedalus: The Living Tree—the Changing Meaning of Being Chinese Today* 120(2): 148–52.

———. 1991b. *China and the Overseas Chinese.* Singapore: Times Academic Press.

Wang, Gung Wu, and Jennifer Cushman. 1988. "Notes on Origins of Hua Qiao." In *Changing Identities of the Southeast Asian Chinese since WWII.* Hong Kong: Hong Kong University Press.

Wang, Ling Chi. 1991. "Roots and Changing Identity of the Chinese in the U.S.A." *Daedalus: The Living Tree—the Changing Meaning of Being Chinese Today* 120(2): 181–206.

———. 1995. "The Structure of Dual Domination: Toward a Paradigm for the Study of the Chinese Diaspora in the United States." *Amerasia Journal* 21(1–2) (spring): 149–69.

Watson, James L. 1975. *Emigration and the Chinese Lineage: The Mans in Hong Kong and London.* Berkeley: University of California Press.

———. 1993. "Rites or Beliefs? The Construction of a Unified Culture in Late Imperial China." In *China's Quest for National Identity,* ed. Lowell Dittmer and Samuel S. Kim. Ithaca, N.Y.: Cornell University Press.

———. 2002. Tracking a Postmodern Diaspora: The Man Lineage in Hong Kong, London, and Beyond. Inaugural Bernard S. Gallin Endowed Lecture in Asian Anthropology, April 12, 2002, Michigan State University.

White, Lynn, and Li Cheng. 1993. "China Coast Identities: Regional, National, and Global." In *China's Quest for National Identity,* ed. Lowell Dittmer and Samuel S. Kim. Ithaca, N.Y.: Cornell University Press.

Williams, Brackette. 1989. "A Class Act: Anthropology and the Race to Nation across Ethnic Terrain." *Annual Review of Anthropology* 18: 401–41.

Williams, Lea E. 1960. *Overseas Chinese Nationalism: The Genesis of the Pan-Chinese Movement in Indonesia, 1900–1916.* Glencoe, Ill.: Free Press.

Wong, K. Scott, and Sucheng Chan. 1998. *Claiming America: Constructing Chinese American Identities during the Exclusion Era.* Philadelphia: Temple University Press.

Wong, Sau Ling. 1995. "Denationalization Reconsidered." *Amerasia Journal.* 21(1–2): 1–27.

Woon, Yuen-Fong. 1989. "Circulatory Mobility: Temporary Migrants in Kaiping City, Pearl River Delta." *International Migration Review* 27(3): 578–604.

——. 1989. "Social Change and Continuity in South China: Overseas Chinese and the Guan Lineage of Kaiping County, 1949–87." *China Quarterly* 118 (June): 324–44.

——. 1990. "International Links and the Socioeconomic Development of Rural China: An Emigrant Community in Guangdong." *Modern China* 16(2) (April): 139–72.

Wu, Chun-hsi. 1967. *Dollars, Dependents, and Dogma: Overseas Chinese Remittances to Communist China.* Stanford: Hoover Institution.

Wu, David Yen Ho. 1991. "The Construction of Chinese and Non-Chinese Identities." *Daedalus: The Living Tree—the Changing Meaning of Being Chinese.* 120(2): 159–79.

Wu, Xing Ci and Li Zhen. 1988. "Gum San Haak in the 1980s: A Study on Chinese Emigrants Who Return to Taishan County for Marriage." *Amerasia Journal* 14(2): 21–35.

Yang, Mayfair. 1994. *Gifts, Favors, and Banquets: The Art of Social Relationships in China.* Ithaca, N.Y.: Cornell University Press.

——. 1997. "Mass Media and Transnational Subjectivity in Shanghai: Notes on (Re)-cosmopolitanism in a Chinese Metropolis." In *Ungrounded Empires: The Cultural Politics of Modern Chinese Transnationalism*, ed. Aihwa Ong and Don Nonini. New York: Routledge.

Yeung, Y. M., and David Chu. 1994. *Guangdong: Survey of a Province Undergoing Rapid Change.* Hong Kong: Chinese University Press.

Yu, Renqiu. 1992. *To Save China, to Save Ourselves: The Chinese Hand Laundry Alliance of New York.* Philadelphia: Temple University Press.

Zhang, Li. 2001. "Contesting Crime, Order, and Migrant Spaces in Beijing." In *China Urban: Ethnographies of Contemporary Culture*, ed. Nancy N. Chen, Constance D. Clark, Suzanne Z. Gottschang, and Lyn Jeffery. Durham, N.C.: Duke University Press.

igration fever (*chu guo re*), 129, 140; as a gamble, 144, 148; mainland Chinese attitudes toward, 156, 158, 206–7

Errington, Frederick, and Deborah Gewertz, 227 n.3

Ethnic ownership, 194

Ethnography, 7, 9–20, 212 n.12; multi-sited, 8

Evans Pritchard, E. E., 213 n.20

Exclusion Acts (Chinese), 4, 12, 47, 98–100, 213 n.18, 217 n.11

Extraterritorial rule, 15, 53, 64, 88, 141

Family history, 12–13, 24, 32, 34–35, 39, 49, 86, 88, 90, 96, 107–8, 186, 193–94. *See also* Genealogy

Faure, David, 120

Feng shui, 127, 155

Flexible citizenship, 63

Floating population, 27, 63, 132, 135. *See also* Immigrants

FOB ("fresh off the boat"), 64

Forged transnationality, 31, 64, 74. *See also* Schein, Louisa

Ganqing, 149, 150, 223 n.14

Gazetteers, 45

Gender, 32, 97–98, 117

Genealogy (*zupu*), 7, 12–13, 29–31, 39–40, 49, 88, 117–18, 120, 186, 193–94, 213 n.21, 216 n.2; exclusion of women from, 117–18; inclusion of women in, 90; and mainland Chinese, 79; transformation of, 32, 35, 90, 96, 110; versus *jiapu*, 177. *See also* Family history; Kinship

Generational naming, 118

Generations, 30; American-born, 11–12, 25, 47; first, 11; immigrant versus American-born, 4, 64; intergenerational conflict, 105; of overseas Chinese, 55, 178; second, 10; third, 10, 117

Gift giving, 149–51, 223 n.14, 224 n.15; by overseas relatives, 154; to overseas relatives, 154, 205, 228 n.4

Glick Schiller, Nina, 89

Globalization, 19, 29, 101–2, 192

Golden Venture, 158

Gold Mountain (Gum San), 45, 140

Gold Rush, 211

Guangdong, 55, 90, 211; economy, 49, 140; history, 42, 129; and Hong Kong, 49, 129, 130; multiple meanings of, 32, 182; and overseas Chinese, 29, 192; as transnational, 43

Guangdong Chinese, 16, 22, 34, 71; attitudes toward emigration, 147–48, 156–57, 209; attitudes toward overseas Chinese, 128, 174, 178, 180; centered-identity, 172; and Hong Kong, 155; ideas about America, 148; ideas about development opportunities, 180, 210; ideas about outside world, 127, 130, 134, 139; new prosperity, 181; relations with overseas relatives, 149, 151; versus inland Chinese, 135

Guangzhou, 129, 205

Guan lineage, 54, 79, 219 n.14. *See also* Woon, Yuen Fong

Guanxi, 223 n.14

Guomindang (Kuomintang), 216 n.5. *See also* KMT

Gupta, Akhil, and James Ferguson, 64, 215 n.33, 216 n.8

Handler, Richard, 120

Heshan County, 213 n.21

He Shang (river elegy), 136, 217 n.14

Heung ha (*mui/jai*), 147, 223 n.13

History: Chinese American, 90; construction of, 35, 108, 202; narratives of, 93, 193

Hmong/Miao, 31, 212 n.12, 226 n.14

Home, 192; conceptions of, 171, 185, 189

Hometown, 15, 226 n.15; associations (*tongxiang hui*), 60; hometown mates (*tongxiang*), 15, 53, 213 n.20; hometown sentiment,(*xiang qing*), 50, 53, 55; of overseas Chinese (*qiao xiang*), 43, 58. *See also* Ancestral village; Native place

Hongbao, 220 n.17

Hong Kong, 43, 129; movies, 195; as tourist destination, 141; transnationals, 41, 97, 102; versus Shenzhen, 208. *See also* Astronauts (Hong Kong)

Hsu, Madeline, 214 n.15

Huaqiao, 213 n.19.*See also* Chinese; Overseas Chinese

Huayi, 47, 61, 161, 166, 169, 176, 213 n.19

Hu Dehart, Evelyn, 103

Identity: consciousness-raising, politics, 104, 194; hyphenated, 103, 186; narratives, 33, 95–96, 98, 203; politics, 33, 103, 123; production, 7–9, 20, 32, 88, 97, 121, 190, 202

Immigrants, 98; from inland China, 55, 63; post-1965 (U.S.), 47, 99. *See also* Floating population

Immigration: illegal, 64, 208; to the United States, 70. *See also* Immigrants

Indian Americans, 195

Japanese invasion, 4

Jin doi, 118–19

Jook sing, 93, 106, 186

Judge Bao Qing Tian, 137

Karaoake, 117

Kertzer, David, 109, 220 n.3, 224 n.1

Kinship, 17, 30. *See also* Family history; Genealogy

KMT (Kuomintang), 46. *See also* Guomindang

Kondo, Dorinne, 14

Kong, Lily, 220 n.20

Kung fu, 85, 91, 99, 130

Kwong, Peter, 158

Labor, 100, 104, 180, 202

Lai, Him Mark, Genny Lim, and Judy Yung, 221 n.7

Lam, Andrew, 101

Language ability: Cantonese dialect, 112, 114–15, 201; Chinese, 99, 106, 111; English, 25, 207; Mandarin dialect, 14, 201

Latin America: family origins in, 47, 98, 114

Lau, Mr. (pseudonym), 57, 136, 142, 177–78

Lineage revival, 54, 79

Lowe, Lisa, 105

Lull, James, 138

Maira, Sunaina, 195–96

Malkki, Liisa, 48, 215 n.33

Manga, 85, 91

Manhattan's Chinese Lady, 142

Man lineage, 31

Mao Zedong, 26–27, 49, 128; post-Mao, 10, 15, 131

Media, 34, 47, 91, 99–100, 127, 172, 222 n.4; advertisements, 137; Hong Kong television., 135–39; images of Chinese abroad, 142; polysemic images, 139

Mobility, 29, 35, 71, 95–96, 140, 190; of ethnographers, 9; and village visits, 81, 218 n.1

Model minority, 24

Modernity, 179; alternative modernities, 172, 180, 214 n.27; mainland-centered, 181; mainland Chinese discourses of, 22, 35, 49, 162, 203; overseas Chinese–derived, 71, 180

Mooncake, 226 n.9

Multiculturalism (U.S), 22, 24–25, 95–98, 101–2, 104, 106, 191, 203